The Wealth of Reality

The Wealth of Reality

An Ecology of Composition

Margaret A. Syverson

Southern Illinois University Press
Carbondale and Edwardsville

02 01 00 99 4 3 2 1

Publication was partially funded by a University Cooperative
Society Subvention Grant awarded by the University of Texas at
Austin.

Library of Congress Cataloging-in-Publication Data
Syverson, Margaret A., 1948–
The wealth of reality : an ecology of composition / Margaret A.
Syverson.
    p. cm.
Includes bibliographical references and index.
            1. English language—Rhetoric—Study and teaching—
Research. 2. English language—Composition and exercises—
Psychological aspects. 3. English language—Rhetoric—Psycho-
logical aspects. 4. Report writing—Psychological aspects.
5. Authorship—Collaboration. 6. Human ecology. 7. Cognition.
I. Title.
PE1404.S92 1999
808'.042—dc21   98-37550
ISBN 0-8093-2251-X (cloth : alk. paper)   CIP

Once more,
for Ben

There was a groping for using everything and there was a groping for a continuous present and there was an inevitable beginning of beginning again and again and again.

Having naturally done this I naturally was a little troubled with it when I read it. I became then like the others who read it. One does, you know, excepting that when I reread it myself I lost myself in it again. Then I said to myself this time it will be different and I began. I did not begin again I just began.

In this beginning naturally since I at once went on and on very soon there were pages and pages and pages more elaborated creating a more and more continuous present including more and more using of everything and continuing more and more beginning and beginning and beginning. . . .

The problem from this time on became more definite.

—Gertrude Stein,
"Composition as Explanation"

Contents

List of Figures   xi

Preface   xiii

Acknowledgments   xix

1   Introduction: What Is
an Ecology of Composition?   1

2   Thinking with the Things As They Exist:
Ecology of a Poem   28

3   "Next Time We're Not Giving Steve
Our Essay to Read": Ecology of Writers   75

4   Desert Storm on the Network:
Ecology of Readers   126

5   Conclusion: Implications and Proposals
for an Ecology of Composition   182

Appendixes

A   Syllabus and Journal Questions for Third College
Writing Program, 1A, Winter, 1989   211

B   Workshop Handout   219

C   Conference Worksheet   221

D   Correlations Between Events of the Gulf War
and XLCHC Messages   223

E   Distribution of Participants by Location, Discipline,
and Gender   235

F   Example of a Completed California
     Learning Record   237

     Notes   247

     References   251

     Index   269

Figures

1. An ecological matrix   23

2. A page from Sarah Reznikoff's manuscript   39

3. A page from Charles Reznikoff's manuscript   41

4. A comparison of Nathan's and Charles's narratives   42

5. A note by Charles Reznikoff   47

6. A schematic diagram of relevant texts   61

7. Emergence of Sarah's texts   62

8. Nathan's manuscripts   63

9. Collaborative writing assignment handout   81

10. Distribution of messages
    on the topic of the Gulf War   144

Preface

It all started innocently enough. I was curious about how writers think about writing, and how writing shapes their thinking; I thought I might study student writers to see what I could learn. The main research problem I encountered was in making thinking manifest in ways that would allow us (teachers and researchers) to observe the process. Talk-aloud protocols seemed to constrain the composing situation too much, and I suspected that there would be cognitive interference in trying to accomplish a verbal task while reporting verbally about it. I hoped to capture some aspects of writers' cognitive processes while they were engaged in ordinary writing tasks in typical situations. It seemed to me that if students were engaged in a collaborative writing task, they might articulate some of their assumptions about writing, and they might reveal some of the cognitive processes that shape their writing. If we could tape their composing sessions, we might learn a great deal about how people think about their composing processes. My initial case study only revealed how much more I had to learn about conducting research. One thing was certain, however: it was fascinating to observe the complex dynamics of people wrestling with a writing task together. I also discovered that these collaborative composing situations were subject to cultural influences at many different levels. At that point, I was still most interested in cognitive processes in individuals, and I was still unsure whether what I was learning was confined solely to student writers.

Anthropology, it seemed, could provide the research methods that would help me work in naturalistic settings and also identify cultural influences. I studied cognitive anthropology with Roy D'Andrade and became fascinated with anthropological methods and inquiry. Questions about the relationship between culture and cognition intrigued me. At the same time, I began to study the archival materials on Charles Reznikoff, the objectivist poet, to try to understand the composing processes of an accomplished writer. At the suggestion of Michael Cole, I also joined a computer forum of social scientists interested in issues of learning, technology, and literacy. Technological transformations of composing processes fascinated me. For some time, these three areas of interest seemed distinct and unrelated.

Then, quite by accident, I stepped into Edwin Hutchins's courses in Everyday Cognition and Distributed Cognition and completely lost my bearings. Suddenly thinking was revealed as not simply a matter of logical processing neatly managed by a brain in splendid isolation but as a complex ensemble of activities and interactions among brains, hands, eyes, ears, other people, and an astonishing variety of structures in the environment, from airplane cockpits to cereal boxes to institutions. More surprising, to me, was the wide range of cognitive activities that seemed to involve no verbal language at all. I had the eerie sensation of someone who has been peering through a microscope for a very long time and then suddenly steps back and notices the vastness of the world. It is safe to say I have not completely recovered from those courses. The introduction to the work in situated cognition of Lucy Suchman, Jean Lave, David Woods, and many others, as well as Hutchins's work in distributed cognition, the new perception of a richly complex, dynamic cognitive "ecology," and the growing recognition of the potential for applying these concepts to composing situations was riveting.

Reading further, in current research on complex systems, I encountered John Holland, Stuart Kauffman, Brian Arthur, Murray Gell-Mann, and others whose concepts of emergence, self-organization, adaptation, criticality, and embodiment provided a theoretical framework that I believed might help us focus on the dynamics of interactions among readers, writers, texts, and their environments.

Immediately it became apparent how my three disparate research interests might be connected. I decided to use these diverse writing situations to test the application of theories of complex systems and distributed cognition in composition studies. In the process, I believed we might gain a deeper, richer understanding of composing, as well as some important theoretical concepts worth exploring in future research. Furthermore, I wanted to argue for the significance of composing situations as productive sites for research in cognitive science by demonstrating that composing is a situated and distributed activity that provides, not a mirror, but a manifest trace of cognitive and cultural processes.

This book, then, is the result of the convergence of ideas from many different fields and from many different sources. These ideas share a common theme: the wealth of reality is richly complex, interdependent, and emergent; we are embedded in and co-evolving with our environments, which include other people as well as social and physical structures and processes. Although composed of many individuals acting independently, the dynamics of processes occurring in these ecosocial environments is irreducible to discrete individuals.

I wrote this book to help explain what, exactly, such a perspective might mean for those of us in composition studies. Our profession has a long and distinguished history of seeking potential applications for the best research methods, theories, and approaches developed in other fields to enrich and inform our own research methods, theories, and approaches while also focusing serious attention on practices grounded in our classrooms, journals, conferences, and workplaces, as well as in the culture at large. Many of our "treatments" and "interventions" have proven to have unreliable or unpredictable outcomes. Many of our best ideas have become trivialized or deformed in practice. Many of our model programs have been sabotaged or diluted to insignificance through malice, indifference, or greed. Technological advances have proven to increase rather than reduce the complexity and difficulty of our work. We cannot hope to understand these situations by studying individuals in isolation; we need an ecological approach that considers the dynamics of systems of people situated in and codetermining particular social and material environments. This book is a first step toward articulating such an approach.

The first chapter introduces theories of complex systems currently being studied in diverse disciplines. Complex systems are described by theorists as adaptive, self-organizing, and dynamic; they are systems that are neither utterly chaotic nor entirely ordered, but exist on the boundary between these two states. Ecological systems are "meta–systems" composed of interrelated complex systems. I propose that we might consider that writers, readers, and texts, together with their environments, constitute one kind of ecological system. In the process, I argue, we might gain a new understanding of composing situations. I describe four attributes of complex systems that provide a theoretical framework for the study: distribution, embodiment, emergence, and enaction. Distribution refers to the concept that processes in complex systems are distributed (in both senses; that is, both "divided" and "shared") among agents and structures in the environment. Embodiment refers to the grounding of complex systems in physical experience and interactions. Emergence refers to the self-organization that arises globally in networks of simple components connected to each other and acting locally—readers, writers, and texts, for instance. Enaction refers to the situated practices and activities that structure the composing situation as it unfolds over time, from microscale (e.g., drawing letters on a page, tapping a keyboard) to global (e.g., the development of the Internet).

Chapter 2 focuses on a single passage taken from "Early History of a Writer," a poem published by Charles Reznikoff. This chapter provides an ecological perspective on text composing as distributed, embodied, emergent, and enactive. The Reznikoff passage, drawing on manuscripts produced by Reznikoff's parents, was distributed both in authorship and in actual texts. It was embodied in different forms in these manuscripts and in Reznikoff's drafts and was also grounded in the physical experience of the poet (including his legendary walks in New York City) and his family. It emerged through forty years of a family writing prose and poetry, reading, talking, editing, translating, and publishing in a specific social and physical environment, which includes not only the literary movements of the time but the Russian Jewish ghetto in New York, the physical work in the garment district, and the politics of assimilation. Finally, the passage was enacted through specific activities and practices, including Reznikoff's law school training, his self-publishing of his poetry, the establishment of the Objectivist Press, and the responses of readers.

Chapter 3 presents a case study of a group of first-year college students composing a collaborative essay. This chapter introduces the concepts of adaptation and coordination in ecological systems. These college students, through their situated activities together, developed a high degree of coordination within the group but struggled in their attempts at developing coordination with readers, including other students and the instructor. The efforts toward coordination were distributed among writers in the group, technologies for writing, and readers, including the instructor. These efforts were embodied in physical states and actions, from the choice of essay topic ("noise in the dorms") to the physical fatigue of the writers as the project evolved. Coordination emerged through the writers' conversations during the composing process, in their response to contradictory responses from readers, and through their struggles with revisions. Further, their efforts toward coordination were enacted in practices and activities associated with the writing and reading tasks, in workshops, and in conferences with the instructor, as well as in general activities involved in college life.

Chapter 4 focuses on an episode of conversation in a computer forum during the Gulf War, an episode that developed into a conflict among members of the forum. This conflict is the basis for an investigation into the situation of readers in composing situations. This chapter introduces the concept of perturbation and its unpredictable effects on complex systems. As the Gulf War conflict unfolded, the four attributes of complex systems were evident through the effects of perturbations in the forum. The conflict was distributed among participants as well as their technologies for composing and communicating. It was embodied not only in the physical manifestation of texts but in the physical references in the messages themselves; this embodiment not only grounded the conceptual development of the message, but also served to define relationships among the participants. The conflict emerged from a brief, scarcely noticed response to a request for course material dealing with psychological issues with Middle Eastern content into a large-scale conflict that ranged over issues of sexism, racism, gay activism, and rhetoric. Finally, the conflict was enacted via the activities and practices of participants, including reading and writing, argumentation, scholarly communication, and use of the computer for reading, composing, and communicating text.

Teachers, researchers, and scholars in our field might wonder how theories of composition as ecological system can inform our everyday practices and institutions. The final chapter discusses some implications of an ecological approach for composition research, pedagogy, and assessment. This chapter describes the Learning Record system, which integrates literacy instruction, assessment, and research, as a practical model that demonstrates how an ecological approach can be productively applied. It presents some challenges to the theory of composing as an ecological system and proposes directions for further research. This chapter argues that technological changes have made new and urgent demands on our theories, methods, and practices of composition and communication. These changes have created new environments for composing and new arenas for research; at the same time, they also suggest the possibilities for reconsidering conventional environments in the light of new theoretical and methodological approaches.

Acknowledgments

There is no such thing as love, there are only acts of love.
—French proverb

This study proved to me that composing is an ecological system. I have depended on a network of scholars, texts, computer hardware and software, friends and family. The entire process has been distributed among countless interactions with people and resources in the environment; it is embodied in this text and in physical interactions with it; it has emerged over time from a few key concepts into a theoretical framework and finally into this extended study; and it has been enacted in a set of practices and activities that range from taking notes in an archive or participating in a lab discussion to formal institutional processes of admission to a discipline. There is a tremendous amount of work involved in composing a book such as this; but one writer cannot accomplish it alone. I owe an enormous debt of gratitude to the many people who have contributed to this work.

My greatest debt and deepest appreciation is owed to Charles Cooper, who has served as the very best example of scholarship combined with good sense and compassion I have ever encountered. No one could ask for a better mentor and colleague. He believed in me when it was not possible for me to believe in myself, he encouraged me to pursue the questions that beckoned to me, he supported me in my moments of confusion and uncertainty, and he pressed me to clarify my vague ideas until they were coherent. I can't hope to return to him the measure of what he has given me; I can only hope to share it with my own students with some fraction of his grace and tact.

I'm also thankful for the generosity of Edwin Hutchins, who, instead of providing answers, introduced me to a better class of questions, and instead of treating me as an interloper from an alien discipline, made me feel welcome. This book is an extended reflection on concepts and questions raised in his own work, a model of passionate inquiry into the ways people think. Meetings of his distributed cognition lab group are lively and thought provoking and contributed a great deal to my thinking about issues in this study.

Many others have contributed their support and encouragement: Michael Davidson introduced me to the work of Charles Reznikoff, read many earlier drafts of my work, and encouraged me to develop and publish my early research in the Archives of the University of California at San Diego (UCSD). His comments were always warmly supportive and insightful.

Mary Barr introduced me to the California Learning Record, read early drafts of chapters, and provided very helpful suggestions that helped me clarify my ideas about the application of complexity theory in diverse composing situations. She authorized permission to reproduce the completed Learning Record in appendix F. As director of the Center for Language in Learning, home of the Learning Record, she is a real inspiration and also a warmly supportive friend.

Other faculty members at UCSD made key contributions to my development of this project: Roy D'Andrade introduced me to the irresistible questions and methods of cognitive anthropology; Kathryn Shevelow and Stephanie Jed drew my attention to the extraordinary in everyday texts and the power of autobiographical writing; and Anthony Edwards made me realize that ancient questions about rhetoric and audience continue to be reappraised and renegotiated. His perceptive comments on an earlier paper compelled me to reexamine my ideas about computer-mediated discourse and its relationship to more traditional forms of discourse.

I also wish to thank the Mandeville Department of Special Collections, Archive for New Poetry, at UCSD, for permission to reproduce the manuscript pages that appear in chapter 2: Charles Reznikoff Papers. MSS9. Mandeville Special Collections Library, UC, San Diego.

I am very grateful to the students in my Third College Writing Program classes, who were generous and good-humored enough to tolerate my intrusion into their lives for the case study in chapter 3.

For the chapter on the Gulf War episode on xlchc, Michael Cole provided valuable insights into the historical, cultural, and technological particulars of xlchc; Valerie Polichar supplied background information on computer forums and email communication; Peggy Bengel and Noah Finkelstein provided archival records of xlchc messages; and Arne Raeithel supplied missing messages to fill the gaps in the archives. Laura Taub suggested the Gulf War episode on xlchc as a potential subject of study. I would also like to thank the members of xlchc, who have constructed their computer forum as an open and public expression of multiple voices and who have consistently supported research into this phenomenon.

My colleagues at the University of Texas at Austin have been enormously supportive; their energy and commitment are inspirational. I am especially indebted to John Slatin for many thought-provoking conversations and helpful advice and to the graduate students in my Minds, Texts, and Technology seminars.

Cindy Selfe and Gail Hawisher have been extremely instrumental in providing spaces in our field for discussions about the relationship between technology and composition, for supporting and developing scholars new to the discipline, and for establishing an outstanding scholarly journal that both showcases and legitimizes professional discourse about computers, networks, and writing. I am very grateful for their inspiration, their warmth, and their support. Extremely influential on my thinking were the many long discussions with, source suggestions by, and encouragement of Martin Rosenberg, who first introduced me to the work of Humberto Maturana and Francisco Varela.

I'd like to acknowledge, too, the members of the Conference on College Composition and Communication (CCCC) committee that selected my dissertation project for the 1995 James Berlin Memorial Outstanding Dissertation Award, as well as the members of the Computers and Composition committee that selected the dissertation for the 1995 Hugh Burns Dissertation Award. These awards were profoundly affirming and deeply appreciated.

Beyond these rich professional and academic resources, however, I have been nourished by the love, encouragement, and strength I have received from my family and extended family, the real wealth of my reality: my sister, Nora Ishibashi, who challenged my thinking and also provided daily encouragement by email, snailmail, and telephone; Lynn Susholtz, Aida Mancillas, and Amy Rosen, more sisters than friends; Reina Juarez; and Joko Beck. I am especially thankful for my mother and my father, whose loving expressions of support take different forms but whose care has always sustained me.

But most of all I am deeply grateful to my son Ben, whose naive and not-so-naive questions propelled much of my drive to understand new discourse arenas, whose explorations of possibilities with the computer convinced me that composing environments are fundamentally and permanently altered, and whose own achievements in this field are already being recognized. His love, his energy, his humor, and his imagination have given me back to life.

The Wealth of Reality

1

Introduction: What Is
an Ecology of Composition?

> The real lesson to be learned from the principle of comple-
> mentarity, a lesson that can perhaps be transferred to other fields
> of knowledge, consists in emphasizing the wealth of reality, which
> overflows any single language, any single logical structure. Each
> language can express only part of reality. Music, for example, has
> not been exhausted by any of its realizations, by any style of
> composition, from Bach to Schönberg.
>
> —Ilya Prigogine and Isabelle Stengers,
> *Order Out of Chaos: Man's New Dialogue with Nature*

Introduction

- In 1929, Charles Reznikoff, the objectivist poet, published *Family Chronicle,* which included a story of his mother's life, his father's life, and his own life in New York's garment district. In 1932, he published an autobiographical novel, *By the Waters of Manhattan.* In 1962, he published an autobiographical poem, "Early History of a Writer." Who wrote these texts?
- In 1989, three college students collaborated to write a single essay in a first-year writing course at a prestigious university. In spite of clear instructions, an intelligent and well-organized composition textbook, good advice from fellow students, ample opportunities for revising, and conferences with the instructor, the essay was disappointing. Why?
- In 1991, a collegial group of social scientists sharing ideas in a computer forum became embroiled in a bitter conflict about the Gulf War, a conflict that threatened to destroy long-standing research partnerships and nearly terminated the group. Three months later, members of the same group enthusiastically contributed to a conversation about refrigerator doors as family communication centers, which ultimately formed the chapter of a book. How?
- In spite of a vast body of research dating back at least to 1890, in

spite of the best intentions of talented instructors, in spite of large-scale institutional commitments to composition programs, and in spite of an unprecedented publishing boom for composition textbooks, manuals, style guides, and anthologies, there is no evidence that students are writing, reading, or thinking better than at any time in the past. What are we missing?

This book is an attempt to address these questions by taking a new look at composition with three questions in mind:

- Why are our present accounts of composing inadequate to answer the questions above?
- How might we develop a richer, more comprehensive theory of composing?
- On what grounds could we argue that such a theory has greater explanatory power than existing accounts?

To address these questions, we will need to consider a different unit of analysis in our studies of writers, texts, and audiences: an ecology of composition. To support and develop this approach, this study draws on current research in fields as diverse as biology, physics, communications, cognitive science, philosophy, and economics; and it suggests how theories developed in these fields might enlarge our understanding of composing. Much of this research focuses on a set of concepts that are generally grouped under the working term *complexity* or *complex systems*.[1] This interdisciplinary effort could be very productive for composition studies: biologist Henri Atlan argues that interaction between seemingly disparate disciplines, with different classification schemes, theories, and methods is crucial in developing new knowledge: "[T]he frontiers of knowledge are found not only, as is often believed, in the very small or the infinitely large, but in the articulations between levels of organization of the real that correspond to different fields of knowledge whose techniques and discourses do not overlap" (qtd. in Paulson 109).

This introduction will define an ecological system as composed of numerous interrelated complex systems, introduce some central principles emerging in studies of complex systems, and explain generally how these principles might be applied to situations involving writers, texts, and readers. This study represents an initial, exploratory attempt to describe what such an ecology of composition might reveal about writers, readers, texts, their environments, and the dynamic process of composing.

The case studies in the chapters that follow analyze in greater depth three specific examples of actual writers and composing situations, including a well-known objectivist poet composing an autobiographical poem, a group of objectivist college students working on a collaborative essay, and a computer forum of social scientists conducting research on learning and development. These cases will allow us to explore the potential for applying theories of complex systems in rhetoric and composition studies, and to suggest their generalizability across diverse composing situations.

What exactly do we mean by *ecology?* And what is a *complex system?* Although these two terms are often used interchangeably by researchers, I would suggest that an ecology is a set of interrelated and interdependent complex systems; and on this basis, we first need to understand what a complex system is in order to define an ecology.

Complex systems have been proposed as an explanation for a wide range of puzzling phenomena, from the human immune system to the economics of the stock market to the rise and fall of a pre-Columbian city-state in the American Southwest, phenomena which share some surprising features. These systems have attracted serious research interest ranging across disciplines, from Nobel laureates (Murray Gell-Mann, Ilya Prigogine, and Philip Anderson in physics; Kenneth Arrow in economics) to graduate students. In a complex system, a network of independent agents—people, atoms, neurons, or molecules, for instance—act and interact in parallel with each other, simultaneously reacting to and co-constructing their own environment. Waldrop explains that in complex systems, the richness of these interactions allows the system as a whole to generate spontaneous self-organization:

> Thus, people trying to satisfy their material needs unconsciously organize themselves into an economy through myriad individual acts of buying and selling; it happens without anyone being in charge or consciously planning it [on a global scale]. The genes in a developing embryo organize themselves in one way to make a liver cell and in another way to make a muscle cell. . . . Atoms search for a minimum energy state by forming chemical bonds with each other, thereby organizing themselves into structures known as molecules. In every case, groups of agents seeking mutual accommodation and self-consistency somehow manage to

transcend themselves, acquiring collective properties such as life, thought, and purpose that they might never have possessed individually. (11)

Complex systems are also adaptive, Waldrop points out, in that they do not respond to events passively, "the way a rock might roll around in an earthquake." Rather, "they actively try to turn whatever happens to their advantage. . . . Species evolve for better survival in a changing environment—and so do corporations and industries" (11).

Finally, complex systems are dynamic, more unpredictable, spontaneous, and disorderly than a machine, more structured, coherent, and purposeful than utter chaos. "Instead," Waldrop argues,

> all these complex systems have somehow acquired the ability to bring order and chaos into a special kind of balance. This balance point—often called the edge of chaos—is where the components of a system never quite lock into place, and yet never quite dissolve into turbulence, either. The edge of chaos is where life has enough stability to sustain itself and enough creativity to deserve the name of life. (12)

There are examples of complex systems at every level of scale, from neurons in the brain to large-scale cultural and social systems such as academic disciplines or nations.

As I have mentioned, complex systems that function this way are the subject of a great deal of current research in a wide variety of disciplines.[2] The term has a specific technical meaning for these theorists; William Paulson, in *The Noise of Culture,* distinguishes complex systems from simple systems and complicated systems:

> It is not hard to conceive of simple systems: a pendulum, a piston, a single logical operator at the level of bits in a microprocessor. We can understand fully the operation of such systems. Complicated systems, such as a clock, a car engine, or a home computer, can be fully understood as the interaction of their component parts, so that whereas knowing them requires much more of one's time and patience, in principle nothing prevents us from explaining their operation just as fully as we can explain that of the simple systems of which they are made up. What distinguishes the complex system, on the other hand, is a discontinuity in knowledge between the parts and the whole. (108)

In other words, because such a system is self-organizing, adaptive, and dynamic, it is not possible to predict its behavior simply by understanding its parts and their relationship to each other; a complex system defies any attempt at a strictly mechanistic explanation.

I would argue that writers, readers, and texts form just such a complex system of self-organizing, adaptive, and dynamic interactions. But even beyond this level of complexity, they are actually situated in an ecology, a larger system that includes environmental structures, such as pens, paper, computers, books, telephones, fax machines, photocopiers, printing presses, and other natural and human-constructed features, as well as other complex systems operating at various levels of scale, such as families, global economies, publishing systems, theoretical frames, academic disciplines, and language itself. For my purposes, then, an ecology is a kind of meta-complex system composed of interrelated and interdependent complex systems and their environmental structures and processes. And my principal question is this: Can the concepts currently emerging in diverse fields on the nature of complex systems provide us with a new understanding of composing as an ecological system?

John Holland, a professor of psychology and computer science and a leading theorist of complex systems, uses the term *complex adaptive systems* to describe what I have termed an *ecological system* (Holland, "Complex"). That is, according to Holland, complex adaptive systems involve "great numbers of parts undergoing a kaleidoscopic array of simultaneous interactions." Further, all of these systems involve a characteristically "evolving structure": "these systems change and reorganize their component parts to adapt themselves to the problems posed by their surroundings" (18). According to Holland, complex adaptive systems share three characteristics: evolution, aggregate behavior, and anticipation. We say they evolve because, as time passes, the parts of the system attempt to improve the ability of their kind to survive in their interactions with the surrounding parts. The systems exhibit aggregate behavior that is not simply derived from the separate actions of its parts, but represents a globally coherent pattern that emerges from the interaction of the parts. And such systems also anticipate changing circumstances in order to predict what adaptations will be required. As Holland argues,

> Because the individual parts of a complex adaptive system are continually revising their ("conditioned") rules for interaction, each part is embedded in perpetually novel surroundings (the changing behavior of the other parts). As a result, the aggregate behavior of the system is usually far from optimal, if indeed optimality can even be defined for the system as a whole. For this reason, standard theories in physics, economics, and elsewhere [I might add composition studies], are of little help because

they concentrate on optimal end points, whereas complex adaptive systems "never get there." They continue to evolve, and they steadily exhibit new forms of emergent behavior. History and context play a critical role, further complicating the task for theory and experiment. Though some parts of the system may settle down temporarily at a local optimum, they are usually "dead" or uninteresting if they remain at that equilibrium for an extended period. It is the process of becoming, rather than the never-reached end points, that we must study if we are to gain insight. (20)

In "Learning in the Cultural Process," Edwin Hutchins and Brian Hazlehurst put it another way:

> One of the central problems faced by biological and artificial systems is the development and maintenance of coordination between structure inside the system and structure outside the system. That is, the production of useful behavior requires internal structures that respond in appropriate ways to structure in the environment. The processes that give rise to this coordination are generally considered adaptive.
>
> Biological evolution, individual learning, and cultural evolution can all be seen as ways to discover and save solutions to frequently encountered problems; that is, they are processes that generate coordination between internal and external structure. (689)

Let's consider a prototypical example of composing: someone writing a book to explain a set of theories, such as this one. We think of this writing situation as involving a writer, an unfolding text, and a potential audience, a reader. The writer transfers "ideas" into written language, the actual text appears on a page, and the audience reads the text and receives the writer's "ideas." This, of course, is an extremely limited and partial view of the composing situation. In considering an ecology of composing, we would try to take into account the complex interrelationships in which the writing is embedded: the people and texts that form a larger conversation in which the writer, text, and reader participate and from which the "ideas" emerge to take written shape. We would consider the writer's interaction with the environment, including the technologies for writing, the memory aids, the tools and instruments that help shape and support the writing. We would consider how the text takes shape as it emerges, how the writer interacts dialogically with the text not only through acting upon it but by responding to it and to its potential readers. We would situate the composing of the text in a nexus of complex social structures, ranging from the personal (the writer's relationship to an editor, a critic, or an academic colleague, for example) to the institutional (the system of publication for tenure, a corporate hierarchy, or a government funding agency, for example) and even global (a genre or an international computer network of scholars in a particular field, for example). We would also attempt to situate the writing in a historical complex, not only as an unfolding process marked by events such as first drafts, revisions, and so on, but within a larger discourse that is historically situated, and involving historically situated technologies, social relations, cultural influences, and disciplinary practices.

Further, we would take a similar approach to the co-construction of the writing process by readers, who are not merely passive recipients of the text in this ecology of composition but active constituents of it: situated, like writers and texts, in a physical, psychological, social, temporal, and spatial network of relations. Even in this extremely abbreviated overview, we can readily admit that such a view of the composing situation is indeed complex.

But it is not enough to simply stipulate that a system is complex. What features distinguish such systems? Recent work by Hutchins, as well as by Varela, Thompson, and Rosch, has provided a theoretical framework for this analysis of composing as an ecological system. I suggest here four attributes of ecological systems often overlooked by current composition theories: distribution, emergence, embodiment, and enaction. These attributes are currently gaining strength in theories of complex systems, such as cognitive processing.

Distribution

In complex systems, processes—including cognitive processes—are distributed, that is, both divided and shared among agents and structures in the environment. As Holland puts it:

> A complex adaptive system has no single governing equation, or rule, that controls the system. Instead, it has many distributed, interacting parts, with little or nothing in the way of central control. Each of the parts is governed by its own rules. Each of these rules may participate in influencing an outcome, and each may influence the actions of other parts. (21)

Complex systems are also distributed across space and time in an ensemble of interrelated activities. Hutchins describes a classic example in his ethnographic study of a navy navigation team (*Cognition*), an example that provides intriguing insights into composing situations.

In this study, Hutchins describes a navy navigation team guiding a ship into San Diego Harbor. On each side of the ship, seamen using an optical instrument called a *pelorus* are positioned to spot landmarks and determine their position relative to the ship. Their readings are recorded in a bearing record log by a third seaman and then relayed by telephone to the navigator, who places a one-armed protractor on a chart, indicating the ship's position relative to the landmark. A series of three bearings is taken, and the navigator inscribes a line on the chart for each one, producing a small triangle that signifies the ship's location. The navigator then calculates the projected path of the ship at its present rate and direction of travel and issues instructions for the time and landmarks for the next reading. This process is repeated at least every three minutes until the ship is safely at anchor or secured to a pier.

This example presents interesting challenges to our understanding of composing. For instance, which individual on this team is really doing the "writing?" Which individual "knows" the ship's position best? Whose knowledge is being represented in the writing? It is clear that in this example, the knowledge involved in "writing," inscribing the marks upon the chart, depends on activities and communication shared in interactions not only among people but also interactions between people and various structures in the environment, from physical landmarks to technological instruments to graphical representations. Composition researchers, by this analogy, have tended to focus their attention on the person inscribing the lines on the page, or on the nature or quality of the lines themselves, or on the activity of inscribing. Our theories of composing have been somewhat atomistic, focusing on individual writers, individual texts, isolated acts, processes, or artifacts.

Recent work in distributed and situated cognition by researchers such as Edwin Hutchins, Jean Lave, Charles and Marjorie Goodwin, Lucy Suchman, and Bruno Latour demonstrates the degree to which cognitive processes are not only dependent on social interactions but also determined by activities situated in specific environments. Situations such as scientific laboratories, ship navigation crews, courtrooms, and classrooms are complex cognitive systems, in which knowledge and practices must be coordinated among groups of people in a way that cannot be defined as contained in any individual mind; further, such knowledge and practices are dependent upon structures and processes in the environment (including, for example, architecture, technological instruments and other cognitive artifacts, texts, institutions, and language itself) that are not merely the tools of cognition, but constitutive of it. Cognitive scientists have termed the operation of such ensembles *distributed* or *situated* cognition, and their work with these concepts has important applications in composition studies. *Distributed cognition* refers to the way cognitive processes are shared, that is, both divided and coordinated among people and structures in the environment. *Situated cognition* refers to the fact that cognitive processes are always embedded in specific social, cultural, and physical-material situations, which determine not only how cognitive processes unfold but also the meanings they have for participants. These two concepts, distributed cognition and situated cognition, are thus closely related and interreferential.

By privileging the individual writer composing in isolation, we have slighted or ignored compelling evidence that writing, like other cognitive processes, occurs in ecological systems involving not only social but also environmental structures that both powerfully constrain and also enable what writers are able to think, feel, and write. Some of these structures are naturally occurring: weather, animals, oceans, mountains, and forests, for example. Others are human constructions: buildings, computer keyboards, monitors, modems, software environments, notebooks, pens, desks, chairs, and so on. For example, teachers recognize the importance of the physical arrangement of a classroom. There is a difference between a room set up theater style, with all seats facing the teacher, and a room set up seminar style, with chairs arranged around a large conference table, or a room with smaller tables and clusters of chairs, and this difference alters the teaching and learning environment in nontrivial ways. Literary biographies abound with explicit and implicit references to the importance of the physical environment for writers: Ernest Hemingway liked to write standing up, pounding the keys of an old Remington portable typewriter; Robert Coover uses a computer equipped with a hypertext program called StorySpace to create new kinds of fiction; some writers insist on a certain pen, a specific kind of paper, a set of bound composition books, a particular arrangement of objects on their desks, and so on. They themselves provide much of the physical structure in their own environment: annotations in books, notes on scraps of paper, lists of sources, files of ideas and correspondence, computer files, phone numbers of colleagues, and tools, such as tape, staplers, rulers, scissors, and so on. Away from this familiar supportive environment, writers think and write differently; when writing while on vacation or at a conference, for example, they may feel either stripped and helpless or liberated and refreshed.

The distribution of cognition in the chart room of a ship, a scientific laboratory, or a classroom is not simply a question of the spatial arrangement of people and environmental structures in a static field, however. Since the process of cognition, and composing, is a dynamic one, we must also consider how these complex processes emerge.

Emergence

In spite of its variety and complexity at almost every level, composition is not an entirely chaotic activity; neither is it a stable, perfectly ordered and predictable one. From a vast ocean of words, phrases, and ideas, writers continue to bring forth texts that organize themselves into more or less coherent and recognizable forms at every level of scale: metaphors, sentences, introductory chapters, lab reports, dissertations, detective novels, and so on. From an incredible range of writers producing mountains of texts, a few writers emerge as influential: the texts they produce not only provoke attention or interest among readers but generate a kind of following. Writers respond with new texts that reflect the influence; and when a certain threshold is passed, a literary movement, a genre, or a style develops genuine force and momentum through the more or less coherent activities of a large number of writers and readers. Or a new term gains widespread currency (*catch-22, Kafkaesque, antihero*), a character joins our cultural stock of types (Pollyanna, Don Quixote, Romeo, Scarlett O'Hara, Walter Mitty), an event becomes "historic" ("What are Caesar's battles but Caesar's prose?" asks Lyn Hejinian). These phenomena are examples of emergence.

The question that drove scientific research on emergence was a simple and familiar one: Why is there something instead of nothing? According to the second law of thermodynamics, in a closed system, entropy will increase to a maximum; over time, the system's ability to produce energy will steadily diminish. Yet through evolution, increasingly complex species have evolved; in nations, increasingly complex and global economic systems have evolved; and on pages and computer screens, texts continue to emerge. How can this apparent contradiction be explained? In their investigations of this puzzling mystery, researchers have theorized that complex systems display a kind of energy for self-organization that seems to defy laws of entropy; they argue that such systems exhibit emergent properties.

Emergence refers to the self-organization arising globally in networks of simple components connected to each other and operating locally. Emergent properties have been proposed as the counter effect to entropy: they are tendencies toward self-organization, order, and structure that emerge from simple components that might be expected to exhibit either random, chaotic behavior or stable, predictable behavior—but that in fact, do neither. Yet, this order is not created or determined by a single, central master "executive" or "brain."

Hendriks-Jansen suggests that the concept of emergence has three different senses. The first, he writes, "amounts to a thesis about the hierarchical organization of entities and processes. It maintains that the properties at higher levels of organization are not predictable from properties at lower levels." In other words, complex systems cannot be adequately described simply by analyzing their simpler components. The second sense of emergence is historical: "This draws attention to the fact that simple traits and forms of organization give rise, in the course of evolution, to more complex and irreducibly novel traits and structures." Finally, Hendriks-Jansen suggests a third sense of emergence, which he calls "interactive emergence."

> I shall argue on empirical and conceptual grounds that all behavior is situated activity, and all situated activity results from interactive emergence. Behavior cannot be adequately described in terms of events that take place inside a creature's head. It cannot be explained by rules that formalize neural activity or mental activity, for it comes into existence only when the creature interacts with its species-typical environment. (30)

This third sense of emergence incorporates the first two senses, and it is in this sense that the term will be used in this study.

Meaning, genre, irony, style, authority, credibility—these are all emergent properties in texts. So is the influence of a particular text or writer in a social, historical, or cultural situation. Emergent properties suggest that all of our classification systems are actually open-ended, explanatory theories rather than closed, deterministic containers. Novels explode into hypertexts, which begin to organize themselves into new genres: cyberpunk novels, literary interpretive webs, multi-authored fiction, and so on. However, the concept of emergence is not in opposition to entropy: it includes it. As new forms or agents emerge, others fall away, break up, dwindle down, rust, decay, or decompose into either chaotic or stable states from which new forms emerge. What deconstruction breaks apart comes together again as elements of new texts—for example, journal articles by literary theorists. The "exhaustion" of postmodernism itself affords novelty.

Embodiment

Writers, readers, and texts have physical bodies and consequently not only the content but the process of their interaction is dependent on, and reflective of, physical experience. In *Reading Minds,* for example, Mark Turner makes the point that the physiological fact that humans are bilaterally symmetrical determines many of our fundamental concepts, causing us to perceive and interpret the world in terms of bilateral balance, binary oppositions, and other forms of symmetrical relations. Thus, we "naturally" construct argument as a battle between two opposing forces that seek a "common ground." Mark Johnson and George Lakoff have also argued that our conceptual schemas and metaphors are grounded in our physical experiences. Since we are bounded by our skins, for instance, and experience the rest of the world as outside of us, we have developed a broadly deployed schema: "Each of us is a container, with a bounding surface and an in-out orientation. We project our own in-out orientation onto other physical objects that are bounded by surfaces. Thus we also view them as containers with an inside and an outside" (Lakoff and Johnson 29). The container metaphor is extended not only to physical space but to events, actions, activities, states, and other abstract entities, including writing situations.

The fact that humans share, to a large extent, similar experiences as a result of their physical being makes both language itself and its content comprehensible. But embodiment does not refer only to our conceptual structures and cognitive activities. Neither writing nor reading can be accomplished without physical activity: clasping a book, moving the eyes across a line of text, using the muscles of the hand, arm, and fingers to handle a pen or keyboard. The nature of that activity may vary: blind people read a text through touch rather than sight, a writer may use voice to dictate a text rather than manipulate a pen or a keyboard by hand. Still, such atypical activities only foreground the inherently physical interaction between writers, readers, and texts. One of the salient features of academic life is the massive suppression of awareness of this physical relationship. (Yet it is tacitly acknowledged in children's books such as *Pat the Bunny* and its successors, as well as in the kinesthetic pop-up books.) Feminist scholars have begun drawing attention to gendered constructions of writers and readers, but this research represents only one aspect of embodiment. The work with metaphors and schemas by Lakoff and Johnson and by Turner provide another piece of the puzzle. Philip Lieberman connects the evolution of language to biological adaptations of the tongue, mouth, and brain. Embodiment grounds our conceptual structures, our interactions with each other and with the environment, our perceptions, and our actions. Just recognizing that readers, writers, and texts are physically embodied, both in their structures and in their interactions is an important step, but it is not enough. To get a comprehensive understanding of composition, we need to understand how distribution, emergence, and embodiment are enacted through activities and practices in composing situations.

Enaction

Enaction is the principle that knowledge is the result of an ongoing interpretation that emerges through *activities* and *experiences* situated in specific environments. Lucy Suchman explains,

> The *situated* nature of learning, remembering, and understanding is a central fact. It may appear obvious that human minds develop in social situations, and that they use tools and representational media that culture provides to support, extend, and reorganize mental functioning. But cognitive theories of knowledge representation and educational practice, in school and in the workplace, have not been sufficiently responsive to questions about these relationships. And the need for responsiveness has become salient as computational media radically reshape the frontiers of individual and social action, and as educational achievement fails to translate into the effective use of knowledge. (xiii)

Jean Lave, Michael Murtaugh, and Olivia de la Rocha have studied the activity of "supermarket shopping," for instance, as an example of cognition in context; William G. Chase has studied how taxi drivers organize their knowledge of a city through their daily activities; Bruno Latour (*Science*) has studied scientific activity in laboratories. These are among many recent studies of situated activity, focusing on how cognition proceeds via the activities of participants in particular settings. But the concept of enaction goes beyond the notion of situated activity: Maturana and Varela define enaction as the principle that "every act of knowing brings forth a world" and "all knowing is doing" (*Autopoiesis* 26). In our perceptions, thoughts, and actions, we are constantly engaged in "bringing forth a world." What exactly does this mean? Two examples might help demonstrate this underlying basis for the concept of enaction. The first example looks at visual perception, and the second example expands on the first to look at special cases of "seeing."

While we might argue about the correlation between language and "reality out there" or about different classification schemes for what we perceive, we generally believe that visual perception itself is unproblematic: in our commonsense model of "seeing," our visual apparatus passively receives the sensory information already existing in a pregiven world. Anyone who happened to be standing in the same place would see the same things because that person would be receiving the same input (in the form of light waves) from the "real world."

In a fascinating study that challenges this model of vision, Oliver Sacks wrote about a man who had his sight restored through an operation at the age of fifty after having been blind since very early childhood. He had functioned well as a blind man, working as a masseur at a YMCA, living independently in an apartment, and getting along capably in the world. We might expect that the restoration of his sight would provide him with wonderful experiences in which the world in all its visual splendor would be instantly and miraculously revealed to him. However, this was not the case. In fact, seeing became a devastating burden for him. In the first place, he found that he had to "learn" how to see, even though his sight was fully restored in the physical sense. The world was a confusing mass of colors, light and shadow, and motion, which he was utterly unable to interpret. He could not establish edges and boundaries, so he had to learn, painstakingly, for each object, to distinguish unities: a chair, a cat, a tree. (We take this kind of "figure-ground" perception quite for granted.) A set of stairs represented an incomprehensible jumble of intersecting colors and lines; he had to be assisted in climbing them, not just the first time, but over and over again. He had no sense of depth or distance; when he entered a room, the furniture seemed to be rushing toward him at a frightening rate, and he couldn't navigate his way through it. Paintings in perspective or a football game on television were visually incomprehensible to him. He could not tell the difference between his cat and his dog except by closing his eyes and feeling them. Further, the projection of perspective was impossible for him; at every change of viewpoint, for example, a chair seemed an entirely different object. The cognitive effort of seeing exhausted him. Even worse were the expectations of his coworkers and friends; they assumed that he was fully functional "now that he could see." His work, once a source of deep satisfaction, now repulsed him as he became aware of the freckles, colors, and imperfections on the bodies of his clients.

This case demonstrates the remarkable degree of cognitive coordination we bring to the seemingly "natural" activity of seeing, and it reveals a great deal about our social and cultural expectations and assumptions about the nature of sight. Since much of this coordination is developed in infancy and very early childhood, we are unaware of the cognitive activity that is required simply to "see." It is not merely our interpretations of what we are seeing that are cognitively coordinated but the activity of seeing itself, as well as what is "seen." Vision is *enacted*—what we see is brought forth (*emerges*) through the coordination of our physical structure and our cognitive and physical activity.

Our vision is also socially and culturally coordinated, as Goodwin and Goodwin demonstrate in another example of enaction in visual perception. In "Professional Vision," they detail how novice archaeologists are socialized into their profession through activities in the field under the guidance of an experienced archaeologist. An important part of this process is learning how to "see like an archaeologist": to distinguish subtle differences in the color and texture of dirt, to discriminate changes in layers of dirt in an excavation, and to associate meanings with these distinctions. Goodwin and Goodwin refer to this process as establishing a "domain of scrutiny," which becomes the field of physical and social activities that creates a "disciplined way of seeing on the landscape they are investigating." They note,

> Through systematic discursive procedures encompassing talk, tools, and writing practices [archaeologists] are able to transform events in that landscape into the distinctive objects of knowledge that become the insignia of their profession: the theories, artifacts and bodies of expertise that are its special domain of competence and set it apart from other groups. The same is true for lawyers, doctors, and linguists, all of whom transform the events that become the objects of their concern into the forms of knowledge that animate the discourse of their profession. (2)

This transformation is not entirely unproblematic, however; in the same report, Goodwin and Goodwin describe how jurors in the first

Rodney King trial were socialized into a particular kind of "professional vision" through the meticulous efforts of police "experts," in which weapons became "tools" and an elaborate coding scheme for potential "aggression" justified police "escalation" or "de-escalation" of force. Millions of people saw the videotape of the incident, which was replayed many times on television, so theoretically they all "saw the same thing." Yet jurors in the case came to *see* the tape very differently as a result of this careful instruction in "expert vision." This example further refutes the simplistic model of vision as passive reception of a sensory stimulus and supports the argument that vision is a classic example of the principle of enaction. Although we are unaware of much of this activity, we are constantly and actively co-constructing our own sensory experiences in the world.

Now we must ask: What are the implications of enaction for our understanding of textual ecologies? Varela, Thompson, and Rosch suggest a possibility when they argue that cognitive capacities are "inextricably linked to histories that are *lived,* much like paths that exist only as they are laid down in walking."

> Yet another way to express this idea would be to say that cognition as embodied action is always about or directed toward something that is missing: on the one hand, there is always a next step for the *system* in its perceptually guided action; and on the other hand, the actions of the system are always directed toward *situations* that have yet to become actual. Thus cognition as embodied action both poses the problems and specifies those paths that must be tread or laid down for their solution. (205)

Texts are also "paths laid down in walking," and they too are always about or directed toward something that is missing (as Reznikoff's texts were "directed toward" his grandfather's missing poetry). In text composing we do not report on a pregiven world "out there" or "inside ourselves"; rather, we *bring forth* a textual world as we are writing it. And we dwell in that world and are defined by its creation as certainly as we dwell in the "real" world.

We might ask then: If enaction constitutes and defines ecological systems, and if we are to consider composing situations as ecological systems, what kinds of activities in composing situations are evidence of enaction? It seems to me that our present view of such activities is seriously impoverished. We conventionally posit composing situations as enacted in a very small set of practices, generally represented as "reading" and "writing." Recent ethnographic studies have enlarged this view to include the role of "talking." In our journals, we have discussed at length the practices of teaching writing, almost invariably in terms of the activities of writing, reading, and talking. We have discussed as well practices related to our institutional involvements, such as job hunting, seeking tenure, and presentations at professional conferences. But we have maintained, in general, a reductionist perspective on actual writing situations. I believe we need to look not more closely, but differently, at any ecological system of composing in order to discover the range and variety of the situated activities that both constitute and define it.

Our activities and practices as readers and writers generate effects in the environment, which includes other people; and, at the same time, the same environment is affecting our activities and practices. Enaction involves "capacities that are rooted in the structures of our biological embodiment but are lived and experienced within a domain of consensual action and cultural history," as Varela, Thompson, and Rosch put it. They add,

> If we are forced to admit that cognition cannot be properly understood without common sense, and that common sense is none other than our bodily and social history, then the inevitable conclusion is that knower and known, mind and world, stand in relation to each other through mutual specification or dependent coorigination. (149–50)

We can see enaction at work as writers interpret their experiences and ideas in texts that emerge from continuing activities and experiences with their environments, on computer screens, on legal pads, with keyboards, pens, and pencils as physical devices for inscription. Composing practices such as freewriting, invention heuristics, diagramming, outlining, sketching, and marking manuscripts for revision also structure the form and content of what is written. The emerging text begins to organize itself into a body, and through the interactive process of its composing, it also specifies its writer—we are shaped by the texts we create as surely as we shape them. The reader interacts with a text through time, in which meaning emerges and organizes itself, more or less coherently, in dialogue with the reader's mind: thus text and reader arise codependently. Sometimes, indeed, as Ornatowski has demonstrated in the writing of government contractors, readers (government officials) actually dictate the form and content of the text (contract proposals). Writers, readers, and texts develop and mutually specify each other in specific situations through physical, social, psychological, temporal, and spatial experience and activity; for this reason, we describe composing as an enactive process. We chat on the phone with a colleague, attend a conference and listen to presentations, construct an assignment for our students, read a journal article, exchange email with a professor in another field, write some notes on a legal pad, map out an outline, open a word-processing file, and choreograph finger movements on a keyboard with a peculiar arrangement of alphabetic keys. These are all situated activities, which derive their meanings from the specific contexts in which they occur.

I will not attempt to argue that the four attributes I have selected for discussion here—distribution, emergence, embodiment, and enaction—exhaust the possibilities for describing an ecology of composition; rather, these attributes are significant in current research across the disciplines that are engaged in studies of mind, language, and technology, and they have the potential to shed new light on our understanding of writers, readers, texts, and composing processes. But how is it that these attributes manifest themselves?

Dimensions of Complex Systems

To better understand how the attributes of distribution, emergence, embodiment, and enaction can be revealed in ecologies of composing, let's look at five analytical dimensions: physical-material, social, psychological, temporal, and spatial.

The physical-material dimension (including technology). Texts emerge through writers' and readers' physical interactions with material structures: pens, paper, computers, typewriters. Texts take physical form as print on paper in books, journals, log books, and illuminated electrons on the screens of computers. Writers and readers are physical beings, too: one of the reasons Hemingway preferred to type standing up was to relieve the pain from an old back injury. Writers physically interact with the instruments of writing in order to produce texts; readers physically interact with texts, not only through visually scanning, but by holding a book, using a keyboard or a mouse to scroll through a document, turning pages of a journal. Writers and readers stop writing or reading when they are hungry, thirsty, sleepy, or physically restless. They are sensitive to type that is too small, books that are too thick, margins that are too skimpy, screen fonts that are too hard to read, computer monitors that are too small, rooms that are too warm or too dim, and to many other physical features of the text or the environment that shape their interactions with the "content" of the text.[3]

The social dimension (inter-individual). The social dimensions of composing have been the focus of a great deal of recent attention, particularly through ethnographic studies such as Barbara Walvoord and Lucille McCarthy's study of college freshmen, Geoffrey Cross's study of collaborative writing in business, and Cesar Ornatowski's studies of textual collaborations between government agencies and contractors. Literary studies have a long tradition of research dealing with social milieus of writers, texts, and readers—new historicist explications of Shakespeare, feminist studies of popular women's fiction, and new interpretations of slave narratives, for example. In this study, the social dimension is not confined to interactions between individuals (such as between the writing instructor and a student) or groups (such as a discussion on a computer forum) but also encompasses a broad range of social structures, practices, and relationships, including cultural and political movements, literary traditions, and institutions.

The psychological dimension (intra-individual). A great deal of research attention—by researchers such as Linda Flower, John Hayes, Carl Bereiter, and Marlene Scardamalia—has focused on psychological aspects of both composing and reading. Thoughts and emotions are widely accepted as the source of writing and the determinant of its reception by readers. Our folk beliefs about writing depend heavily on psychological theories, which have given us concepts such as "writer's block," "problem solving," and "decision making" for describing individual experiences of composing. In fact, this dimension has dominated discussions of composing to such an extent that our assumptions about it have become almost invisible to us. Is writing really the result of simply transferring what's inside an individual's head onto paper? Students complain that they can't *think* of a topic, that they don't *know* enough to write about their subject; writers provide a heroic narrative to explain how they came up with a plot, or they offer psychoanalytic explanations for their inability to meet a deadline; readers despair over the difficulty they have grasping the ideas in a text. Recently, there have been attempts to bridge the psychological and the social dimensions of composing (Berkenkotter;

Brandt). This rapprochement demands an entirely new perspective on research agendas, methodologies, and modes of inquiry, however, and it remains to be seen whether it can be effected. Further, such a combined approach still neglects several important dimensions of composing. For example, as a discipline we have paid little attention to current research on the neurophysiology of attention, language recognition, and text comprehension.

The spatial dimension. Text composing has some unusual spatial properties. Texts are constructed across a bounded space—words on a page or a computer screen, on a billboard or a sign, even a single word scrawled in lipstick across a mirror. Texts fill books and take up space on bookshelves, in libraries, on computer disks, in bookstores, and in warehouses. But texts also cross unbounded spaces, unimagined and unpredictable spaces between their original construction sites and their readers: they are sent out by truck, by plane, by ship, and by computer networks, and, of course, they are passed from hand to hand, to destinations far from their makers. Their writers are situated in particular spaces—a familiar kitchen, an office, a library, a laboratory, a hillside—and so too are readers, who cross the space of the text word by word, sentence by sentence, like travelers in another land. Texts allow writers to travel where they may never go, and readers to be where they've never been. We speak of them as breaking new ground, covering a subject, taking us into familiar territory, as uphill reading; readers are engrossed in another world, far away, lost in the story, struggling over the rough spots, skipping around, or halfway through. These metaphors reflect some of the spatial dimensions of the relationship between writers, readers, and texts. And, like other forms of space, textual real estate usually entails a cost: there is a generative cost (paper, pencils, computers, software), a publication cost (print runs of books or journals, computer media, networks, CD-ROM publishing), and a cost for readers, as well. Sometimes this cost is explicit (books, subscriptions to journals, online charges), and sometimes it is masked ("free" access to the Internet for academics, review copies of textbooks, advertisements, government funding). A nontrivial cost for both writers and readers is temporal: the time consumed in preparing, composing, producing, distributing, seeking, and reading texts.

The temporal dimension. Composition theorists have recently embraced the concept that all discourse is historically and culturally situated. Beyond programmatic assertions, however, there has been little real development of the concept itself. Indeed, such statements tend to be both theoretically oversimplified and themselves ahistorical. That is, they serve to flatten the real historical dimensions of any event, activity, state, or process.

Hutchins points out that every person, collective, piece of structure in the environment, and activity has a distinct and different historical trajectory (*Cognition*). He projects these trajectories in three-dimensional space along three temporal axes, which we might term the social, the environmental or technological, and the unfolding activity itself.

Consider a routine event—in his example (*Cognition*), the navigation of a ship into a harbor. On the social axis, we might note that the career of a naval officer on a navigation team, for example, occurs typically on a scale from zero to thirty years. There will also be, at any given moment, several people on the navigation team at different loci on that scale, and the team itself has a history of interactions. Furthermore, the entire process is embedded in a cultural system, the navy, which has its own history dating back to earliest human attempts to navigate the seas. On the environmental/technological axis, we observe that some members of the team may use a piece of structure in the environment, such as a natural landmark, whose history evolves on a scale of thousands of years, but the task will also involve various man-made technological instruments and practices, some new and some older, whose usefulness spans perhaps hundreds of years. On the activity axis, people interact with these environmental structures and each other to accomplish a specific navigational task that unfolds over a few minutes or even seconds.

Many other social, technological, and environmental elements are involved, whether centrally or peripherally, in this navigation moment, each situated on its own historical trajectory. What is the historical situatedness of this complex ensemble? At any moment of observation, as Hutchins notes, we can only take a slice that captures the momentary position of participants but that cannot account for all of the dimensions of their historical relations. Such a view refutes the simplistic notion of "historical situatedness" as some sort of linear progression, an inevitable unfolding of sequences of large and small events, and argues instead for a more complex sense of a network of historical relations in dynamic interaction with each other.

This more complex sense of the historical dimensions of an activity has a direct application to the writing situation, in which relationships among writers, readers, and texts unfold over distinct historical trajectories in a landscape of historical relations—the emergence and reception of genres, styles, and topics; the politics of race, gender, and class; economic cycles; cultural trends; life cycles of writers and readers; particular writing tasks or reading episodes. For example, let's consider a writer engaged in a composing task and manipulating a piece of equipment, a personal computer, that would have been as unimaginable as a "personal space shuttle" even a few years ago and that could easily be superseded by some newer technology a few years from now. But the textual form or genre, such as a dissertation, for instance, might date back hundreds of years, to the development of the university system in Europe. The writer is a particular age—8, or 19, or 45, or 78—and this fact makes a difference not only in terms of the life experience, skills, and strategies for writing that the writer brings to the work but also in terms of how the text will be viewed by readers. The text has a certain lifetime, too: perhaps a few seconds if it is scrubbed out on the computer screen before it is printed, perhaps centuries if it is cherished and preserved. The style may become dated; the genre might fall out of fashion; universities could come to view dissertations as quaint relics of the past, or they could replace them with new forms—virtual-reality constructions, book or journal publications, or videos of candidates in action. There are intellectual and social trends as well: ethnographic studies come into favor, empirical studies fall from grace; women and minorities are celebrated, white males drop out of the spotlight; it's a good year for studies of composing in early childhood, it's a bad year for studies of college students revising; Bakhtin is in, Derrida is out. Meanwhile, the institutions in which all of this activity is embedded are themselves changing: budget crunches forcing the closure of whole departments; new disciplines emerging, gaining prestige, or falling from favor; publishers starting up or closing their doors; funding agencies shifting their priorities.

The five dimensions outlined here are not categories or classes of objects; they are five aspects of every object, process, fact, idea, concept, activity, structure, event, and so on. Thus, although we can distinguish these dimensions, they cannot be "separated out" because they are interdependently specified. As in geometry, single-dimension objects can only exist theoretically, in the imagination.

Each of the four attributes mentioned above shares the properties of the five dimensions, so we can speak of the distribution of cognition (or text composing) across physical, social, psychological, spatial, and temporal dimensions. Further, each of the properties can be deployed across all four attributes. For example, the social dimensions of composition are distributed, embodied, emergent, and enactive (see fig. 1).

These dimensions and attributes can be observed at every level of scale, from neuronal structures and processes in the brain to population genetics, geophysics, and global economics; in composition studies, from a poet's tiny editorial correction on a draft of a poem to a global literary movement—poststructuralism, feminism, hermeneutics.

Much research in complex systems theories has used the formal language and modeling of mathematics to express and validate concepts in the field. I am not arguing for a mathematical approach to composing, but I *am* trying to get at complexities in ecological systems that have not been addressed by theorists in rhetoric and composition. This may be why so many existing theories are so unsatisfactory and partial. Typically, composition research has posited a triangle of writer, text, and audience and has tended to single out the writer, the text, or the audience as the focus of analysis. Once, rhetoric and composition theories focused on text features alone, tropes, modes, argumentation, coherence, transitions, and so on; texts were artifacts. Other than the related issues of reaching one's "audience," usually considered as a purely textual exercise, there was little theoretical consideration of the psychological, social, temporal, or physical dimensions of writing.

	Physical	Social	Psycho-logical	Spatial	Temporal
Distribution					
Embodiment					
Emergence					
Enaction					

Fig. 1. An ecological matrix

In the 1970s, Janet Emig, Sondra Perl, Nancy Sommers, and others introduced the concept of writing as a process, foregrounding the temporal dimension in which composing unfolds not only as specific writing tasks are accomplished, but also over the longer-term developmental stages of writers. Later, in the 1980s, Linda Flower, John Hayes, and others introduced theories from psychology into composition studies, foregrounding the psychological dimension. In their cognitive models of composing processes, writers draw on long-term and short-term memory as they make plans, solve problems, and develop goals and strategies for writing and revising a text.

At about the same time, ethnographic projects by Donald Graves, Lucy McCormick Calkins, Lee Odell and Dixie Goswami, Shirley Brice Heath, and others began to illuminate the social dimension of writing, acknowledging the importance of social interactions and structures in composing, and arguing for the significance of collaborative writing. Recent ethnographic studies of classrooms and other composing situations (Chiseri-Strater; Walvoord and McCarthy), studies of co-construction of texts (Gere; Lunsford and Ede), and case studies of "real-world" writing (Doheny-Farina and Odell; Odell and Goswami; Ornatowski) have complicated the picture, introducing into the triangle an additional member, often referred to as *context* or *culture*. The construction of context or culture, in much of this research seems, however, primarily social; there is little discussion of the material or physical world as a significant component of composing activity.

There are hopeful signs that our discipline is growing aware of the need to enlarge its sphere of inquiry. In "The Ecology of Writing," Marilyn Cooper quotes Richard C. Lewontin, the biologist:

> All organisms—but especially human beings—are not simply the results but are also the causes of their own environments. . . . While it may be true that at some instant the environment poses a problem or challenge to the organism, in the process of response to that challenge the organism alters the terms of its relation to the outer world and recreates the relevant aspects of that world. The relation between organism and environment is not simply one of interaction of internal and external factors, but of a dialectical development of organism and milieu in response to each other. (368)

In spite of the promise in Cooper's title and the Lewontin quote, however, the ecology of writing in the article is still rather sketchy and limited to social interactions via ideas, purposes, interpersonal interactions, cultural norms, and textual forms.

Until very recently, in fact (e.g., see Haas, *Writing*), there has been surprisingly little attention directed to the physical, material circumstances of writing, although Michael Davidson argues persuasively for the value of such study through, for example, research in archives on poetic drafts and manuscripts. Davidson points out that the archive "returns a quality of voice and physicality to work which may seem, in its published version, hermetic and isolated" (317). And finally, researchers such as Cynthia Selfe, Gail Hawisher, Andrea Herrmann, Paul LeBlanc, Stuart Moulthrop, George Landow, and others studying computers and composition have drawn attention to some aspects of the physical dimensions of writing using new technologies. Martin Rosenberg, Paul Taylor, William Paulson, and Katherine Hayles have for some time explored chaos and complexity theory in relation to literary theory and to some extent composing situations. But we do not yet have a comprehensive theory of composing as an ecological system of interrelated structures and processes that are at once physically or materially, socially, psychologically, temporally, and spatially emerging in codependent activities.

It seems that composition researchers, even those working with collaborative composing, are still constrained by some common cultural assumptions about mind, language, and society. Central to these assumptions is the idea of cognition as uniquely the property of individuals, as computational activity of the brain. Second is the assumption that language represents thought, which somehow precedes it. Third is the assumption that a group can be treated simply as a gathering of individuals, who make individual plans, decisions, contributions, and "moves" in enacting the group process. Fourth is the assumption that text composing can somehow be isolated from the physical and material conditions of its production and use. A collateral assumption is that we can understand composing atomistically, as distinct entities (texts, individual writers, genres, strategies, tasks, decisions, problems, and "processes"), rather than as an ecological system with a high degree of integration among its components.

This study presents a challenge to current assumptions about the nature of composing. Working with concepts developed by Ed Hutchins, Jean Lave, Bruno Latour, John Holland, Stuart Kauffman, Lucy Suchman, Francisco Varela, Evan Thompson, and Eleanor Rosch, I argue that composing, like many other human cognitive processes, is irreducibly social and inextricably embedded in specific environments that are not merely supportive of but integral to the processes of thinking, writing, and reading. Further, I argue that our goals for improving or even understanding reading, writing, and thinking cannot be achieved without a careful consideration of the ecological systems within which these practices occur.

Pat Churchland, a philosopher of science, has raised an interesting issue for theorists of complex systems. When asked whether it is reasonable to think of the human brain as a complex dynamical system, she replied, "It's obviously true. But so what? Then what is your research program?" (qtd. in Lewin 164). For composition theorists, this challenge presents itself as two related questions: How can we determine whether theories of complex systems are relevant to composing? And if they are relevant, what is our research program? This book suggests both the possibilities and the necessity for such research.

New technologies, while they have expanded the horizons for discourse, have also made manifest the inadequacy of our present approaches to composition. Ethnographic methods are confounded by the time and distances involved in highly interactive computer communication. Discourse analysis is tailored to conversation, but analysis of turn-taking, timing of pauses, and interruptions is impossible with email discussions. Revisions are no longer necessarily separate drafts with handwritten corrections, but fluid processes of change, including correction, deletion, and elaboration on the computer screen. Electronic manuscripts have elastic properties of font size and style, margins, footnotes, and other features that make it difficult even to establish an authoritative text for analysis. Since our present analytical approaches are inadequate to the task of understanding new technologies for composing and communication and their transformational impact on cognition and culture, our best hope of developing new analytical approaches lies in careful observation and interpretation of the discourse as people are presently using it in a wide range of applications, in classrooms and corporations, in campuses and laboratories, in government agencies, and in commercial information services.

We need to discover who and what are the agents interacting in an ecology of composition; how these agents organize themselves into a more or less coherent whole—a word, a sentence, a poem, a literary genre, a collaborative writing group, a movement such as "romanticism" or "modernism"; how they situate themselves; how they interpret their environments; and how they use their interpretations to engage in purposeful activities and interactions. And specifically, we need to gain a better understanding of how composing systems are distributed, embodied, emergent, and enactive across physical, social, psychological, temporal, and spatial dimensions.

Among the problems with attempting to enlarge the unit of analysis beyond the individual, the unit with which we are so familiar, is that such a change confronts us with a seemingly overwhelming amount of information. Ethnography presents researchers with a dramatic example of this predicament: among the vast mass of collected observations, interviews, notes, and interpretations, how does one sort out the telling details from the inconsequential? It is no use saying that all details are significant; time, space, and writers' and readers' patience are finite. As a discipline, we have not yet developed a useful method for recognizing, sorting, classifying, recording, or interpreting significant features that emerge from the complexity of the context in which they occur.[4] Further, we have not developed a generally accepted (even within our own discipline) means of moving beyond descriptions of complex writing situations toward explanation. Until we are able to do so, our status as a discipline is open to question. Such a project is beyond the scope of a single book, of course. I can only sketch out here some of the dimensions of the task and argue for its importance and urgency.

Our view of composing has been greatly simplified as a consequence of our methodological procedures. In the process, however, we have simply dropped out some rather large and complex components that may be significant for our understanding of what is involved in actual composing situations. As contexts and technologies for writing continue to change at an ever accelerating pace, we cannot cling to our familiar, comfortable assumptions about writers, readers, and texts, or we will find ourselves increasingly irrelevant and even obstructive. We must not only develop new instruments and new tools for analysis; we must also develop entirely new disciplinary ways of seeing, thinking, and sharing knowledge. In the process of reconstructing our disciplinary thinking, there will be many failed attempts, blind alleys, wrong turns, and bloody battles, but the alternatives are worse.

In the chapters that follow, we will look more closely at the four attributes of an ecology of composition mentioned above, distribution, emergence, embodiment, and enaction, by examining specific writing situations, while keeping in mind the central question: What can we learn about readers, writers, and texts by considering composing as an ecological system?

2
Thinking with the Things
As They Exist: Ecology of a Poem

Writing occurs which is the detail, not mirage,
of seeing, of thinking with the things as they exist.
—Louis Zukofsky

Introduction

In this chapter, we look at the ecology of composing from the point of view of the text. In doing so, we are not attempting to separate texts from their readers, writers, or environments. Instead, we are examining the attributes of texts within the context of an ecological system, looking specifically at the structures and processes by which texts are distributed, embodied, emergent, and enactive, and using a particular text as an example. The chapters that follow build on this analysis, using different writing situations as examples and focusing in turn on writers and readers to further illustrate the concept of an ecology of composing.

The Context of the Texts

The text that concerns us here is a selection from a much longer autobiographical poem titled "Early History of a Writer," first published by the objectivist poet Charles Reznikoff in 1969, in a collection titled *By the Well of Living and Seeing and the Fifth Book of the Maccabees.* "Early History" is drawn from a prose manuscript titled "Notes for an Autobiography." The manuscript and several annotated drafts of the poem, as well as other manuscripts and letters relevant to the poem are held in the Archive for New Poetry (Reznikoff, MSS 9). Selections from "Notes for an Autobiography" were originally published in 1963 as an "autobiographical novel" titled *Family Chronicle,* described by Reznikoff in a letter to his wife, Marie, as "a presentation of three major characters, my mother, my father and myself, a period in American Jewish history, and the pilgrimage among the changing circumstances of the world" (Syrkin 47–48). It is telling that Reznikoff, the "solitary" poet, centers his "autobiography" on three major figures rather than on the conventional one.

"Early History of a Writer" presents sections of the prose manuscript that were not incorporated into *Family Chronicle,* including the passage that concerns us here. The subject of the entire poem is the poet's life from his early childhood until the end of World War I, the story of a boy growing up in New York City, the child of Russian Jewish immigrants who had fled the czar and found work in New York's garment trade at the turn of the century. The passage describes a significant family event: the arrival of the boy's grandparents from Russia. As told through the young boy's eyes, the incident is as clearly rendered as a snapshot in the family album.

> When my grandfather was about fifty, he fell sick,
> and my grandparents thought it best to go to America
> where my father and their other children were.
> My father went to the pier to bring his parents to our home
> and could hardly recognize his father—
> the face was swollen
> and the man could hardly move his hands and feet.
> I had been watching from the window
> and my brother and I ran downstairs
> to meet them. My father turned to my grandfather
> and said: "These are my sons."
> My grandfather looked at us with his bleary eyes,
> whose rims were red,
> and turning to my father murmured in Hebrew
> what the patriarch Jacob had said to his son Joseph:
> "I did not think to see your face
> and God has shown me your sons also,"
> and, putting his swollen hands slowly on my head,
> began to bless me. Even as he did so,
> my grandmother who was standing beside him
> poked him in the ribs and said sharply in Yiddish:
> "Well?"
> My grandfather hurriedly brought the blessing to a close.
> Shoving his fist into his pocket he took out a gold coin
> and put it in the hand I had stretched out to greet him.
> "No, no," I said
> and would have given the coin back,
> for I had been brought up to think it disgraceful
> to take money from my elders: the purpose of the instruction

was that I should not ask for pennies,
as ill-bred children did; in good Talmudical style
the prohibition was wider than the evil.
But this time my father smiled and said:
"Keep it—to remember your grandfather by."
As they went into the house,
I stopped to glance at the coin
and saw the monstrous eagle of czarist Russia,
with two open beaks,
from which my father and mother and so many others had fled.

(*Complete Poems* II: 146–47)

Here is an excellent example for our purposes, presenting serious challenges for a theory of texts as distributed, embodied, emergent, and enactive within ecological systems of composing. The most common objection to ecological approaches to cognition, often marshaled in support of individualist approaches, raises the question of undeniable "genius." This passage, then, allows us to test the explanatory power of an ecological approach against paradigmatic individualist assumptions about literary "genius." There is little doubt about the authenticity of the poetic passage. It offers itself as a single text, written by a singular poet, describing a specific scene drawn from his own memory, for the solitary appreciation of an individual reader. Because Reznikoff is very nearly contemporary, we are not far removed from his life and times. We have ample documentary evidence in the Archive for New Poetry of his letters, his drafts of this text, and other papers, including writings by his father and his mother.

Further, he is viewed by critics and biographers as a prototypical solitary soul, who spent hours walking alone in the city, poring over law cases and old records, and keeping very much to himself as he composed his poems, novels, histories, and plays. While he had friends, even other poets, he did not seem to associate with an artistic community of like-minded writers. He declined to adapt himself to his family's wishes, a professional law career's demands, or the conventions of marriage so that he could pursue, with single-minded commitment, his poetic calling. Reznikoff seems as unlikely a candidate for the concept of "an ecology of composition" as any artist we might find and perhaps one of the closest to the romantic image of the solitary poet. Certainly he had influences, our literary concession to the extra-individual dimensions of composing, but they are only seen as shadows in the background of his singular achievements. How can we reconcile this image of the solitary poet with current research in composition claiming that "all writing is socially constructed?"[1]

One way to reconcile these seemingly contradictory views is to look closely at this passage to discover exactly how it is embedded in an ecology of composition and, in the process, discover how its composing was distributed, embodied, emergent, and enactive.

The Context of the Writers

The poetic passage above was written by Charles Reznikoff, a man often described by his own wife, his biographers, and his admirers as a classic example of the solitary poet.[2] Reznikoff was born in 1894 in the Jewish ghetto of Brownsville, in Brooklyn, New York. His parents, Sarah Yetta and Nathan Reznikoff, had emigrated from Russia to escape the oppressive political and social conditions for Jews during the late 1800s. They found work making wrappers (housedresses) in the garment district of New York's Lower East Side, work that was physically exhausting and economically precarious and unrewarding. Eventually, Sarah learned to make hats and started a millinery business, which soon included her husband and her brother. The Artistic Millinery Company became fairly successful before a disastrous loft fire and lengthy lawsuit with the insurance company ruined the business and left the family once again impoverished.

Charles was an extremely bright child who graduated from grammar school at the age of twelve and high school at the age of fifteen. He had started writing poetry when he was about thirteen or fourteen, and by the time he graduated from high school, he was determined to become a writer (Sternburg and Ziegler). While in high school, he had also begun his lifelong practice of taking long walks about the city, jotting poetry and observations in a notebook he carried. After he graduated, Reznikoff enrolled in the new school of journalism at the University of Missouri but found that "journalism is most interested in news and in the second degree writing—and I was only interested in writing, I wasn't at all interested in news" (Sternburg and Ziegler 127).

Reznikoff returned home after one year and worked for his father for a year before enrolling in New York University (NYU) Law School ("a poor man's law school," as he put it), where he graduated second in his class three years later, at the age of twenty-two. He practiced law unenthusiastically for a few months (attracting only "the kind of cases that others wouldn't take because there's no money in it"

[Sternburg and Ziegler 127]); then the First World War gave him a perfect excuse to give up the practice of law and apply to officer's training camp at Columbia.

Meanwhile, he had sent some of his poems off to *Poetry* magazine, where Harriet Monroe selected some for publication and rejected others, yet after one year she still had not published any. He decided to print his poems privately, in a collection entitled *Rhythms*. He liked the independence of privately printing his work so much that he continued to print and publish it this way throughout his life.

The war ended before he saw any action, and when he returned, he did not resume his law practice but worked instead for his father as a salesman; he found that this work left his mind free for writing. Later, during the Depression, he worked for *Corpus Juris,* analyzing and summarizing law cases for this legal encyclopedia. At the age of thirty-six, he married Marie Syrkin, a high school teacher who was later to become a distinguished professor at Brandeis University. The couple became friends with George Oppen and Louis Zukofsky, poets who shared a commitment to Ezra Pound's imagist poetics and his sense of objectivism. Together with William Carlos Williams, a friend of Louis Zukofsky, they formed the Objectivist Press. Marie maintained that, although the objectivists are often described as a school or a movement, their relationships were in fact more complex, and their aesthetic practices were hardly uniform:

> Though they all shared the same literary values, scrupulous fidelity to the subject or idea, in practice each interpreted these values in his individual fashion, as a comparison of Zukofsky and Reznikoff would indicate. Yet Zukofsky greatly admired Charles who was as transparent as Zukofsky was intricate. Whether the Objectivists should be characterized as a movement or more simply as a cooperative of poets who shared the same literary ideals and who sought to circumvent the uncertainties of commercial publication is debatable. (Syrkin 43)

Reznikoff himself commented, when asked about his conversations with Oppen and Zukofsky on objectivist poetics,

> Well, I hate to take any aura from our talks as I remember them, if they have any to begin with, but we talked about something quite practical. We couldn't get our poetry accepted by regular publishers, so we thought it would be nice if we organized our own publishing firm, with each of us paying for the printing of his own book. We picked the name Objectivist because we had all read Poetry of Chicago and we agreed completely with all that Pound was saying. We didn't really discuss the term

itself; it seemed all right—pregnant. It could have meant any number of things. (Dembo 101)

The Objectivist Press published three of Reznikoff's books during the 1930s, as well as the work of Louis Zukofsky, George Oppen, and Ezra Pound. But it was a work by William Carlos Williams that attracted the most critical attention, with a review on the second page of the *New York Times Book Review,* resulting in sales of nearly all of the five hundred copies printed (101).

In 1938, Reznikoff was offered a job in Hollywood by an old friend, Albert Lewin, but his two-year stay was singularly undistinguished: he was paid a pittance (by Hollywood standards) of seventy-five dollars a week and given minimal responsibilities. When he returned to New York, he decided to abandon further efforts to find a job and concentrate on writing full time. This decision created tension in his marriage; and in 1950, when Marie was appointed to the English Department at Brandeis in Massachusetts, they separated and lived apart for seventeen years. However, they continued to work together on a journal called the *Jewish Frontier,* after Marie arranged for Charles to get a job there, and Charles continued to share his writing with her. In 1966, when Marie retired from Brandeis, they reunited in New York and lived there until Charles's death from a heart attack in 1976 (Syrkin).

The Context of the Readers

Throughout his life, Reznikoff had sustained his poetic mission through difficult times by a patchwork of jobs chosen to provide him the time and energy to pursue his writing. His work was warmly appreciated by a small but distinguished audience of fellow poets, by some influential critics, and by the everyday people about whom he wrote (Shapiro; Weinberger). He published his own work until 1929, when his collection of poetry titled *By the Waters of Manhattan* attracted the notice of the publisher Charles Boni. In 1930, Boni published Reznikoff's autobiographical novel by the same title. The novel was very well received by reviewers, and Reznikoff began to attract critical attention, which was strengthened by Zukofsky's influence and admiration.

He wrote novels, plays, and historical accounts, as well as the poetry that was his main interest. Among his most arresting works are *Family Chronicle,* an autobiographical account of his parents' lives and his own life in New York's garment district, published in 1963; the massive two-volume *Testimony: The United States 1885–1890, Recitative* (1965), and *Testimony: The United States 1891–1900, Recitative* (1968); and *Holocaust* (1975). In both *Testimony* and *Holocaust* he adopted an unusual poetic approach: after sifting through thousands of pages of legal records of court cases, he would select a particular case or episode and strip away what he considered extraneous, leaving the bare bones of a story in its original, but pared-down words. Then he would provide line breaks to create poems from this original wording. While *Testimony* focuses on legal records from the early days of the United States, *Holocaust* is drawn from testimony at the Nuremberg trials and the Karl Adolf Eichmann trial. The result is harrowing and pitiless, and at the time the books appeared, neither the public nor the critics were appreciative (Hindus). Even Marie said, "Though the stark style of *Testimony* won a number of distinguished and discerning admirers I confess that a little *Testimony* went a long way with me. Like any Philistine I saw it in the main as chopped up prose" (Syrkin 64). After its publication, Reznikoff was once again reduced to self-publishing his work until 1962, when New Directions issued a volume of his selected verse, *By the Waters of Manhattan*. Finally, at the age of sixty-eight, he began to receive recognition from a much wider audience. Throughout his lifetime and afterwards, Reznikoff's work has continued to attract new admirers and exert a powerful influence on poets from contemporaries and near-contemporaries, such as Lorine Neidecker, Carl Rakosi, George Oppen, and Louis Zukofsky, to recent poets, such as Allen Ginsberg, Robert Creeley, and Lyn Hejinian.

The Critical Problem

The theme of solitude is recurrent in much that has been written about Reznikoff. Hindus returns to this concept often in descriptions of the poet: "The refusal to become competitive also explains his delight in the discovery of writing, which for him from the beginning was a solitary activity." He closes his introduction to *Charles Reznikoff: Man and Poet* by reiterating the mythology of the writer as solitary genius.

> Emerson once noted that the best writers of any age often seem to have the briefest biographies, because the genius "draws up the ladder after him" and the world, which had consigned him to relative obscurity during his lifetime, "sees the works and asks in vain for a history." What-

ever judgment is ultimately passed upon Charles Reznikoff, not much more than his works is ever likely to become known of him. The record which he wished to be preserved is the one made by himself, and it will have to suffice for the curiosity of those rare readers who have learned to treasure his works and his memory. (33)

Mary Oppen, wife of the objectivist poet George Oppen, concurred. She talked of how they would meet Charles on Saturdays to walk along the Hudson River: "We walked to Astoria, again Charles knew of a good cafeteria where we ate. I wonder, did he always feed us not knowing what else we might like? We'd have appreciated talk about his poetry, about the world of poetry that was, uniquely and in a solitary way, his" (Oppen 80).

Reznikoff's wife, Marie Syrkin, also contributed to the prevailing individualist image of the poet. After discussing their friendships with Louis Zukofsky and Mary and George Oppen, she remarked, "Though we had a small social circle, Charles was essentially a solitary figure" (Syrkin 43). Even Reznikoff himself wrote,

> A hundred generations, yes, a hundred and twenty-five,
> had the strength each day
> not to eat this and that (unclean!)
> not to say this and that,
> not to do this and that (unjust!),
> and with all this and all that
> to go about
> as men and Jews
> among their enemies. . . .
> But I am private as an animal.
>
> I have eaten whatever I liked,
> I have slept as long as I wished,
> I have left the highway like a dog
> to run into every alley . . .
>
> (*Complete Poems* II: 25)

The contrast between traditional social structures and the solitude of the poet is strongly marked here, as it is in much of Reznikoff's work, reinforcing both the romantic model of the artist as individual genius outside of social conventions and Reznikoff's image as a solitary figure, walking, thinking, and writing about what he witnesses. Among our most cherished folk beliefs is the concept of the literary work as a clearly bounded object, the product of a solitary individual whose genius is immutable and largely independent of social, environmental, or physical influences. Recent critical theories have occasionally succeeded in displacing the focus onto the reader or onto the literary critic; but here again, the individual remains the unit of analysis for textual production and reception. Literary biographies, literary movements, academic disciplines, composition and rhetoric courses, commercial publishing, and writers themselves help sustain this model of the solitary literary genius, a model that instantiates the larger cultural bias toward individualism. Even when we acknowledge the significance of social context, textual collaborations, material conditions, and historical events, for example, we still maintain our individualistic assumptions about literary writers, readers, and texts. It is clear that any attempt to apply theories of complex systems to such a powerful cultural schema is a real test of their robustness. How can we possibly explain literary works as embedded in ecological systems in which they are distributed, embodied, emergent, and enactive?

Distribution and the Poem

Science and literature have shared a common romantic belief in individual cognition. Hagiographic accounts of scientific geniuses and their solitary achievements as well as brilliant authors and their individual creative oeuvres abound. However, Ludwik Fleck's long-unappreciated book, *Genesis and Development of a Scientific Fact* (1935), contesting this notion in the evolution of medical knowledge, has in recent years been joined by a substantial literature on the collective construction of knowledge in science, including important contributions from Thomas Kuhn, Robert Merton, Philip Kitcher, Bruno Latour, and Edwin Hutchins. Indeed, this concept has become something of a commonplace in the sciences, while the humanities and the social sciences have tended to cling adamantly to the romantic view privileging individual thought. B. Chandrasekaran observes,

> It is easy to conceive of distributed computing in the case of what are evidently communities of individual processors, such as ants building hills, armies, corporations, or the scientific community. What is less obvious is the utility of this conception in understanding the information processing of an individual human being. (4)

We are wedded, it seems, to the individual as the unit of analysis, and it is difficult to imagine how to expand our concept of mind and text beyond that boundary. Yet, it is clear that this individualistic model is inadequate to explain how "thinking gets done" or "text gets composed." What exactly does it mean to describe a text or a composing situation as "distributed"? Jerome Bruner offers one explanation:

> As Roy Pea, David Perkins, and others now put it, a "person's" knowledge is not just in one's own head, in "person solo," but in the notes that one has put into accessible notebooks, in the books with underlined passages on one's shelves, in the handbooks one has learned how to consult, in the information sources one has hitched up to the computer, in the friends one can call up to get a reference or a "steer," and so on almost endlessly. All of these, as Perkins points out, are parts of the knowledge flow of which one has become a part. And that flow even includes those highly conventionalized forms of rhetoric that we use for justifying and explaining what we are doing, each tailored to and "scaffolded" by the occasion of use. Coming to know anything, in this sense, is both situated and (to use the Pea–Perkins term) distributed. To overlook this situated-distributed nature of knowledge and knowing is to lose sight not only of the cultural nature of knowledge but of the correspondingly cultural nature of knowledge acquisition. (106)

What are the implications of such a perspective for the study of text composing? In looking at a text, we might consider what agents are involved in constructing the text; what physical, material, or technological structures in the environment are integral to its production; what kinds of processes and interactions are involved; and how the text is distributed. In other words, how is the generation of the text distributed across our five dimensions: the physical, the psychological, the social, the spatial, and the temporal?

We encounter Reznikoff's poetic passage about his grandfather's arrival on pages 146–47 of a book titled *Poems 1918–1975: The Complete Poems of Charles Reznikoff,* published in 1989 by Black Sparrow Press, and edited by Seamus Cooney. This paperback volume was designed by Barbara Martin and printed for Black Sparrow Press by Graham Mackintosh and Edwards Brothers, Inc. The quoted passage begins in the fifth stanza of the eighth section of a long (pp. 137–78) poem titled "Early History of a Writer." But this is not the first appearance of this poem. It had first appeared in print in 1969 in a volume titled *By the Well of Living and Seeing and the Fifth Book of the Maccabees,* published by Charles Reznikoff in New York and revised, expanded, and reprinted in 1973. But before it was printed, it underwent several drafts, typewritten by Charles Reznikoff and meticulously revised in minute handwritten corrections and additions. And if we look further back, the text undergoes a startling transformation: before it took shape as a poem, it was typed as prose, as part of a manuscript titled "Notes for an Autobiography," with handwritten marks added to the typescript to indicate poetic line breaks. So far, we have implicated a poet, an editor, a designer, a publishing house, two printers (at least), and an undetermined number of distributors and booksellers, without even considering the tools, vehicles, presses, typewriters, and other equipment, in the construction of this passage. But even if we ignore the "nonpoetic" members of this ensemble and cast our net just a little wider and a little farther back, we discover a still earlier set of manuscripts, which contain elements taken up in the poetic passage describing the arrival from Russia of Charles Reznikoff's grandparents (Reznikoff, MSS 9). And here the text takes another surprising leap—in authorship. One of these manuscripts was typed, in prose, and it appears to be an English translation of an autobiographical account written by Charles Reznikoff's father, Nathan. The original for this typescript is a manuscript of several hundred pages handwritten in Yiddish on the back of stationery for the Artistic Millinery Company, the family business. Another set of handwritten manuscripts was apparently produced by Charles Reznikoff's mother, Sarah, interspersing formal exercises of letterwriting with episodes of her life story as she painstakingly taught herself to read and write English. If we take our investigation even further back, we leap from New York to Russia, include yet another author, and encounter a set of texts that are meaningful in their absence: Sarah's father, Ezekiel, had written poetry in Hebrew for some thirty years while traveling as a salesman in Russia. When he died, far from home, his belongings, including his poems, were shipped home in a trunk. As Sarah reports in *Family Chronicle,*

> Mother opened it, and on top she found a bundle of long sheets of paper, carefully wrapped. They were covered with verse in Hebrew, and Abram was the only one of us who could read it at all. Father had been somewhat free in his speech, and Mother was afraid there might be something Nihilistic in his writing that would get us all into trouble. She was afraid to ask an outsider what the writing was about. In those days it was enough to say of a family, "They are Nihilists," to have them arrested at once; the police investigated at their leisure. There was too much to burn at one time, so Mother burnt a few sheets every morning until all were gone. As she put the first into the fire she said, "Here's a man's life." (56)

This incident is retold in Reznikoff's poetry and fiction, and it came up often in interviews. He attributed his "predisposition" for poetry to it, and it probably accounts for his determination to publish his own work and distribute it. (He put a printing press in his parents' basement, printed his own books, and sent copies of every volume to the British Museum.) Certainly his mother must have told Reznikoff this story in his early childhood, and it undoubtedly contributed to his determination to become a poet himself.

So we begin in the grandparents' generation with absence and loss of texts, and with reunion in other texts; the trail goes no further back. Sarah's autobiographical manuscript was probably written sometime before 1929, when Charles Reznikoff first published an edited version of his mother's story in *By the Waters of Manhattan: An Annual*. By then Reznikoff had already been writing and publishing his poems for eleven years. He published his edited version of his father's autobiography in 1936 as *Early History of a Sewing Machine Operator*. In the unpublished sections of their manuscripts, both Sarah and Nathan mention the incident of the arrival of Nathan's par-

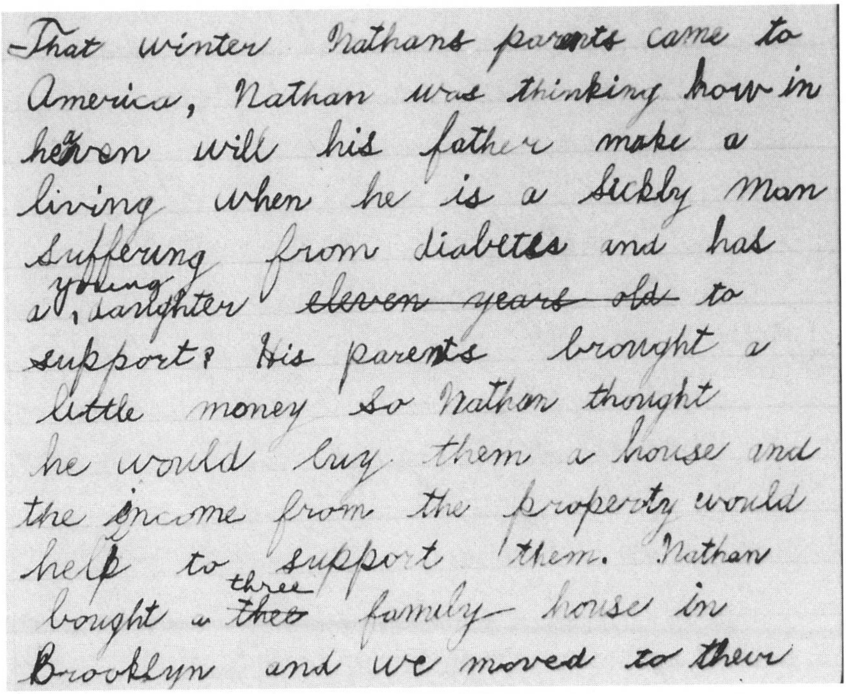

Fig. 2. A page from Sarah Reznikoff's manuscript

ents from Russia described in Reznikoff's poetic passage above. I have written extensively elsewhere about these manuscripts (Syverson, "Community," "Sarah Reznikoff") so I discuss them only briefly here, to characterize the complexity of their intertextual relationships. Sarah's description of the arrival of Nathan's parents is brief (see fig. 2).

> That winter Nathans parents came to America, Nathan was thinking how in heaven will his father make a living when he is a sickly man suffering from diabetes and has a young daughter to support? His parents brought a little money so Nathan thought he would buy them a house and the income from the property would help to support them.

Nathan's version is much longer, rich with allusions to biblical stories, emotional expression, and poetic diction.

> He didn't recognize me nor did I him. His looks were terrible—swollen up that he hardly moved with his hands or feet—A changed man—nothing remained from that beautiful man I had left with 14 years back. The impression that it made on me I could only express in a stream of tears.

When he brings his parents home, he mentions that Sarah and the children, and also his sisters and brothers-in-law, were waiting.

> When we came over to the house and my boys noticed through the window our approach, they ran down the stairs to meet us. I said to my father "Father, those are my sons." He smiled to them and became serious. He lifted his eyes and said to me in Hebrew [sentence x'd out] "To see your face I had not hoped, and lo God has shown me thy seed." [A reference to the story of Jacob and Joseph in the Bible.]

He then makes a longer speech blessing the boys "in the name of my fathers, Abraham, Isaac, and Jacob." Nathan comments, "This scene looked so noble and sacred and it was said with such earnestness that it seemed like Jacob of old himself said it to the children of Joseph." The moment is so moving for Nathan that he writes, "This day the yoke of a livelihood was not in my thoughts. My head was occupied with other thoughts. My heart was full with such feelings that I am not able to express."

Reznikoff typed Sarah's manuscript and edited it, as I mentioned, for publication; however, the incident of the grandparents' arrival is not mentioned in the published version of *By the Waters of Manhattan* (1929). Nathan's manuscript was written in Yiddish and then typed in an English translation, which was probably a collaboration between

Charles and Nathan. Again, the grandparents' arrival does not appear in the version of Nathan's memoirs published in *Early History of a Sewing Machine Operator*.

The next appearance of the incident is in Charles's manuscript "Notes for an Autobiography," apparently begun sometime in the 1940s while Charles was working in Hollywood (see fig. 3).

But the incident does not appear in *Family Chronicle*, where, in 1963, Charles published his mother's account and his father's account

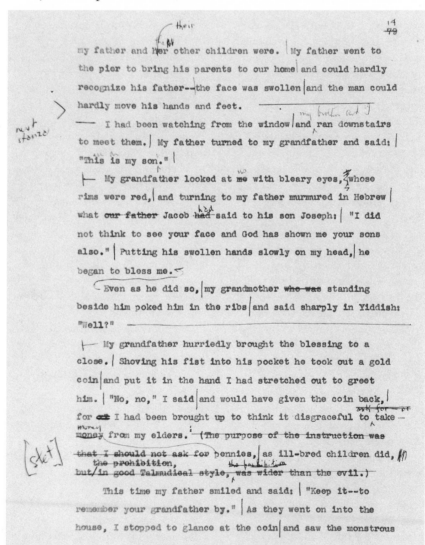

Fig. 3. A page from Charles Reznikoff's manuscript, "Notes for an Autobiography"

Fig. 4. A comparison of Nathan's and Charles's narratives

Nathan's Account	Charles's Account
At the time that we moved downtown my parents made a bigger move. They left Russia and went to America. . . . the letter that we received a few days before they arrived explained to us the reason of their decision—as all their older children were already in America, they only remained with the baby, a girl of about 10 yrs. old, and my father was sick on diabetes, they thought that he wouldn't last very long, my mother feared God knows what could happen to her too—it might be a pogrom or some other thing that takes away strong people unexpectedly—then who will take care of the child, who will bring her up; and my father carried around a thought that there is one thing that he asks of God—that once before he dies he should be able to see his children— then he would be satisfied to die peacefully. . . . I recognized my mother. The little sister whom I had never known didn't interest me very much. It is possible because my whole interest was in my father. He didn't recognize me nor did I him. His looks were terrible—swollen up that he hardly moved with his hands or feet—A changed man—nothing remained from that beautiful man whom I had left with 14 years back. . . . By the time we came home I calmed myself. Sarah Edith and the children, also my sisters and my brother-in-laws were waiting impatiently for the welcome guest. When we came over to the house and my boys noticed through the window our approach, they ran down the stairs to meet us. I said to	When my grandfather was about fifty, he fell sick, and my grandparents thought it best to go to America where my father and their other children were. My father went to the pier to bring his parents to our home and could hardly recognize his father— the face was swollen and the man could hardly move his hands and feet. I had been watching from the window and my brother and I ran downstairs to meet them. My father turned to my grandfather and said: "These are my sons." My grandfather looked at us with his bleary eyes, whose rims were red, and turning to my father murmured in Hebrew what the patriarch Jacob had said to his son Joseph: "I did not think to see your face and God has shown me your sons also," and, putting his swollen hands slowly on my head, began to bless me. Even as he did so, my grandmother who was standing beside him poked him in the ribs and said sharply in Yiddish: "Well?" My grandfather hurriedly brought the blessing to a close. Shoving his fist into his pocket he took out a gold coin

(Continued on next page)

Fig. 4. Continued

Nathan's Account *(Continued)*	Charles's Account *(Continued)*
my father "Father, those are my sons". He smiled to them and became serious. He lifted his eyes and said to me in Hebrew "To see your face I had not hoped, and lo God has shown me thy seed." And then he turned around to the children and put his hands over their heads and proceeded "May the Angel who redeemed me from all evil bless the lads, and through them be recalled my name in the name of my fathers, Abraham, increase abundantly in the midst of the earth. With these shall Israel bless saying God make them as Ephraim and Menasseh". This scene looked so noble and sacred and it was said with such earnestness that it seemed like Jacob of old himself said it to the children of Joseph. This day the yoke of a livelihood was not in my thoughts. My head was occupied with other thoughts. My heart was full with such feelings that I am not able to express.	and put it in the hand I had stretched out to greet him. "No, no," I said and would have given the coin back, for I had been brought up to think it disgraceful to take money from my elders: the purpose of the instruction was that I should not ask for pennies, as ill-bred children did; in good Talmudical style the prohibition was wider than the evil. But this time my father smiled and said: "Keep it—to remember your grandfather by." As they went into the house, I stopped to glance at the coin and saw the monstrous eagle of czarist Russia, with two open beaks, from which my father and mother and so many others had fled.

together with a section of his own autobiography drawn from "Notes for an Autobiography." By the time the poetic description of his grandparents' arrival was finally published in 1969, Charles had had forty years of reading and rereading, translating, typing, editing, selecting, and publishing material from his parents' autobiographical writings; and even before that there were certainly oral accounts of the family history told and retold. Elements of his mother's and father's accounts emerge in Reznikoff's passage in a way that makes it impossible to distinguish what young Charles witnessed from his parents' experience (see fig. 4).

Throughout a reading of both Sarah's and Nathan's memoirs, we are struck by their function as a kind of bearing record log, like that used by Hutchins's navigators; in observing landmarks and recording their bearings, these texts served a central role in Charles's own textual navigation. He drew on them repeatedly throughout his life in poetry, nonfiction, autobiography, and novels, as he charted his course in the unfamiliar waters of the Great Depression, World War II, and the decades beyond.

We cannot call this *collaborative writing* in the sense that we have become accustomed to using the term; Reznikoff's parents had no control or authority over the final text. Although Charles and Nathan probably collaborated on the translation of Nathan's memoirs, they did not work together as he was drafting or revising his poem. On the other hand, we cannot quite consider this the work of a single individual. Even what we consider uniquely internal to us as individuals, our psychological processes, are compromised in this text. It seems that memory is not simply an individual possession, a map or a film of lived experience, but rather a distributed process; researchers are only beginning to recognize how much of it is co-constructed in this way.

David Middleton and Derek Edwards have done extensive research on this subject. In their discourse analyses of conversational remembering, they observe,

> There seemed in these data to be evidence of a social discursive basis for metacognition itself, of the sort hypothesized by various theorists, such that the very notion of mind, of mental life, of memory and experience as objects of reflective awareness, is given shape and occasion by discursive practices in which versions are being compared, conjoined and disputed. (28)

Consequently, we discover that even a text that seems to record a moment of singular vision is distributed materially, psychologically, and socially across time and space. Its construction is distributed among other texts and members of a family in a way that cannot be reduced to a single individual. In many other works, as well, Reznikoff's poetry and prose are created in collaboration with existing texts: in *Testimony,* poetry is constructed from the actual language of law cases recorded in the early days of the United States, in *Holocaust,* poems are constructed from testimony given at the Nuremberg and Eichmann trials, while a wide range of Reznikoff's other work draws on historical records and biblical stories.

Perhaps the image of Reznikoff as a "solitary" poet is really a function of our enculturated view of what it means to be "creative." Perhaps it is too simplified to allow us to see the richer context in which writing is really accomplished. In fact, there are as many clues to Reznikoff as an intensely social being, if we look closely enough; it is all there in his work. The passage we are considering here is a rich tapestry of social structures and dynamics: family interactions between father and son, grandfather and grandsons, husband and wife; religious traditions; and political oppression.

Then there was the poet's separation from his wife, Marie; even when they were living apart, there was no discussion of divorce. They continued to work together companionably on a journal, the *Jewish Frontier,* and Reznikoff continued to share his writing with Marie. As Marie insists about their separation: "Nevertheless, despite the lack of a common household, for seventeen years, we maintained a common life" (Syrkin 54).

Even while they were still living together, Charles's sociability was evident. Charles and Marie could never agree about getting a maid to help out with the housecleaning:

> An added complication was his genius for getting involved in the personal difficulties of whoever was doing the cleaning. One statuesque Greek, who looked as if she had stepped out of the chorus of *Medea,* had various dietetic requirements that could only be met by Charles' running to various stores for their purchase. He was also a patient listener to tales of wrongs endured. (56)

According to Marie, even his walks were never as solitary as we might imagine. "In their course he acquired a number of acquaintances, elderly, retired gentlemen who followed the same route and regaled him with anecdotes of former days" (58). He was not simply a magnet for other lonely souls, however:

> Often, as with the problems of the maids, Charles would get involved in an act of simple helpfulness that would expand beyond the original intent: a wilful blind man who would not release his arm after Charles had led him across the street but would insist on his company till he had reached his destination; a crotchety old woman who asked for directions kept a firm hold on him till he had delivered her to her friends some distance away. (58)

He took a young black man who had been injured to the hospital by taxi; he helped a child who was struggling with a heavy bicycle, carrying it up five flights of stairs in an unsavory tenement, and was unfazed when the boy's father gave him a suspicious look and slammed the door in his face. Marie concludes, nothing could check the irrepressible fellow-feeling to which his verse bears witness, be it an old man glimpsed in an automat "slowly eating with reverence, food, the great comforter" or poor folk sitting before books they do not read in libraries to which they had come "for warmth, not light." (59)

Even reading, generally thought of as a solitary activity, was a distributed one for Reznikoff, not only because he and Marie read aloud to one another, but because his reading often involved an ensemble of translations and even assistance from Marie.

> Each evening he read a few pages of the Old Testament in the original Hebrew and in two translations, English and Luther's German. He would also be re-reading some other work. One winter it was the *Iliad*. As he did not know Greek, a comparison of German and English translations gave him a better approximation of the original. Since I had studied Greek at college my reading of the text aloud enabled him to hear the dactylic hexameter and consider the merits of Pope's couplets, blank verse or freer versions. Sometimes he would be plunged in Icelandic sagas. European poets he read in whatever bi-lingual texts were available; and in view of his stylistic predilections, our bookshelves were crowded with Haikus and Chinese poets. (59)

I think the perception of Reznikoff as a solitary soul is based on our inability to acknowledge the deep and varied social interactions in which his life was embedded, and upon which his texts depended, simply because so many of those interactions did not reflect the conventional expectations of his time (or even ours). Yet if we pay careful attention to the texts among which our poetic passage is situated, we are struck by their steady focus on human beings, their interactions with each other, and their struggles with their material and historical conditions; by the texts' implacable observations of social structures and processes; and by their meticulous recording of the dynamics of the relationships between individuals and their communities.

These compassionate observations of the "minute particulars" of human beings and their behaviors testify to Reznikoff's deep sense of connectedness with others, even as he refused conventional social roles. He explains it himself in a typewritten note (see fig. 5).

But the poetic passage is not merely "socially constructed" or socially distributed, it is also distributed via a material environment that is not simply background to the writing but constitutive of it. Charles's typewriter and the printing press he installed in his parents' basement rendered his parents' stories and his own poetry suitable for publica-

I was--and am--very much interested

in communities--as well as in individuals.

After all, man is a social animal. And

I wrote and write about Jewish x

communities because I think I know most

about that kind of a community and its

problems

Fig. 5. A note by Charles Reznikoff

tion and further distribution; his parents provided material support by providing Charles with a job as a salesman in the family business and continued to pay him for some time after he left the business to try to make a living as a writer. The texts themselves became structures in the environment that could be revised or altered by handwritten marks on the page, and the languages of English, Yiddish, and Hebrew provided yet another kind of environmental structure, which shaped not merely the form but the very fabric of the thought and writing in this text. The dynamic process of working through the translation of Nathan's memoirs from Yiddish to English inescapably transformed the possibilities of what could be written. Furthermore, the nature of this text's distributed composing process is profoundly dependent on physical experience, a fact that becomes apparent as we consider, in the next section, the attribute of embodiment.

Embodiment and the Poem

Hutchins has pointed out that conventional cognitivist approaches in cognitive science, in positing the brain as a computer and the computer as a brain, have "dropped out" of their conceptual approaches any consideration of the eyes, the hands, the ears, the legs—in short, the rest of the human body (*Cognition*). This is also true of our taken-for-granted beliefs about "thinking." And I would argue that in studies of composing we have suffered from the same blindness. The poetic passage has a body, is a part of a larger body, and is produced by a body. We have already seen, however, how the production of the "solitary" text was actually distributed over several "bodies." What is the nature of the relationship between the text and bodily experience?

If we look carefully at this text, we notice it is largely composed of descriptions of physical conditions, actions, perceptions, and interactions: the grandfather is of a certain age ("about fifty"), and because he "fell sick" (a metaphor relating a physical condition—illness—to a physical action—falling[3]), the grandparents physically transport themselves to America. Nathan "could hardly recognize his father" (visual perception) because "the face was swollen and the man could hardly move his hands and feet." Charles "had been watching from the window" and "ran downstairs to meet them," and so on in virtually every line throughout the entire passage, which ends

> I stopped to glance at the coin
> and saw the monstrous eagle of czarist Russia,
> with two open beaks,
> from which my father and mother and so many others had fled.
> (*Complete Poems* II: 147)

In this final phrase, we have nested physical experiences, the "stopping," "glancing," and "seeing" activity of Charles, the visual recognition of the image of the "monstrous eagle," and the physical actions of Charles's parents fleeing czarist Russia.

In fact, both Nathan and Sarah left Russia in order to escape different forms of physical bondage: Nathan out of fear that he would be conscripted into the czar's army, where Jews were viciously abused by their own troops and officers; Sarah in rebellion against the traditional system of arranged marriages, which often imprisoned women in loveless relationships and condemned them to lives of physical and material hardship. They joined the growing numbers of Russian Jews leaving their homeland to forge new lives in America.

It is difficult to imagine the physical and social impact of this wave of immigrants from eastern Europe flooding into New York in the 1880s. In his essay, "The Educational Alliance: An Institutional Study in Americanization and Acculturation," historian Joseph Dorinson writes,

> From 1880 to 1910, East European Jews flooded into the United States. About 1,119,000 came from Russia. . . . About 70 percent settled in

New York city, where the Jewish population rose from 85,000 (including Brooklyn) in 1880 to 850,000 in 1907. By 1914 the Jewish population in New York City had risen to 1,335,000, with the already highly Americanized Jews of German origin representing only 10 percent of this total. Adjacent to the central factory area, the tenth ward throbbed with more than 700 people per acre in 1900, making it the most densely populated spot in America, if not the world. In 1910 the Lower East Side bulged with 542,061 inhabitants. (93)

This massive influx not only resulted in enormous physical crowding, it also created a great deal of controversy among American Jews, some of whom opposed large-scale immigration from Russia on the basis that it would create a drain on existing charities and cause tensions in the community. Dorinson notes,

> Only a small percentage of the newcomers . . . either knew English or were becoming naturalized citizens. Resistant to assimilation, East European Jews exhibited an "exotic" and conspicuously different life-style. Those who observed religious rites clearly preferred Orthodox to Reform Judaism. In secular pursuits, they engaged in peddling, garment work, trade unionization, radical agitation, and a few even turned to crime. For the already Americanized Jews, these newcomers with their boorish manners, Yiddish jargon, and herd-like clannishness came like a shock of recognition that triggered anger as well as anxiety. (93–94)

Overcrowded, struggling for a foothold in a foreign land, and discriminated against even by American Jews, the new immigrants found themselves in a chaotic environment that demanded all of their physical strength, energy, and resourcefulness. Reznikoff's parents closely matched this profile of Russian Jewish immigration. Arriving in New York City at the crest of the wave, in 1891, they immediately began working in the garment trade, sewing wrappers as piecework. The work was physically exhausting, and the hours were long. Sarah Yetta, however, unlike many immigrants, was fiercely determined that English would be spoken at home and insisted that her husband learn to read and write it, even though she herself would not have the time to do so until she became too ill to work. In fact, Jewish community leaders were also soon exhorting immigrants to become acculturated to their new home:

> At the [Educational] alliance's twenty-fifth anniversary fete on March 21, 1915, an event attended by many dignitaries including Mayor John P. Mitchell, Friedlaender spelled out his version of a genuine educational

alliance. Speaking in Yiddish, Friedlaender commended the Russian Jew without rationalizing his faults. He exhorted the immigrant to adopt the best in his new environment without surrendering the best in his old setting. A cultural synthesis, that is, acculturation, was the solution espoused by Friedlaender. . . .

In the Old country, Friedlaender observed in another context, Jewish learning and piety had given shape to social structure. In this country, Friedlaender maintained, religious observance and talmudic scholarship "were 'not only valueless' but were a 'hindrance, and sometimes a nuisance.' " (Dorinson 93, 101)

This is the milieu from which the poetic passage emerged, the world in which the young Charles Reznikoff grew up and which so profoundly shaped his worldview and his aesthetics. By the time he was twenty-three, enormous historical changes were reshaping the world:

> That halcyon year, 1917, signaled the high point of cultural synthesis between "fathers and sons," or acculturation. . . . It also brought sweeping change in its wake. Revolution visited Russia—the principal source of Jewish immigration—in two stages: first moderate, then radical. The United States entered the war at President Wilson's behest "to make the world safe for democracy" and in that process unleashed an orgy of hatred, superpatriotism, and ultimately—the "red scare." All Jewish organizations were affected. . . .
>
> Restrictive immigration legislation reduced the flood tide of newcomers to a mere trickle. With the advent of rapid transit subways and improved economic conditions, which contributed to social as well as geographic mobility, the congestion of the Lower East side began to dissolve. In 1916 there were 353,000 Jews living in the neighborhood. The number dipped to 257,832 in 1920, to 121,000 in 1930, and to 98,400 in 1948. (102–3)

Sarah and Nathan's flight from Russia to New York perfectly illustrates the dynamics of complex systems: as the Russian political system and traditional Jewish community life imposed a more and more rigid social order, individuals—such as Sarah and Nathan—began to break away in various ways, emigrating to America in a movement that started as a trickle and developed the critical mass to become a flood. These forces contributed, finally, to a collapse of order at home, culminating in the Russian Revolution of 1917. In their flight, Nathan and Sarah found themselves at the very edge of chaos in the teeming ghettos of New York City, and again the dynamic properties of complex systems came into play: they drew back from chaos toward order, keeping to the narrow edge between the two where complex systems thrive.[4] This they achieved by finding familiar work in the garment district, arranging to be married by a rabbi (Sarah remarked, "A Rabbi Levine married us. Some of our friends, who were radicals, made fun of Nathan and me for having a wedding, but I said, 'I am not going to be among the first to jump away from the old customs: who knows where I'd land?'" [*Family Chronicle* 94]), working very hard to establish a family millinery business, and raising a family of children who went on to become educated and successful.

Because Reznikoff's poetic passage depends so heavily on the accounts, both in texts and stories, of Nathan and Sarah, it becomes apparent that what appears to be a simple memory of an individual experience grows more complex and depends upon the embodied experiences of Reznikoff's parents as well, mediated through language and culturally and historically situated not just in one moment but in a much larger space and time. Interestingly enough, it seems that even "individual" embodied experience is much more distributed than we have imagined.

We tend to think of time as a disembodied, abstract concept, even though the evidence clearly refutes this notion. We are, as living beings, walking clocks, and so are all of the embodied structures we encounter in the environment. In this textual ecology, time is embodied in the aging grandfather (although we hardly think of fifty as aged now); in the two boys flying down the stairs, frozen in the space of the text at eleven or twelve years old long after their human counterparts have aged and died; and in the gold coin, a link to family and cultural history. Time is palpable here, as it is in the archive among the papers and manuscripts in the collection. Our sense of the physicality of time is reflected in our obsession with dating these bits of textual evidence: we are frustrated that Charles, Sarah, and Nathan seldom dated any piece of writing.

Did Sarah write her pages from her own memory, and was Charles's typescript copied from these pages; or was it the other way around? Did Nathan begin his autobiographical manuscript before Charles began writing seriously, or after? The lines of mutual influence are blurred beyond our reconstruction. The real point is that our sense of time is indeed embodied in these physical artifacts, which we struggle to order in time so that we can better understand this composing situation. Further, our own embodiment as readers constrains the amount of time we can engage the texts and their mysteries.

In fact, our meaning structures neither precede nor follow upon our sensory experiences—they arise codependently in collaboration with our environment, which includes the other people in it. This process is not as simple as it may seem when we consider that the environment is constantly changing as a consequence of our own behaviors, so that adaptations are always aiming at a moving target (Holland, *Adaptation*). Young Charles Reznikoff, growing up in the crowded Jewish ghetto and an equally crowded household (to which his grandparents and their daughter had now been added), and observing the grinding physical labor of his parents' work, adapted by discovering solutions that provided him space and freedom, both physically and psychologically: he began writing poetry, and he began his lifelong practice of taking long walks in the city. It would not be quite accurate to say either that Charles's poems resulted from this physical interaction with New York or that his poetic vision shaped his physical experience of the city. Rather the poetry and the physical experience of the city arose codependently. Marie explains,

> The role of walking in Charles' life went far beyond the jogger's mechanical therapy; it was a spiritual as well as physical exercise. Unless he walked a number of miles, dwindling through the years from twenty to six daily, he suffered psychic deprivation. "I did not walk today," he would announce with an air of tragic loss that the simple fact did not seem to justify. The obsession had started in his boyhood . . . Charles never wearied of assuring me that his walks were a major source of experience: he saw, he felt, he wrote. The small notebook he always carried to jot down lines that occurred to him testifies to this productivity. . . . That he called one of his books, *Going To and Fro and Walking Up and Down* was no casual choice. (Syrkin)

In *By the Waters of Manhattan*, Reznikoff himself had described walking as "that sober dance which despite all the dances man knows, he dances most." In an interview with Reinhold Schiffer he clarifies his sense of the interdependence of poetry and physical motion:

> When I began to write, rather seriously, I wrote in prose. I was dissatisfied with prose: it didn't have the emphatic music that I wanted, which I found in free verse. Now if we reverse it, and say "reverse" (I don't mean that as a pun!) but if we reverse it, people would say, "Yes, and he's still writing prose!" And maybe they don't feel the rhythm, the stops. You

stop, you break it up, you reverse it in the middle, as I said, comparing it to the turn in the dance, instead of walking straight on. (115)

He expressed similar views in an interview with L. S. Dembo (98). And in a handwritten note found among his papers in the archive, Reznikoff sets out a schedule for completing several projects he was working on, together with the comment "revise while walking." The process of walking was not merely to provide "material" for his texts, but rather provided a direct physical interaction with the city in which texts emerged in coordination with embodied experiences. It is clear, in fact, that any account of Reznikoff's composing process would be incomplete without acknowledging this central relationship. Our conceptual world is grounded in our experiences and activities as physical beings situated in physical environments. Varela, Thompson, and Rosch argue that we must not cling to objectivist assumptions of a pregiven world that exists "out there" and is internalized in a "representation." Rather, we must recognize that our experience of seeing, for example, inevitably involves at minimum three inseparable elements: the seer, that which is seen, and the activity of seeing. These three elements mutually specify each other in what they term "dependent coorigination."

We see this mutual specification, or dependent co-origination, in the intertextuality of these writing processes. Sarah's and Nathan's lived experiences are translated into textual forms that become a part of Charles's physical experience as he types and translates them, then transforms them into his own texts, which assume various physical forms at different stages, from autobiographical prose to poetic drafts to published poetry; and eventually, many of these texts come physically to reside in the Archive for New Poetry of the UCSD Library, where they are once again physically encountered by scholars and researchers who translate them into new texts that also incorporate the researchers' embodied experiences, including the experiences of reading and writing this and other texts.

Yet texts, because they are embodied and only exist as embodied entities, are susceptible to the physical dynamics of birth, survival, age, and environment. Scrawled on cheap composition paper, Sarah's manuscript is frail, aged, and crumbling. It has been photocopied to preserve the text, but in the process, much of the physical qualities of the original text are lost. Nathan's Yiddish manuscript, written on the back of stationery from the Artistic Millinery Company, has fared better because the quality of the paper is higher, yet this manuscript, too, is at risk: only a few people can read and understand Yiddish, and this manuscript is inaccessible to most of them because of physical distance. Most of these people are elderly now, and their own physical processes, including failing eyesight, make it difficult or impossible for them to decipher Nathan's tiny script. There is some hope, however, in recently renewed scholarly interest in the study of Yiddish. The English translation is typed on cheap paper as well, and it, too, is fragile.

Because these manuscripts are unpublished, they do not have a very stable physical life; yet books, too, are physical beings prone to environmental damage, neglect, and physical abuse by readers. They can be dropped on the floor, crammed into backpacks, caught in the rain, chewed by dogs, destroyed by fire. They can be overlooked and forgotten, tossed into boxes, sold off at rummage sales, or used to prop up furniture. When the physical embodiment of the text is gone, can we say the text itself exists any longer? Perhaps we take comfort in the existence of the archive to preserve the existence of texts such as these, texts we have decided are extraordinarily valuable. Such conditions are not permanent: the social structures that preserve texts can also change as a consequence of budget cuts, increased demand for storage, and political changes, for example. Further, the archive itself is tied to environmental structures: architectural structures, geological structures, climate, and so on. It is subject to natural and unnatural environmental forces—earthquakes, floods, explosives, failure of the electronic environmental controls that monitor the temperature and humidity to preserve the paper, leather, and cardboard in which texts are embodied. Even when preserved on acid-free paper, in a climate-controlled archive, the body of a text is subject to the ravages of time; fashions change; people move or die; the guardianship of texts depends on an economy of scale. When there are too many texts, some have to go. They may be sold, warehoused, or destroyed, but the ultimate result is the same—the loss of the connections between texts, their readers, and their writers. The same changes might leave the texts physically present but untouched and abandoned.

We tend to think of text as eternal, and it is true that many texts have outlived their original authors and readers by hundreds, even thousands of years; many others have been lost because they were physically destroyed. Others are lost because there are no longer enough readers who can comprehend them, as is happening with Nathan's Yiddish manuscript. Changes in the physical form of text significantly alter the entire ecology of composing. Reznikoff printed and bound his work to make it physically more enduring; through this process, we have come to value not only the writing we think of as his but also his parents' texts, which are physically embedded in his own. The point is not that these texts are in imminent danger of destruction; the point is that texts are embodied and subject to the same physical conditions as other embodied beings, including those who both write and read them.

These texts are spatially embodied across the pages on which they are scrawled, typed, and typeset; they cover page after page in loose sheets filed in folders, in composition books stored in boxes, and in published books arranged on bookshelves. They have been removed from their original places and transported across the country to a place set aside for acquiring and preserving texts. Because of their physical embodiment in a particular space, the Archive for New Poetry, these texts acquire significance, and readers approach them in a different kind of spatial arrangement. To reach this space, readers have to leave behind their personal belongings; they must request a meeting with the texts in writing on a special form; they move into a specially constructed room with carefully monitored temperature and humidity, in which they can be watched at all times; and finally the texts are brought to them. All of this careful guardianship serves not only to protect fragile documents but to construct a spatially defined relationship between the reader's body and the physical body of the text. Papers that earlier in their existence were crammed into drawers, stuck in filing cabinets, stacked carelessly on desks and tables and largely ignored are treated with reverence here—as a consequence of the space they inhabit.

It hardly needs saying that the text is grounded upon the physical experiences of Charles, Sarah, Nathan, and Nathan's parents; these physical conditions, activities, and interactions are described in the passage. However, this text and the other texts in this ecological system are also embodied in their production and their reception. Sarah's labored scrawl, Nathan's minute Yiddish script, Charles's typescripts with their painstaking handwritten revisions all testify to the physical effort involved in making text visible on the page. The consequences of the particular tools and materials used are also evident: Charles's typewriter greatly eases the effort of constructing text, and this fact may testify to the much greater volume of text he is able to produce. By contrast, Sarah's use of pencil and, occasionally, fountain pen, combined with her illness and her struggle to learn to write in English, makes even a brief personal letter seem a heroic physical effort. The coupling between our own physical architecture and the materials and tools we take up for use constrain our activities (and our texts) in nontrivial ways: no one picks up a broken brick and begins to scrawl on a sidewalk "It was the best of times, it was the worst of times . . ." In fact, one of the most interesting features of text is the way it instantiates a point of contact between our internal structures and external structures and makes visible our struggles to coordinate the two.

Indeed, texts often become a representation of the physical body of their writers, just as writers become the embodiment of their texts: Sarah Reznikoff's mother says, as she puts Ezekiel's poetry onto the fire, "Here's a man's life" (not "Here's a man's writing").[5] Reznikoff was marked by Sarah's telling of this incident; before he enlisted in the army in 1918, he made sure that he had privately printed up a book of the poems he liked. He sent this book, *Rhythms,* out to friends and reviewers, clearly hoping to ensure that, even if something happened to the physical Reznikoff, the textual Reznikoff would survive, in a physical form. One reason for the great robustness of complex systems (including text composing) is that the body of the system can generally survive the loss of embodied individuals. Thus distribution and embodiment are also interdependent attributes.

Reznikoff himself seems to have recognized that sense of distributed embodiment. When Marie, an ardent Zionist, made a trip to Palestine in 1933, Charles declined the opportunity to go with her because "he had not yet explored Central Park to the full." But he wrote to her in Palestine:

> I feel a compulsion, which I shall not resist, to write my lament for Israel. I am thinking of nothing else in my spare time, and though nothing may come of it, I must do what I can. . . . I wish you to see everything and enjoy everything slowly, unhurriedly, to soak in as much as possible. Somehow, I feel as if I as well as you am in Palestine, that is that you are my alter ego, and so I know that we have really become one flesh. (Syrkin 44)

Although the physical bodies of Sarah, Nathan, Marie, and Charles are no longer present, their textual bodies continue to generate new ideas and new texts. This process demonstrates yet another attribute of complex systems, *emergence,* which we will consider in the next section.

Emergence and the Poem

Emergence is a simple yet powerful concept. Theories of emergence in complex systems research provide an account for the self-organization of a system in which the parts of the system are interacting locally, without the imposition of a central control or "boss." It addresses questions such as, How does a single cell, dividing repeatedly, generate the structures that develop into a human being, with all of its differentiated cells, organs, and systems contributing to a coherent whole? How do individual people moving about in the world and trying to meet their physical and social needs begin to form communities, cities, and nations with many differentiated systems that work together to create a (more or less) coherent whole? And, in terms of texts, How do the simple components of written language develop into larger, meaningful wholes, from metaphors to proverbs to descriptions to autobiographies to libraries?

In the study of complex systems, such questions have provoked a great deal of research—research that has challenged some powerful paradigms. Susan Oyama, for example, refutes the widely held belief that genes carry "information" that "programs" the developmental change from egg to embryo to infant to adult. Instead, she argues, these changes emerge in complex interactions between developing cells and their environments, including neighboring cells, which are also developing and changing over time.

> It is my contention that information does develop, not by special creation from nothingness, but always from the conditional transformation of prior structure, by ontogenetic processes. Depending on the level of analysis, such transformation can be described as interaction among systems or entities, such as cells or organisms, or as a change within a system or entity, such as an embryo or a family; since sets of interactants are nested, a change in focus is sufficient to shift from one perspective to the next. (4)

Once again, as with embodiment, we have a compelling argument for co-evolution of organism and environment in dependent co-origination. Roy Bhaskar warns, however, that talk of emergence "can easily become vague and general, if not indeed laced with frankly idealist or romantic overtones" ("Emergence" 283). In fact, in the physical and cognitive sciences, researchers studying emergent properties have struggled with the ghost of "vitalism," working to demonstrate that emergent properties are not dependent on mystical concepts of

"spirit," "soul," "homunculus," or other insubstantial element. Instead, Stuart Kauffman, Stephen Wolfram, Ilya Prigogine, and other
scientists provide compelling evidence that in complex systems order
arises for "free."[6] Varela, Thompson, and Rosch remark, "In fact, it
seems difficult for any densely connected aggregate to escape emergent properties; thus theories of such properties are a natural link for
different levels of descriptions in natural and cognitive phenomena"
(90). Modeling complex phenomena using cellular automata or
connectionist networks or mathematical equations, as these researchers do, is a fascinating exercise in theory building, but we may well
wonder how these theories apply to concrete writing situations. What
exactly is emergence in texts?

In the first place, we must recognize that in composing situations
meaning does not reside solely in the text (à la new criticism), nor
does it reside solely in the writer (à la psychoanalytic schools of criticism), solely in the reader (à la reader-response criticism), nor even
solely in the "context" (à la cultural studies and new historicism). It is
not an entity that exists prior to the writing or reading of the text that
instantiates it. Rather, meaning emerges as a dynamic process among
these participants, a process that changes each of them even as it is
unfolding. Meaning is an emergent property of the relationships
among texts, writers, readers, and textual environments.

We are not looking for causes, then, so much as emergent properties in our poetic passage. We cannot say that Nathan Reznikoff's
memoirs "caused" Charles Reznikoff's "Early History of a Writer,"
nor that Sarah's stories of the loss of her father's poetry "caused"
Charles to commit to his poetic vocation, nor that the historical law
cases "caused" *Testimony*. The evidence is much more complex. In
fact, it is possible to consider at least ten aspects of text that manifest
emergent properties.

1. Social relations in the writers' and readers' environments; for ex-
    ample, Reznikoff's relationship with his mother was woven in life
    stories—her father's life, her own life, Charles's life. As the stories
    continued to be told and retold in talk and texts, they shaped the
    lives they were describing, and the relationship itself emerged in
    the context of these texts.
2. The material object or artifact; that is, words written on paper
    generate other words in response, continuations, revisions, drafts,
    galleys, books, critical reviews, bibliographic citations, scholarly
    papers.

3. Local meanings, such as the emergence of words from groups of letters or clauses and sentences from groups of words, as writers construct them and as readers visually (or tactilely) perceive them.
4. Global meanings, such as the emergence of genres, as well as mood, organization, style, and other coherent structures.
5. Significance, the connection to writers' and readers' experience.
6. The image of the writer in readers' minds that continues to emerge as readers interact with the writer's texts.
7. The image of the text and of readers in writers' minds.
8. Transformational effects on social structures, as when texts, such as Reznikoff's poems, provide alternatives to traditional ways of "being Jewish."
9. Transformational effects on environmental structures, including other texts; for example, the influence of Sarah's and Nathan's texts on Reznikoff's poems, the influence of Reznikoff's poetry on other poems by other poets.
10. The justification or rationalization of the text's existence, or its role in either reproducing or transforming social structures. This includes the critical apparatus that develops around the text as readers respond, interpret, and analyze the text in new texts.

We might think of emergence as a process in which disparate individual entities and relations undergo transformations or deformations that bring them into increasing coordination with each other. This process is not necessarily what we would call *collaboration* or *cooperation,* although mutual transformations play a key role; the entities or relations may actually be conflictual or predatory. The system as a whole, however, reflects an emerging, dynamic coordination. There occurs what theorists of complex systems term a *phase transition,* a qualitative global change in the system; an assortment of individuals suddenly transforms itself into a collective with distinctive global properties irreducible to its individual parts. This transition is effected through relationships and processes in densely connected networks.

Emergence is a phenomenon that foregrounds the temporal dimension of our ecology of composing, since it posits a qualitative change in the system over some span of time. For example, a phase transition occurs when we read along word by word and suddenly we "have" the sense of a sentence, not by parsing each word or phrase additively, but through a global shift to the meaning of the whole. Idiomatic expressions, metaphors, and proverbs are some other examples of emergent phenomena in which the meaning of the whole is irreducible to the sum of its parts. In texts, we see emergent properties at many levels of scale.

Rather than elaborate on each of these possibilities, however, it might be more instructive to focus on a concrete example and ask, How does the poetic passage from "Early History of a Writer" demonstrate emergent properties? Physically, there are (at least) ten versions of the incident described in the passage (see fig. 6).

There are two handwritten manuscripts by Sarah, plus a typed version of one of them; there is the manuscript in Yiddish by Nathan, as well as the typed translation of it; and there are five typescripts of Charles's drafts of the poem. These texts exist in a network of relationships that are nearly impossible to untangle. For the most part they are undated. The logical conclusion is that the typescript of Sarah's memoirs was prepared from her handwritten manuscript, and that may be true. However, one of the manuscripts is found in a bound composition book bracketed by personal letters written as handwriting exercises or rough drafts, and these letters were dated between 1933 and 1935. The typescript very closely matches this manuscript. Yet Charles Reznikoff first published "Early History of a Seamstress," based on the typescript, in 1929. Sarah's other manuscript, slightly different from either the typescript or the bound manuscript, is on loose, undated pages (see fig. 7).

Where does this leave our textual chronology? The most likely explanation seems to be that Charles prepared the typescript from the loose pages, revising or editing them as he went along, and then his mother actually copied her second manuscript into the bound composition book by copying the typescript. Or perhaps the typescript is based on an oral transcription of Sarah's story, which she later committed to print in her struggle to learn to write and read English. The translation of Nathan's manuscript from Yiddish to English is another puzzle: Did Nathan dictate a translation to Charles, who then typed it; did Charles provide the translation; or did they collaborate to construct it as they went along? (See fig. 8.) These textual mysteries may be unresolvable, but they do reveal the emergent properties of these texts unfolding in the context of a densely connected network of relations.

In this example, we see how Sarah's rambling, fragmentary journals or Nathan's more elaborate memoirs studded with biblical allusions are drawn into Charles's texts, as disparate family memories are coordinated in the "Notes for an Autobiography" and then, through

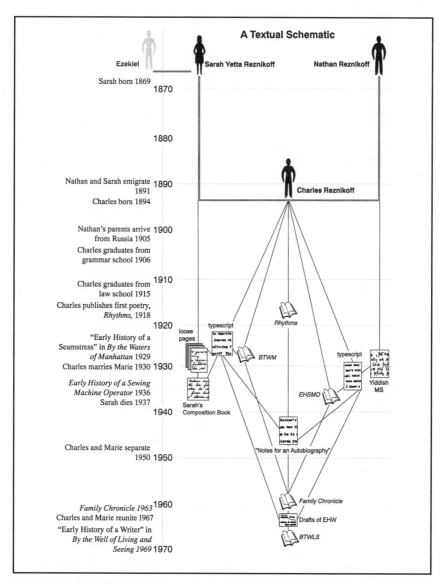

A Textual Schematic

Ezekiel

Sarah Yetta Reznikoff

Nathan Reznikoff

Sarah born 1869
1870

1880

Nathan and Sarah emigrate 1890
1891
Charles born 1894

Charles Reznikoff

Nathan's parents arrive 1900
from Russia 1905
Charles graduates from
grammar school 1906

Charles graduates from 1910
law school 1915
Charles publishes first poetry,
Rhythms, 1918
1920

Rhythms

"Early History of a
Seamstress" in *By the Waters
of Manhattan* 1929
Charles marries Marie 1930 1930

loose
pages

typescript

BTWM

typescript

Yiddish
MS

*Early History of a Sewing
Machine Operator* 1936
Sarah dies 1937
1940

Sarah's
Composition Book

EHSMO

Charles and Marie separate
1950 1950

"Notes for an Autobiography"

Family Chronicle 1963 1960
Charles and Marie reunite 1967
"Early History of a Writer" in
*By the Well of Living and
Seeing 1969* 1970

Family Chronicle

Drafts of EHW

BTWLS

Fig. 6. A schematic diagram of relevant texts by Sarah, Nathan, and Charles Reznikoff

the process of reading, walking, and revision, emerge as the "walking" or "dancing" verse form of "Early History of a Writer." Sarah's hesitant scrawl, Nathan's minute Yiddish script, Charles's typescripts with their meticulous revisions, page after page of textual memory emerges to construct the story of everyday activities in a life, a family, a cultural mix, and a geography, and to illuminate the historical

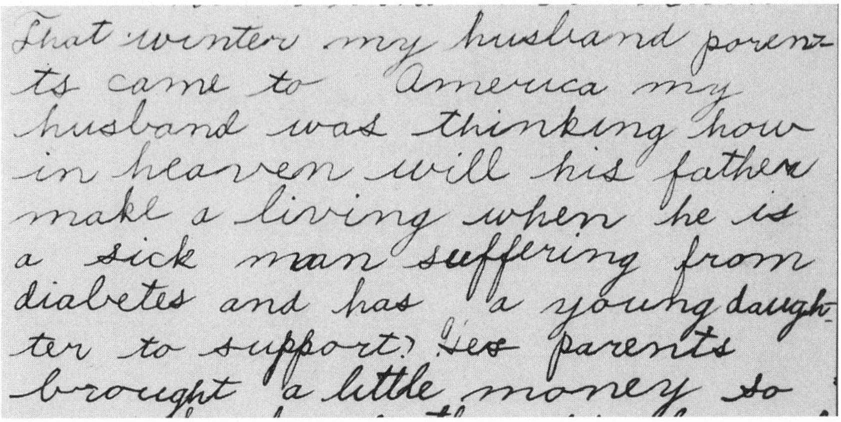
That winter my husband porenz-
ts came to America my
husband was thinking how
in heaven will his father
make a living when he is
a sick man suffering from
diabetes and has a young daughter to support? ~~Les~~ parents
brought a little money so

A. *Selection from Sarah's loose manuscript pages*

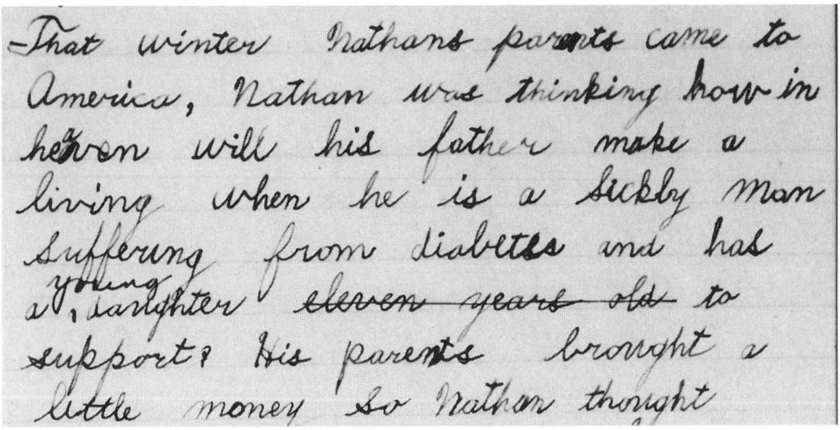
That winter Nathans parents came to
America, Nathan was thinking how in
heaven will his father make a
living when he is a sickly man
Suffering from diabetes and has
a young daughter ~~eleven years old~~ to
support? His parents brought a
little money so Nathan thought

B. *Selection from Sarah's bound composition book*

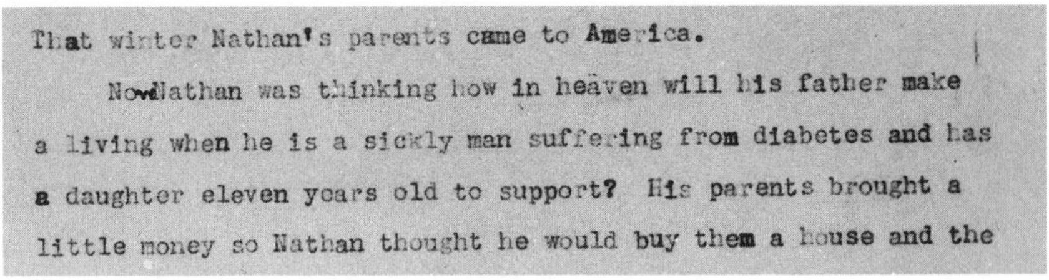
That winter Nathan's parents came to America.

NowNathan was thinking how in heäven will his father make
a living when he is a sickly man suffering from diabetes and has
a daughter eleven years old to support? His parents brought a
little money so Nathan thought he would buy them a house and the

C. *Selection from typescript of Sarah's autobiographical writing*

Fig. 7. We tend to think of writing as evolving over time into more finished and polished texts at every stage. But perhaps that is not always the case. Which is the real chronological order of these texts: A, B, C or A, C, B or even C, A, B? We can't be sure. In textual ecologies, even emergence is not a simple phenomenon but a complex one.

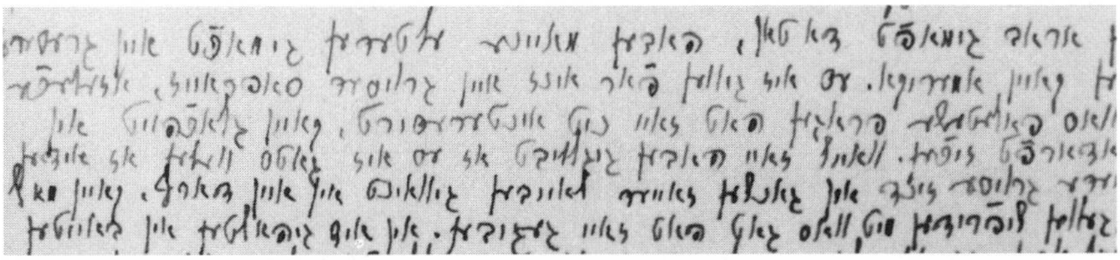

A. Selection from Nathan's manuscript in Yiddish

At the time that we moved downtown my parents made a bigger move. They left Russia and went to America. It was a big surprise to us--such people as my parents--as political questions didn't interest them. Equality and freedom they didn't have to look for as they firmly believed that it is God's will the Jews should suffer in captivity for their gross sin. All their lives they lived in a village, never had any big demands, were satisfied with what God gave them and kept on praying to him 3 times a day that the Redeemer should come and redeem all the Jews including them from the deosferer and bring them to the Land of Israel, and not only prayed for it, but believed and hoped for it. People with such observations should all of a sudden leave their home where they lived and strived and brought up their children and to let themselves emmigrate in another world with a new exile where the customs are different and the Jewish life especially is not the same that they are used to conducting; but the letter that we received a few days before they arrived explained to us the reason of their decision--as all their older children were already in America, they only remained with the baby, a girl of about 10 yrs. old, and my father was sick on diabetes, they thought that he wouldn't last very long, my mother feared God knows what could happen to her too--it might be a pogrom or some other thing that takes away strong people unexpectedly--then who will take care of the child, who will bring her up; and my father carried around a thought that there is one thing that he asks of God--that once before he dies he should be able to see his children- -then he would be satisfied to die peacefully. One thing and the other brought them to make an end of

B. Selection from English translation of Nathan's manuscript

Fig. 8. Nathan's manuscripts

process of lived experience in New York's garment district in the early 1900s.

What about the larger textual environment in which these texts are situated? Long before Sarah and Nathan wrote their memoirs, and before Reznikoff began writing his poems, both fictional and autobiographical writing about Jewish immigrant life had become a well-established genre. Stanley Brodwin writes that by 1893, when Edward Smith King published his novel of Russian Jewish immigrant life in New York City, *Joseph Zalmonah,* "the American literary scene, already profoundly affected by the radical social changes following in the wake of the Civil War, was still rife with debate over the esthetic theory and practice of realism and the 'school' of Zolaesque naturalism" (121).

Brodwin argues that there was a tension between traditional aesthetic techniques and the values of romantic idealism on one hand and impulses toward a socially democratic or "commonplace" realism on the other, the result of what Brodwin calls "the failure of American fiction and poetry, in general, to reconcile what appeared to be the 'commonplace' homogeneity in American social life with the profound diversities—and often harsh inequalities—that seethed underneath an 'idealized' national surface." Consequently, "The task of reconciling these tensions was, in a sense, bequeathed to the so-called naturalistic writers such as Crane, London, Norris, and Dreiser" (122). Still, this unreconciled and perhaps irreconcilable tension persists even today.

The critical theories of Frank Norris, detailed in an essay titled "A Plea for Romantic Fiction" (1901), helped define the genre, according to Donald Pizer,

> Norris . . . placed realism, romanticism, and naturalism in a dialectic, in which realism and romanticism were opposing forces, and naturalism was a transcending synthesis. . . . [W]e can follow Norris's critical thrust in his attempt to rescue the term realism from its pejorative attachment to the "stinkpot" school of Zola and romance from its connotations of the unsubstantially "unreal," the abstract, the world of the Beautiful Ideal. . . . He wrote: "Romance does very well in the Middle Ages and the Renaissance Chateaux, and she has the entree there and is very well received. This is all well and good. But let us protest against limiting her to such places and such times. You will find her, I grant you, in the chatelaine's chamber and the dungeon of the man-at-arms; but, if you choose to look for her, you will find her equally at home in the brownstone house on the corner and in the office building downtown. And this very day, in this very hour, she is sitting among rags and wretchedness,

the dirt and despair of the tenements of the East side of New York." (qtd. in Brodwin 124)

Reznikoff, born just one year later, would echo these sentiments in poems such as "Scrubwoman," "Ghetto Funeral," "The Burden," and, of course, "Early History of a Writer." Whether or not Reznikoff ever read widely in the genre of naturalistic immigrant fiction, he was certainly not immune to the same social, cultural, and aesthetic forces that gave rise to it.[7] In fact, these forces were so powerful that Reznikoff found himself still caught in their grip some seventy-three years later, when he finally published "Early History of a Writer." And it is telling that already, by 1893, the romance of the "poor but noble immigrant who struggles and eventually triumphs" was being challenged by books such as Stephen Crane's *Maggie: A Girl of the Streets,* and Abraham Cahan's *Yekl: A Tale of the New York Ghetto.* Brodwin notes,

> These two works are now historically and esthetically regarded as the forerunners of a new wave of literature that deromanticized the "tenement tale" tradition of presenting the urban poor as noble, long-suffering, but spiritually triumphant victims of their slum-ghetto lives. *Yekl* has the special distinction . . . as being the first truly realistic account of Jewish immigrant life and the bitter consequences of assimilation. (126)

While the plight of immigrants and the urban poor struggling to adapt to their material conditions was emerging into a mature genre in fiction and autobiography, it was not simply confined to a literary trend. As I have discussed elsewhere ("Community"), by the late 1920s and 1930s, when Reznikoff began publishing his mother's and his father's stories, the documentary movement was becoming a powerful influence in the arts, in intellectual circles, and in popular culture. Suddenly intellectuals, social scientists, and artists were taking note of the "common American"—exemplified by laborers, poor people, racial and ethnic minorities, immigrants, farmers, and others who had been historically excluded or marginalized. A very wide range of work attests to this interest, from ethnographic studies to photographs for the Works Progress Administration (WPA) to magazine articles to autobiographies to post office murals (Stott). The influence was inescapable, and the movement was clearly co-constructed by audiences and by artists, writers, and scholars who were turning away from the excesses of the jazz age and its infatuation with the wealthy, glamorous, and powerful. The profound effects of the Depression altered the textual environment across genres, from scholarly articles to poetry and fiction to articles and advertisements in popular magazines and newspapers.

These large-scale historical forces undoubtedly shaped Reznikoff's poetic mission in important ways. But the emergence of the poetic passage describing his grandfather's arrival from Russia has a particular resonance across levels of scale. At crucial stages during its construction, the poignant moment of family reunion must have seemed especially compelling. During the Depression, when Reznikoff was editing and publishing his parents' memoirs, families were being torn apart by economic pressures; millions of men literally walked away from their families in shame and despair.

Later, as Reznikoff worked on his "Notes for an Autobiography" in the forties, World War II was wrenching young men from their families, and still other families in Europe were being separated or destroyed by the war and by Nazi persecution. He was about the same age then as his grandfather had been when he arrived in America.

In 1969, when Reznikoff published "Early History of a Writer" in *By the Well of Living and Seeing,* his own family had only been reunited for two years after he and Marie had lived apart for seventeen years. And at this same time, there was a large-scale fracturing of families; ironically, over the same issues that had separated Nathan from his own family—the unwillingness of young men to serve in the army and fight for an oppressive government. Some children of the 1960s even fled the country to avoid the draft, much as Nathan had fled Russia and come to America in 1891 to avoid conscription by the czar's army. But in the 1960s, there was a conflict between generations that families in the 1800s had not confronted: parents in Russia had sent their sons to America with their blessings not their curses. With demonstrations and protest marches, sit-ins and campus shutdowns, communes and concerts, American teenagers raged at the "Establishment," and many broke with their families.

At different levels of scale, then, from the personal to the global, the emergence of this text seems to be fueled by specific temporal conditions. In each case, a rupture opened in a relatively stable social system, driving the system toward chaos (the disruptions of the family through immigration, economic chaos, the chaos of war, the chaos of personal conflict, and the chaos of political and social divisions). This poetic passage exerts its small force in the opposite direction as if to move the system back toward order, bounding separation with reunion and family divisions with reconciliation.[8] It is this force that marks the passage as a kind of adaptive response, although characteristically Reznikoff does not appear to have been thinking of the potential large-scale effects of his text. *By the Well of Living and Seeing* was printed in only two hundred copies, which his handwritten note, found in the archive, allocates: "Two hundred copies have been printed: of these a few for libraries and friends; none for sale." Yet, later, *By the Well of Living and Seeing* was incorporated into the body of *The Complete Poems of Charles Reznikoff*, which was commercially published, and the appreciation of a wider audience is evidence of the text's further emergence.

From Sarah's scrawl on lined composition paper, Nathan's painstaking Yiddish script, and Reznikoff's lifetime interactions with these texts as he constructed his own autobiographical writing, we can see the emergence of the poetic passage that serves as our example. Emergent properties are evident in the way Sarah strikes out the words "eleven year old" and replaces them with "young," in the English translation of Nathan's manuscript, and in the typescript text's evolution from a prose memoir to a carefully crafted poem and into published form, where it assumes its final material manifestation. Over a period of forty years, these diverse texts became organized into a coherent poetic moment and consequently increased their potential for survival in a larger textual environment: from family to tiny circle of admirers to a larger critical and scholarly audience.

The emergence of this text also demonstrates a psychological dimension in its profound illumination of the role of family relationships and family memory in shaping our own identities. We think of children as shaped by family stories, which are told and retold by their parents and older relatives: how we came from the old country, what kinds of people our fathers and grandfathers were, our struggles and hard work in a new land. But the example we have here shows that the family dynamic is much more complex. Parents, too, are shaped by their children and their children's questions; their memories are crafted to provide a lesson, soothe a fear, or strengthen a bond. The family stories, as we see here, are collective affairs in which both children and parents share an active, constructive role. As Reznikoff grew older and more independent, determined to write, his father and mother became writers too and collaborated with him in telling their own stories. In such a psychodynamic set of relationships, emergent properties are clearly not confined to individual psychologies.

Enaction and the Poem

Ecological systems are distinguished not only by their distributed, embodied, and emergent properties but by the activities that constitute and define them. Throughout these systems, agents are engaging in activities to coordinate themselves with each other and with their environment. These activities are interrelated and interdependent; in the process, the agents are constructing their world, as well as responding to it. As Holland puts it in "Complex Adaptive Systems," agents in adaptive systems are constantly attempting to make predictions (such as which strategies are likely to be successful in finding food), and they are constantly evolving; that is, they are actively moving into coordination with each other and their environment (such as moving toward the place where they predict they will find food). Yet they exist and operate not as isolated individuals but in a network of relationships structured by the activities of other agents in particular situations. Our question might be, therefore, What kinds of activities and situated practices are evident in the composing situation of the texts we have been considering in this chapter? How are these texts enacted?

Historically, the activities involved in Reznikoff's poetic passage begin in the composing practices of a traveling salesman in Russia in the 1800s, and they are interwoven with the practice of Judaism, as well as political activism: the texts of Ezekiel's poetry were eventually destroyed out of fear that they might contain something nihilistic, which would have caused the family persecution. Later, this set of practices probably became nested in an activity we might characterize as "family storytelling"; presumably Sarah would have told Reznikoff about this incident at an early age, "bringing forth" a world lost to her and unknown to her son. We can only guess about that possibility, however, because we have no physical record of oral practices in the family. However, Reznikoff demonstrated a very early interest in the practice of writing poetry. He graduated very young (at twelve) from grammar school and, by the age of thirteen or fourteen in high school, had found two friends who shared his enthusiasm for writing ("which for us then, still in high school, meant mostly reading"):

> Eugene and I, outside, would be talking about poetry,
> especially the poetry of the new men—new to us—
> Francis Thompson, Arthur Symons, and Ernest Dowson.
> This was not in our English course,
> and Eugene and I felt superior because we read them,

and were proud of ourselves because we, too, were writing verse,
and trying our hands at sonnets
and the French confectionary Austin Dobson—for one—was good at.

(*Complete Poems* II: 160)

Note that the activities described here, reading, writing, and talking about poetry, are enacted in the context of other activities. There is, for example, the "hanging out" of teenagers; these friendships emerge among three young men feeling the harsh discrimination against the children of Jewish immigrants at school. There is the English course at school, which the boys are proud to be "reading beyond," and there is the publication of contemporary poets, such as Thompson, Symons, Dowson, and Dobson. At the same time, Reznikoff was beginning his regular practice of walking and writing for hours in the city, bringing forth both an experiential world and a textual one.

While Reznikoff developed an early sense of his mission as a writer, he soon discovered that some writing practices were not for him. He returned from the journalism school at the University of Missouri after only a year, disappointed that journalism, as noted earlier, "is most interested in news, and in the second degree in writing—and I was only interested in writing" (Sternburg and Ziegler 127).

It is clear that his later experiences in law school actually played a major role in shaping his poetic practices. Consider the wide variety of activities involved in the study of law. Reznikoff remarked that he decided to start law school because Heinrich Heine and Johann Wolfgang Goethe had studied law; and since NYU had only two hours of studying, "the rest of the day I'd be free." However, "The first thing I knew the two hours required six hours of adequate preparation. I stood second in the class, and that too encouraged me, not to study law but to study" (128). In the first place, there is an enormous amount of a very specialized kind of reading, involving material that is primarily historical records embodied in the conventions of the legal genre. In the process of dealing with vast quantities of text, law students learn to take notes that distill cases down to their barest fundamentals.

I soon had no time for writing or reading anything but law
and spent my days in the law library
diligently reading cases and memorizing sentences that seemed meaty;
reading each page as often as I liked
with nothing to jog my elbow or step on my heel;

sifting the facts of each case until I had only the hard essentials;
underlining words and phrases
until I had plotted the judge's reasoning;
and digging for the bedrock of law on which the cases stood—
or did not stand.

(*Complete Poems* II: 169)

Law students learn to challenge and to argue the facts of a case; they learn what constitutes legal evidence and proof; and they are also socialized into a particular kind of language construction that seemed far from the poetry Reznikoff had been immersed in.

I found it delightful
to climb those green heights,
to bathe in the clear waters of reason,
to use words for their daylight meaning
and not as prisms
playing with the rainbows of connotation:
after the dim lights, the colored phrases, the cloying music,
the hints of what the poets meant
and did not say

(*Complete Poems* II: 169)

In enacting these practices, Reznikoff was creating (bringing forth) not only himself but a new and different world (building on, yet moving away from, an old one).

The noise of the street was far away—
ten storeys below;
far away, too, the worry and noise of my parents' shop . . .

(*Complete Poems* II: 169)

In the process of learning to see and to think like a lawyer, he adopted as a poetic persona the role of the witness. The impact of his legal training on his understanding of the role of the poet, the text, and its readers is evident in many of his poems and discussions about poetry and is particularly striking in his interview with L. S. Dembo:

By the term "objectivist" I suppose a writer may be meant who does not write directly about his feelings but about what he sees and hears; who is restricted almost to the testimony of a witness in a court of law; and who expresses his feelings indirectly by the selection of his subject-matter and, if he writes in verse, by its music. Now suppose in a court of law, you are testifying in a negligence case. You cannot get up on the stand and say,

"The man was negligent." That's a conclusion of fact. What you'd be compelled to say is how the man acted. Did he stop before he crossed the street? Did he look? The judges of whether he is negligent or not are the jury in that case and the judges of what you say as a poet are the readers. That is, there is an analogy between testimony in the courts and the testimony of a poet. (99)

It seems, however, that the connection between his legal training and his poetic practices was not self-evident, even to Reznikoff. When he began practicing law, he was sending his poetry out for publication, and he showed some of his poems to a friend (who had been to Harvard and had studied Shakespeare with George Lyman Kittredge), with unexpected results:

> but he read my verse as I had never read verse before,
> scrutinizing it, phrase by phrase
> and word by word, thought and image, thought and sound;
> and much, if not all, that had seemed good to me
> now had the dead sound of a counterfeit coin
> on his marble good sense.
> That was the way he had read Shakespeare at college—
> without such effect, of course—
> and so, except that I gave little thought to image or sound,
> was how I had read my law cases.
> (*Complete Poems* II: 172)

Reznikoff was not devastated by this slash-and-burn critique, but gratified:

> Now doing just what Al did,
> I saw that I could use the expensive machinery
> that had cost me four years of hard work at law
> and which I had thought useless for my writing:
> prying sentences open to look at the exact meaning;
> weighing words to choose only those that had meat for my purpose
> and throwing the rest away as empty shells.
> I, too, could scrutinize every word and phrase
> as if in a document or the opinion of a judge
> and listen, as well, for tones and overtones,
> leaving only the pithy, the necessary, the clear and plain.
> (*Complete Poems* II: 172)

This interesting example demonstrates how, in the process of en-acting ourselves and our world, we use whatever resources we can bring to bear on our situation, including our past experiences, our present resourcefulness, and our interactions with others, which inevitably reflect their past experiences as well. Writers (and readers) are notoriously opportunistic in the kind of bricolage that seizes upon any experience or interaction that can be useful for enacting their textual worlds.

Meanwhile, as Reznikoff was establishing his poetic practice as a witness, he was also developing an interest in narratives and impressions of everyday life, particularly those of his own family. This interest and his own autobiographical writing undoubtedly had an effect on Nathan and Sarah, both of whom began writing their life stories. Sarah had grown too ill to work any longer when she began teaching herself to read and write English. Her texts are spare and direct and speak matter-of-factly about everyday activities. Nathan's texts are infused with allusions to biblical stories, which seem to structure his everyday experiences into richly historical, spiritual, and communal narratives. Reading texts by these three writers together, one is hardpressed to recognize that their writers inhabited the same world, and indeed they did not; yet there are correspondences where space and time on the page are shared. In the process of enacting a world, these texts emerge in a coordinated complex web.

But that's not all. To fully account for the enaction of Reznikoff's poetic text, we would have to consider many other activities and practices, which I can only touch on here. I have already noted his comprehensive and collaborative reading of poetry with Marie (a largely unacknowledged collaborator/audience/critic/supporter), his research and editorial work on the legal encyclopedia, his translating, and his editorial work on the journal the *Jewish Frontier*. Also significant is his self-publishing and self-distribution, which included *By the Well of Living and Seeing;* to ensure the preservation of his texts, he even bought a printing press, installed it in his parents' basement, and learned to operate it himself. Consequently he developed meticulous page layout and proofing skills. Marie recalled that, at the *Jewish Frontier,* "he proof-read the material and pasted the dummy with a degree of precision unfamiliar to our printer accustomed to more haphazard preparation. His galleys and dummy were works of art with carefully ruled red and black lines to guide the typesetter" (Syrkin 54). The meticulous corrections and annotations on the draft versions of the poetic passage give evidence of the care given to his editorial practices. Then too, activities involved in establishing the Objectivist Press with

Zukofsky, Oppen, and Williams, including the discussions of both business and aesthetic principles, the preparation of manuscripts, the production of physical copies, the distribution of copies to reviewers and bookstores, the bookkeeping, and other related activities were certainly important to the evolution of Reznikoff's poetry.

Beyond these activities in the production of the text, however, audiences are also involved in the enaction of texts. Through his poetry readings and correspondence, Reznikoff maintained a lively conversation with audiences, including a surprising number of other poets. The activities of readers—such as Louis Zukofsky, George Oppen, David Ignatow, Michael Davidson, and others—who not only read enthusiastically but respond with public appreciation and emulation actually help build an audience that will in turn enact and preserve the texts not only in memory, but physically, in libraries and archives, in syllabi and publishers' lists of books in print. Also significant are the activities of other readers, editors of poetry magazines, critics, publishers, and so on, whose lack of appreciation for these texts has constructed the "context of neglect" from which Reznikoff's texts are continually being "rediscovered" and "rescued." Thus the practice of scholarship also plays a role in the enaction of the text, particularly the tradition in literary scholarship of recuperating little known or underappreciated texts.

It should be clear, then, that writers, readers, and texts, as well as their environments, interact codependently in enacting a textual world and that this enaction is necessarily distributed, embodied, and emergent as well. These attributes help define the ecology of composition in which Reznikoff's poetic passage is embedded.

An Ecology of Text

In this chapter, I have argued that an ecology of composition, like any ecological system, depends on an intricate web of interactions and processes involving both living and nonliving entities. Their relationships cannot be reduced to single individuals acting independently of others and their environment, or to single artifacts residing in books or archives.

Texts are distributed across social and environmental structures; they are embodied in their writers, readers, and material structures; they are emergent through a wide range of self-organizing processes; and they are enacted through the codependent activities of readers and writers and texts interacting with their environments to bring forth the textual world.

This study of the ecology of a text takes us beyond a social constructivist theory of composing by incorporating the material, physical processes and structures involved in text production. In the same way, it takes us beyond the Bakhtinian concept of intertextuality, which focuses attention on the multiple voices and other texts evident in the content of a text. The poetic passage in "Early History of a Writer" is a physical, as well as social, ensemble, depending on material texts produced by Reznikoff and his parents and brought forth in Reznikoff's physical interactions with them: typing, marking corrections on the page, operating the printing press, stacking books in boxes for storage, and so on.

As we direct our attention across the space in which a textual ecology is situated, we need to determine the salient features, relationships, and processes of the ecosystem for the questions we are trying to answer. This discursive arena is precisely what we have begun to map in our analysis of a specific poetic passage. The view of the complex ecology of texts as distributed, embodied, emergent, and enacted should be just a little clearer. It is obvious that the composing of this poetic passage occurred under unique circumstances, a convergence of historical, social, psychological, and environmental processes that cannot be reproduced and is extremely unlikely to recur. However, it should also be obvious by now that features of this composing situation—including its distribution, embodiment, emergence, and enaction—might be evident in other composing situations. Have we been able to treat the text apart from its readers, writers, and environment? No. Can we say that we have exhausted the dimensions of this textual ecology in its physical-material, social, psychological, spatial, or temporal terms? It is obvious that we have not. We have only made a start. The next chapter extends and tests our understanding of the ecology of composing by focusing on a group of college-student writers working collaboratively to compose a single essay.

3

"Next Time We're Not Giving Steve Our Essay to Read": Ecology of Writers

Knowledge and error flow from the same mental sources;
only success can tell one from the other.

—Ernst Mach

Introduction

Like immigrants in a new land, college students find themselves thrust into a completely different ecology from the familiar families, schools, neighborhoods, and communities in which they have spent much of their early lives. To survive in this new environment, they need to draw on their prior experience and also quickly develop new skills, resources, and relationships. Suddenly the system demands that they read, think, and write in unfamiliar ways. To help students deal with these immediate demands, most colleges and universities offer a first-year composition course. These courses are often the only courses routinely required for all students. Unlike content-based courses, such as those in history, literature, or economics, first-year writing courses typically do not focus on knowledge in a subject domain: they are intended to help students develop practices and strategies that will enable them to coordinate their reading and writing activities with the increasingly sophisticated demands of new discourse arenas both in college and beyond. In that sense, a class such as this, although typically situated in an English department, is closer to a chemistry lab than a survey course in American literature. It provides a bridge for students' adaptation to a new ecological environment. Consequently, such a course can offer an excellent opportunity to examine how complex systems of readers, writers, and texts emerge and develop in a rapidly changing environment. This chapter looks at how students writing collaboratively adapt as writers in a first-year composition course at the University of California at San Diego (UCSD).

Holland, Oyama, Kauffman, Hutchins, and others have suggested that learning is an example of adaptation in complex, distributed systems. In any ecological system, agents are actively seeking to improve their fitness in a given environment. As noted earlier, Hutchins considers that learning is one way to discover and save solutions to frequently encountered problems, an adaptive process that generates coordination between internal and external structures. This process can be observed in many different kinds of environments, from biological systems to economics to organizations and institutions. According to Holland, adaptation raises similar questions across disciplines, including,

> To what parts of its environment is the organism (system, organization) adapting?
> How does the environment act upon the adapting organism (system, organization)?
> What structures are undergoing adaptation?
> What are the mechanisms of adaptation?
> What part of the history of its interaction with the environment does the organism (system, organization) retain?
> What limits are there to the adaptive process?
> How are different (hypotheses about) adaptive processes to be compared?
> (*Adaptation* 2)

These questions are especially pertinent to the situation of teaching and learning in college-level composition courses. In this study, I refer to *adaptation* as a process of enduring structural transformation resulting from interactions between an organism or system and its environment. *Coordination* refers to any accommodation between an organism or a system and its environment, including both transitory and enduring accommodations. Therefore, coordination necessarily includes, but is not restricted to, adaptation.

The problem for students is how to retain the useful parts of their prior reading and writing experiences (solutions to previously encountered problems) yet gain new skills and strategies in the process of adapting to the demands of a new environment. The problem for instructors, textbook authors, and program administrators is how to support students in this transformational process. Students may, for example, manage a temporary, situated coordination with a specific composing situation yet be unable to make necessary adaptive changes (more stable, lasting changes that can be transferred to other composing situations) in their conceptual structures or in their use of social or environmental resources for composing.

This chapter examines how students work toward coordination with their peers and their instructor, as well as with structures in their environment, including the course texts and the computers on which they compose. The study looks closely at three students working collaboratively to compose a single essay and, in particular, at the development of the group as a complex ecological system that is distributed, embodied, emergent, and enactive.

Context of the Study

During the winter quarter, 1989, I conducted case-study research to explore what happens as students write collaboratively. I was interested in collaborative writing, which was the focus of considerable attention in composition studies at that time (Bruffee; Lunsford and Ede; Reither and Vipond), but I was also interested in how writers think about the composing process as it unfolds. Considerable research had already been conducted using talk-aloud protocols (Flower and Hayes, "Cognitive," "Images"; Hayes and Flower), but I felt these studies were too contrived and mechanistic to reveal much about how writers make sense of composing situations. Rather than training writers to talk aloud while writing, creating an extraordinarily artificial, self-conscious, and overcomplicated writing situation, I wanted to audiotape writers working together. I believed that the process of writing collaboratively would compel writers to make some of their normally tacit thinking about composing explicit in their naturally occurring conversations with each other. It seemed to me that if we could capture these conversations as writers were engaged in a writing task in the normal course of instruction (as opposed to a "laboratory" setting), we might gain a better understanding of the cognitive models and processes of student writers. And in the process we could learn a great deal about the adaptive properties of ecological systems of readers, writers, and texts. In addition to audiotaping students' group meetings, I observed students during class time and in their conferences with me; and I collected their journals and workshop critiques, as well as their writing for the course.

Although I still prefer a naturalistic setting for studies of composing, I soon realized that my method of audiotaping writers as they collaborated introduced its own set of constraints. David Woods contrasts this method with talk-aloud protocols: both methods are included in what he calls *process-tracing methods*, referring to a group of techniques intended to externalize internal processes or produce external signs that support inferences about internal workings.

> One common technique is to transform the target behavioral situation into one that requires cooperation between two people. . . . This manipulation generates protocols based on verbal behavior that occur as part of the natural task behavior, rather than having participants produce concurrent verbal reports as an additional task. Note how the choice of manipulation in the test situation—change the task to a cooperative one versus ask for concurrent verbal reports—represents a tradeoff in sources of uncertainty about how the externalized cues relate to internal processes. (233)

The course. The students were enrolled in a first-year composition course in Third College at UCSD. The course, TCWP 1A, was the first quarter of a two-quarter sequence in the Third College Writing Program (TCWP), where I was the instructor. Class size was small, with a maximum of sixteen students per section. We met in a modern college classroom furnished with large tables, generally pushed together to make one very large table with chairs arranged around it. A smaller table at the front of the room, intended for the instructor, was usually used only as a temporary rest stop for handouts and for student work as it was turned in. One wall was entirely windows, and blackboards covered two of the remaining walls. There were no decorations, books, computers, or other furnishings or equipment. The class met for an hour and fifty minutes twice a week for ten weeks. Students also met outside of class to work on collaborative reading presentations, journals, and essay assignments. During this quarter, students wrote four essays: an essay making an evaluation, an essay analyzing the causes of a trend, an essay proposing a solution to a problem, and an essay of literary interpretation, analyzing a short story. While the type of essay was specified for each assignment, students chose their own topics. Their other writing included weekly responses to journal questions that focused on various aspects of their reading and writing for the course and responses to the drafts of other students in class workshops. (See appendix A for a copy of the course syllabus and the journal questions for this quarter.)

The text. There were two required texts: *The St. Martin's Guide to Writing,* 2nd ed., by Rise Axelrod and Charles Cooper, and the short-story collection *Ellis Island and Other Stories,* by Mark Helprin. Writing instruction closely followed the activity sequences in *The St. Martin's Guide* for each essay type. Because instruction in the TCWP 1A and 1B courses was structured around this text, it is here worth summarizing a typical chapter. During the case study, students worked with chapter 7, "Proposing Solutions" (216–55). The chapter is divided into three main sections: "Readings," "A Guide to Writing," and "A Writer at Work." In "Readings," students read examples of published essays proposing solutions to problems: Adam Paul Weisman's "Birth Control in the Schools: Clinical Examination"; David Owen's "Testing and Society: What Can Be Done?"; and Carol Bly's "To Unteach Greed." They also read an essay written by first-year college student Wendy Niwa, "A Proposal to Strengthen the Language Acquisition Project." Each essay is followed by some questions for analysis directed toward rhetorical features of the essay and commentary about the essay. Following these readings, the chapter suggests some important considerations about purpose and audience in writing this type of essay; it then discusses the "basic features" of effective proposals, including "a well-defined problem," "a clear proposed solution," "a convincing argument," and "a reasonable tone."

In the second major section of the chapter, "Guide to Writing," students (and instructors) are provided with various activities designed to assist them with the stages of the project.

"The Writing Task" defines the assignment:

> Write an essay proposing a solution to a particular problem. It should be one you are familiar with or can research. Choose a problem faced by a group to which you belong, and address your proposal either to one or more members of the group or to an outsider who might help solve the problem. (241)

"Invention and Research" provides extensive heuristics for choosing a problem to write about, finding a tentative solution, testing the topic choice, identifying readers, defending a solution, listing and developing reasons for adopting the proposal, comparing the solution to alternative solutions, and researching the proposal.

"Planning and Drafting" helps students organize and draft the proposal through questions and suggestions for seeing what they have, setting goals, outlining the proposal, and drafting the proposal.

"Reading a Draft with a Critical Eye" gives suggestions for providing feedback on a classmate's draft, with a series of questions focused on a range of rhetorical issues, from the definition of the problem to the tone of the argument. This section of the chapter was commonly used as a guide during student workshops on first drafts.

"Revising and Editing" suggests possibilities for incorporating workshop feedback, as well as for revising to strengthen the argument and revising for readability.

"Learning from Your Own Writing Process" suggests that writers reflect on the work done for the proposal and on what they have learned about their own composing process in the process of writing it.

The third major section of the chapter, "A Writer at Work," focuses on how a student writer, Wendy Niwa, analyzed her audience as she was developing her essay (presented as one of the readings in the chapter).

By the time students were ready to begin the proposal essay assignment, they were quite familiar with the text and the structured composing process for essays in this course (readings, invention activities, planning and drafting, workshops, revisions, final submission, and self-evaluation). Following the same process, they had previously written two essays, "making an evaluation" and "analyzing the causes of a trend." The second essay assignment had also formally introduced students to library research at UCSD, documentation, and citation conventions. The main difference between the third writing task and previous essay assignments was that students would be writing the proposal essay collaboratively, in groups of two or three, rather than individually. The evaluation given for the essay would be shared by all members of the group. To ensure that students would not feel penalized or disadvantaged by this unusual arrangement, I modified the customary evaluation procedures so that, at the end of the quarter, students could select three out of the four essays assigned that quarter for their final course evaluation. If a student felt the collaborative essay was problematic, he or she could drop it from consideration; on the other hand, if the group produced a strong essay, the student could drop one of his or her other, weaker essays. Further, students had the option of writing the final essay, the literary analysis, either collaboratively or individually.

In this course, individual essays were not given grades; instead, instructors provided extensive comments, responding to each essay. Students were given an estimate of their current grade at midterm, and then they received a final grade, together with a written commentary on their progress and achievements in the course.

The activities. Students formed collaborative groups of three at the beginning of the quarter, and each group was responsible for presenting and discussing one of the essays of the text for each assigned chapter. I had modified the writing task to provide students with some experience working and writing collaboratively. Figure 9 shows the assignment handout provided to students after we had discussed the collaborative assignment extensively in class.

Fig. 9. Collaborative writing assignment handout

The Proposal Essay
a Collaborative Writing Task
TCWP 1A

The Task: Write an essay proposing a solution to a particular problem. It should be one you are familiar with or can research. Choose a problem faced by a group to which you belong, and address your proposal either to one or more members of the group or to an outsider who might help solve the problem. This essay should be between 6–8 typed, double-spaced pages.

Basic Features of the Proposal Essay (from the *St. Martin's Guide*):
A well-defined problem. The essay must convince the reader that the problem exists and is serious enough to warrant attention. The essay must demonstrate an awareness of the problem's causes and consequences, its history and past efforts to deal with it.

A clear proposed solution. This constitutes the thesis of the proposal. The proposed solution should be thoughtful and realistic.

A convincing argument. The essay demonstrates (1) that the proposed solution will solve the problem; (2) that it is a feasible way of solving the problem; and (3) that it is better than other ways of solving the problem.

A reasonable tone. Because the essay hopes to engage the reader in implementing the solution, the proposal must show respect for the reader's point of view, and for possible counterarguments and alternative solutions.

Collaborative Component: This essay is to be written collaboratively, by your reading/writing group. Working together as a group, you will produce a single essay. Your group will share the evaluation for this essay.

Submitting Your Package. Each group will submit a single final package containing all invention work, a first and second draft, workshop responses, a completed conference worksheet, a final revision, and each group member's self-evaluation.

continued on next page

Fig. 9. Continued

Schedule of the Work. The schedule for completing the work is as indicated on the Course Schematic which I provided you at the beginning of the quarter. Each member of the group is equally responsible for meeting the deadlines for preparing the first draft, workshops, final revisions, and so on.

Managing the Writing Task. Every collaborative writing group works differently. You will need to decide for yourselves how to plan and accomplish your work. Some groups like to assign individual tasks and then bring the various parts together; others prefer to work together on every phase of the work. Some groups work best with a strong leader who directs the work; others work best as equal partners, sharing leadership responsibilities. It's up to you to decide what will work best for your group.

Note: There are two factors which are essential to your success: careful planning, and respect for each individual's ideas and contributions.

Conferences. The conference for this essay will be scheduled with your writing group. However, I am always happy to discuss the work with you individually, as well. Call for an appointment.

Workshops. Drafts will be discussed in the workshop in this way: each group member will bring two copies of the draft to be discussed in small groups which do not include other members of the group. In other words, we will treat the workshop as if the drafts are individually written. This will give you and your group an opportunity to get more responses to each draft.

Reviewing Your Own Experience. I hope you will be aware of your own thoughts, feelings, problems, and pleasures during this experience. It is an excellent opportunity to learn something important about how you function within a group, and to discover new writing strategies that you might use in the future. I will ask you to describe some of your reactions in your journals.

When the assignment was first introduced, I suggested that the class engage in some focused brainstorming, as we had done for previous essays. Students reviewed the invention and research section of chapter 7 in the *St. Martin's Guide,* and then each student listed on a piece of paper five problems that might make potential topics. Students took turns reading their topics one at a time while a student volunteer listed and numbered them on the blackboard. They also added to the list as they thought of additional topics. In this way, close to one hundred topics were generated. We discussed several of these topics in order to "walk through" how a writer might proceed to develop a proposal essay based on that topic. During this discussion, I was also able to point out difficulties or challenges presented by specific topics or their development: logistical problems, methodological problems, rhetorical problems. I also attempted to point out problems of scale: topics that seemed too large and unwieldy for the purposes and time constraints of this assignment (drug abuse, terrorism); topics that seemed too trivial, fleeting, or personal for a college-level essay or not worthy of their efforts (a sloppy roommate, an argument with a parent). And I reminded writers that even this list was not exhaustive but only suggestive; they might choose a topic from the list, or they might think of another topic altogether. The goal was to make their possibilities as expansive as possible yet still provide some examples so that they would not find the possibilities overwhelming. The only restriction was the program-wide policy that students may not select topics that would put themselves or others in physical jeopardy or engage them in illegal activities. In the remaining class time, students met with their collaborative groups to arrange a time and place to work together and to discuss possible topics.

The next step for students was to meet with their collaborative group outside of class to complete the invention work in the chapter and then plan and prepare the first draft of their essay. Each student was to bring two copies of the draft for the in-class workshop the following week.

During the workshop, each student exchanged drafts with two other students, read each others' drafts, and commented in writing, using a handout as a framework for their responses (see appendix B). The purpose of the handout was to help students focus their comments on specific issues in the development of the draft and on particular features of the essay in order to make their critiques more useful and helpful to writers. Because these comments were in written form, writers had something more concrete than their memories of what was said about the draft as they sat down to revise. After readers had written individual responses to the drafts, the workshop group discussed each draft, often elaborating on the comments they had written. In this way, each collaborative group actually received feedback from six readers.

Following the workshop, collaborative groups met again to revise the draft, drawing on the suggestions of readers from the workshop and the chapter in the text. They prepared a second draft to bring to a conference with me. They also completed a short handout to prepare for the conference (see appendix C), giving me an overview of the group's plans and problems involving the essay. Conferences were held with each group in my office; typically I would read the draft silently, or one of the students would read it aloud; then we would review the conference handout together and discuss the progress of the draft.

The collaborative groups then met to prepare the final revision of the essay and gather all of the invention work, drafts, and workshop comments for inclusion in the final package to be submitted to me. Each student also included an individually authored self-evaluation, an informal memo to me reflecting on the student's writing and learning process over the course of the assignment. This provided an opportunity for students to share with me their individual opinions and reflections, both positive and negative, about their experiences writing collaboratively.

The study. I asked for volunteers to participate in the case study from among the collaborative groups that had been formed at the start of the course; nearly every group volunteered. I selected several groups of students for the study and asked them to tape-record their meetings outside of class as they engaged in collaborative work; from these groups, I chose the group composed of Rick, Dana, and Annie for this case study. These students were typical of UCSD students, who represent the top 12 percent of the graduating classes in California high schools and tend to be middle class or upper middle class (the median family income for UCSD students during this year was fifty thousand dollars). They were eighteen to nineteen years old, first-year students, and living in the Third College dorms.

The group recorded one session in which they prepared a collaborative reading presentation and then recorded all of their meetings during the preparation of their collaborative writing assignment. I also taped the group's second-draft conference with me. Otherwise, their participation in the class and its activities was typical of that of all other students in the course. I decided not to tape class meetings: distinguishing individual voices in a group this size is almost impossible, and the alternative, wiring individual students, seemed too intrusive. My goal was to create an environment as normal as possible for this class.

For a new instructor, the textbook provided an organized, coherent framework that made it relatively easy to plan activities and provide support for student writing. Students seemed to find it a rich resource for their writing as well; few students sold their textbooks back after the quarter, and it was common for students long out of the program to tell instructors that they were still using the book as a reference for their writing. I had taught TCWP 1A for the first time the previous quarter, and I felt fairly confident and well prepared for the course.

Rationale for the collaborative writing assignment. I had designed the collaborative writing task to give students some experience with a kind of writing situation fairly common both within the academy and beyond it.[1] Although in Lunsford and Ede's study of collaborative writing, 87 percent of professionals in a wide variety of fields reported that they sometimes write as members of a team or group, 81 percent of those surveyed reported that they had not received any on-the-job training to prepare them for group writing, and 61 percent felt that their high school and college English classes did not adequately prepare them for writing collaboratively. In light of these findings, my goal was to give the students some experience with the challenges and the pleasures of writing with others. To prepare them for the essay assignment, I planned a sequence of journal questions focusing on issues of collaboration and an assignment to prepare a collaborative presentation of a reading from the text. We also discussed in class some typical issues or problems that arise when people write together, from scheduling the work to coordinating different writing styles to working with disagreements. In general, the students in the class expressed their enthusiasm for the collaborative essay assignment, both before they began working together and during the process; no student protested it, either in class or privately.

The workshop on the draft. During the workshop on the first draft, I stayed out of the way and observed the students' interactions; in my experience, if I joined a group or hovered nearby, the students would begin to focus their attention toward me rather than toward the writer or the draft, expecting me to provide the "right answer." But even from my position on the sidelines, it was clear that the case-study group had generated an impassioned response from one of their readers. At the end of class, I asked Rick, one of the group's writers, about it. He said that the topic of their essay was "noise in the dorms" and that one reader, Steve, had argued vehemently that people had a right to listen to their music as loud as they liked, that noise in the dorms was not a real problem, and that any attempt to control his music was an infringement on his personal freedom.

I was a bit surprised that the group had chosen this topic; I felt it was roughly equivalent to several of the topics that, during the brainstorming session, I had suggested were too trivial for this assignment. Topics chosen by other groups in the class included a proposal for a commuter rail system to alleviate the problem of traffic congestion in San Diego and a proposal for the formation of "neighborhood watch" groups in the dorms to reduce theft, which was becoming a serious problem. I asked Rick how his group could convince readers that the problem of noise in the dorms was serious enough to warrant their attention. He responded by assuring me that the problem was really serious; I was not aware at that point that during the workshop several students had agreed that noise in the dorms was a real problem. I reminded Rick that the group could still change topics. (In an earlier class, we had discussed situations in which students discovered that the topic they had chosen was not workable and then returned to the invention work to develop a new topic.)

This should have been a second sign to the writers that they should plan a change of topic. The first sign, however, provided by one of their workshop readers, had come from a person markedly different from the rest of the class and generally treated as an outsider, although I thought he was a real asset. He had long hair, wore T-shirts advertising heavy metal bands, and offered outspoken, often combative opinions in class discussions. His collaborative group was proposing the legalization of marijuana as a way of reducing the problem of drug abuse. In contrast, the other students in the class were polite, conservative in their dress and opinions, agreeable, and cooperative to a fault. It's not entirely surprising that the collaborative group discounted Steve's opinion. It's a bit more unexpected that the second sign, from me, the instructor, was also ignored; while I had tried to tactfully frame my suggestion of a change of topic as a possibility, I assumed the group would recognize it as a compelling need.

Conference with the instructor. When the collaborative group met in my office for a conference on their second draft, I was even more surprised to discover that their topic was still unchanged. Worse, the draft seemed very superficial and the reasoning thin. Not only did the problem of noise in the dorms after quiet hours seem trivial, but the proposed solution (ask the residence halls dean to press the resident advisers [RAs] for stronger enforcement) seemed obvious and hardly worth arguing. The draft did not present any alternative solutions that either had been tried or might be tried to resolve the problem; consequently, there was no real argument that the proposed solution was the best among alternative solutions. Considering and rejecting alternative solutions is presented in the text as a basic feature of the proposal essay, under "Developing a Convincing Argument": "the writer has to convince readers that his or her solution is preferable to other solutions. This is done by examining alternative ways of solving the problem" (240).

In spite of Steve's vigorous, well-defined objections during the workshop, the draft made no gesture toward counterargument, another aspect of a convincing argument in the text: "An important part of arguing that a proposal is feasible involves anticipating counterarguments. Counterarguments consist of any objections or reservations readers may have about the proposed solution" (240).

The conference stands out in my memory as one of my least successful efforts. The tape of the conference shows that, during the first half, I struggled to say something positive about the draft ("Well, you make a fairly good case for the seriousness of its effect on students . . ."). In the second half, I alternated between trying to think out loud about how it could be improved ("Well, you need to think of this as a letter, and that your solution . . . you're proposing is one you expect that the person you're writing this letter to—and think of it as a single person, either it's a single student who represents people living in the dorms or people on campus or whatever, or it's the dean—think specifically about how you can interest that person in this problem.") and trying to reassure them that they could still change their topic and complete the essay on time ("I had one group this morning, which has changed its topic four times and changed it again in the conference, but I think they finally have a good one"). In fact, I was entirely unnerved; it seemed incredible that the group could produce such a weak effort, given the course context and their previous essays. I clung to the faint hope that the writers would reconsider the draft and mount a heroic effort on a new essay topic.

The essay. The final revision was a disappointment, all around, although the writers had made a major change in their proposed solution to noise in the dorms. Their new solution was the creation of "quiet dorms" in a set of buildings separated from the other dorms. Under this proposal, when students filled out residence hall applications, they could specify a preference for the quiet dorms. This was an improvement over "calling the dean," since it was slightly less obvious. There was a more elaborated argument for the seriousness of the problem (students cannot study effectively; loss of sleep makes them more susceptible to contagious illnesses; and once they are ill, it takes them longer to recover), and there were brief vignettes to frame the essay at the beginning and the end. But in spite of our class discussions and the discussion and activities in the text about purpose and audience, the essay showed general confusion about who was being addressed and what the purpose of the essay might be. The framing vignettes were in the second person, addressing a reader who is clearly a fellow student:

> Imagine lying in bed on your back as your face gets covered with white specks of what used to be the ceiling. Tenants above you are playing a heated game of basketball and are determined to finish their four-hour game. Glancing over at the clock, it is now two thirty-three AM and there are about five hours left before your eight AM calculus class.

However, the body of the essay seemed to be addressed to the residence halls administration, arguing for the detrimental effects on students of noise in the dorms and proposing the creation of the quiet dorms. Of course, I (the instructor) was the actual audience, although in class discussions I had urged writers to address these proposals to those people who had the ability to implement their solutions, and even to send them as letters.

The actual text of the unsatisfying essay is not our concern here. As an unfortunate outcome it might be of interest in some other time or place. Instead, we are interested in the struggles of this ecological system of readers and writers and texts to come into coordination, and in the critical dynamics of adaptation.

Distribution and the Writers

Composition courses foreground the mutual efforts of coordination by which students are socialized into the larger discourse arenas (upper-division courses, academic and professional writing, public discourse, and so on) of the cultures in which they live. Student writers are (more or less actively) attempting to adapt to the expectations and demands of new composing environments, while instructors, text-books, assignment sequences, academic institutions, and other students are actively trying to enable them to do so. Resources in the environment—computer labs, copy centers, tutoring centers, and second-language assistance—are made available to assist in coordination. Consequently, it should be obvious that composing situations in such environments are necessarily distributed, as are the efforts aimed at coordination within the system.

The writers in the collaborative group decided to distribute the work by sharing rather than dividing: they agreed to work on the essay only when they were all together in the same room, generally with one person keyboarding texts and changes while the group discussed the work as it unfolded. This decision (which created its own set of problems) was reflected in the responses to journal questions collected during the second week of the collaborative writing assignment.

1. How did your group go about planning the work? How did you decide how you would schedule your meetings?

> Dana: Our group (my group) just called each other and planned to meet. We decided that our meetings would be in the evenings.
>
> Rick: Our group decided how to schedule the work by comparing our class schedules and finding a date and time that we could meet. Sometimes we found that there just wasn't enough time in the day, so we meet over dinner or lunch.
>
> Annie: We met at a specified time and just jumped right in. We didn't really plan the work. We always seem to distribute it evenly without even trying. The meetings were scheduled just by discussing the most convenient times for all of our schedules.

2. How did your group divide the workload?

> Dana: We decided to work on the paper as a whole, not to divide it into parts.
>
> Rick: The division of the work was based on general consensus of the group. We all are equally involved in the mental aspect of the writing (invention, outlining, research, etc.). The physical aspect, such as the actual writing, is based on each person's abilities and time restraints.
>
> Annie: We didn't divide the workload. It's all done by a group effort.

Although the notion of dividing up the work was briefly mentioned, it was never seriously considered, as tapes of the first meeting show:

> Dana: Oh, it should be six to eight pages, typed double-spaced.[2]
> Annie: Six to eight? We'll have trouble getting four pages!
> Rick: Two pages a person, if we each take part of it . . . two pages isn't bad.
> Dana: We could each write a part of it . . .
> Annie: Oh, I'd rather do it all together, I think.

This method proved problematic when one or more members of the group was unavailable. During those times, work on the essay stopped entirely. In response to the week-seven journal asking students to describe some of the obstacles or problems faced by the group during the collaborative writing assignment, Annie wrote,

> Our main obstacles have been the time period that this essay fell on. During the time period before the first draft was due, Dana went on a trip. Rick and I felt that she shouldn't miss out on choosing a topic so we waited until the night before it was do to work on it together. Then when the 2nd draft was due, I was going out of town so, yet again, we waited and did it together.

Beyond the group itself, however, the writers were also dependent upon, and causally motivated by, the textbook, other students in the class, me, the institutional structure of TCWP, competing demands of their other classes, the physical environment of the classroom and dorm rooms in which the writing was accomplished, and the technologies for writing, including the computer hardware and software on which the writing was actually composed and another system of hardware and software on which I composed course materials and responded to student writing.

It was not always clear to the writers, however, how to manage or draw on the resources that were available to them. During the invention work, they referred to the textbook invention activities primarily as a way of reducing uncertainty and simplifying the complexity of the task rather than as a way of expanding possibilities for topic choices, as I encouraged students to do. They first reduced the list of nearly one hundred topics from the in-class brainstorming to a handful by summarily dismissing topics without consideration, as the tapes of the group's first meeting reveal:

Dana: OK forget the family, forget TCWP, forget that UCSD is dull, forget that there's no there's lack of spirit, you can't write on that . . .

Hazy memories of the class discussion on topic selection eliminated other topics:

Dana: OK bad building architecture's out because she said about the costs and all that—

Annie: But we can say about how there's—no, because you still can't change—

Dana: We could talk about, like the plumbing system and the heating system and all that—

Annie: It's still going to cost to fix it . . .

Dana: Oh, we're not supposed to bring up things that can—that will cost, you think?

Rick: Some people said they could . . .

Annie: You could, but like, we can't change the building, we can't rip them down, but we can change the heating system . . .

The distribution of the composing situation expanded during the workshop on the first draft, when the group first encountered the diverse responses of readers. Below are some of the written responses of their fellow students, following the guidelines on the workshop handout (see appendix B); I have reproduced them here at length to provide a sense of their diversity and scope, as well as to demonstrate some of the difficulties faced by the writing group in deciding how to manage the revising. In addition, these responses give us a good sense of the efforts made by readers to assist in the coordination of the composing process.

1. **General impressions.** Write a few sentences stating your immediate reaction to the draft.

   CL: good topic, although solution is not solid. I do realize, however, that this is a rough draft.

   SS: 1st there are several problems which I immediately see with your proposal. There will be more conflict between students if they get written up. I believe if there is a noise complaint the people making the noise can find out who complains. Also, security guards are needed at night to deter parking lot theft. I don't want another babysitter watching me. Also, I would argue that our quiet hours are too restrictive. A compromise should be made. Quiet hours should be extended and then if people make to much noise after those hours show no mercy and write them up. Another problem is that our dorms have no insulation at all in them and were not constructed to contain noise. When students move into the dorms they do have to respect other peoples rights. But also people give up many of their rights to privacy. If someone needs a lot of silence move to a quiet apartment off campus. Our dorms are actually quite conservative compared to many universitys and people don't realize how nice they have it here.

EB: The draft is very "rough." It's a great topic because the problem definitely exists but you need to expand and give specific examples. (I'm sure you were planning to do that anyway.[)]

2. **Audience.** Is it clear to you who is the audience for this essay? Describe the audience the writer is addressing. Does the writer's tone seem persuasive for this particular audience? Does it seem to you that this audience can take action to solve the problem?

CL: It seems as if the paper is addressing students to become motivated themselves and then pushed the campus police.

SS: I guess your audience should be towards Third College Adm. because they have the power to make the switchs. So make sure its written towards them.

TW: Audience would be Yolanda. Mail essay to her, eh.

MB: Audience is 3rd College Dorm residents and administration. I think tone could be much more persuasive but that should come as you write it out. Yes audience can take action.

EB: The audience puts the paper in the perspective that the reader is in this situation. This is a great angle to take because the reader becomes annoyed (as if he/she is in this situation) and would like a proposed solution for the problem. I would suggest really making the problem sound annoying in the first paragraph. (Overstress)

3. **Defining the Problem.** Is the problem clearly defined? Are you convinced that the problem exists? Write down in one or two sentences exactly what the problem is.

CL: The problem is clear and obviously exists (unfortunately). The problem is noisy recreational activities of Third students, after quiet time.

SS: You have stated your side of the problem, but remember there is already a movement in the dorms to lengthen quiet hours, so you should deal with that.

TW: Problem will be defined well. Are you sure problem is widespread, though? A general feeling? I have no noise problem . . .

maybe prove it is a wide-spread problem.

MB: I live the problem—it exists! The problem is loud noise after quiet hours that no one does anything about.

EB: The problem (lack of enforcement of quiet hours) definitely exists and is clearly stated.

4. **Convincing the Audience of the Seriousness of the Problem.** Has the writer presented the problem in a way that will convince *the identified audience* that the problem is serious and that something should be done about it?

CL: I am convinced the problem is serious, but through experience rather than persuasion from the paper. I'm sure the problem will seem more serious after 1. lack of sleep 2. missing of classes 3. sickness and 4. conflicts between students is elaborated upon.

MB: The problem will be more convincing after you add affect to dorm members.

EB: The problem is stated with some effectiveness but I feel that if you state examples magnifying the seriousness of the problem it will be much more effective. show some results of what happens when students can't study or sleep.

5. **Proposed solution.** Has the writer clearly presented a way the problem could be solved? Is this solution described in enough detail so that the readers will be able to take action on it? Does the solution seem reasonable?

CL: Although the solution seems easy enough, I don't think the security will comply. They don't care if you don't sleep.

SS: Your solution is going to be very disliked by a majority of the residents. They will probably retaliate by majority and make your life worse.

TW: Solution seems a little shallow. Do you really want Armahn & the R.A.'s running in giving tickets every time you laugh a little too loud. What is definition of *quiet?* Cut-off? One persons quiet is not necessarily someone elses idea.

MB: Your proposed solution seems reasonable but be sure and find out how much is already being done—like, can the guards or RA's hear the noise (thumps, bumps, etc.) that bother you? They might not be able to.

EB: You have proposed a solution but I feel that it has been described in a vague fashion. It's also a bit to obvious. Supposedly they are enforcing these hours now. Maybe you could propose a new enforcement system

6. **Argument and Counterarguments.** Has the writer argued well for the proposed solution? Does the writer provide enough evidence in the form of reasons, examples, facts, statistics, and so on to support the proposed solution? What other evidence might be provided? Has the writer anticipated the audience's counterarguments?

> TW: Alternative: What about implementing quiet dorms for those requiring more quiet? Have more places for "loud" people to "hang-out" at night. Don't all students, louder & quieter have equal rights to living area, since everyone pays same amount? Why do those requiring what some would consider unnecessary quiet deserve prefriential treatment.
> MB: You haven't stated any alternative solutions.

The distribution of reading and response presented new problems of coordination for the collaborative writers: How should they think about the varied responses to the draft, and how could they implement the diverse suggestions they received? The week-seven journal asks, "How did your group decide which revisions to make? Who actually made the revisions?"

> Annie: We read the responses and kept the general ideas in mind while revising. We had to make major alterations in our proposal so we didn't worry about the small suggestions given to us. . . . It seemed pretty obvious what needed to be done. The class clearly told us to find a better solution and a different audience. We made the revisions as a group. It was done in the same manner as the first draft.
> Rick: We read the various comments offered by the class and looked for common "motifs" in their responses. Once we had a mental list of the problems, we then began to write the second draft of the paper.

The audiotapes, however, reveal that during the revising of the first draft there was little discussion of the feedback from readers. The night before the second draft was due at the conference, the group met in Rick's dorm room. There was only one reference to the workshop:

> Dana: . . . So far we've found out that our topic was not pleasing to everyone—
> Annie: And that our audience must be a dean maybe?
> Rick: Yeah. Unless we can get somebody higher. That'll make it easier to back up.

Annie: Next time we're not giving Steve our essay to read.
Dana: Yeah . . .
Annie: Obviously he must be a very loud person . . .
Rick: Yeah, since he took offence.

The distribution of the composing task was further extended to include me, both via the class discussions of the work and the conferences with the collaborative groups. In a larger sense, the distributed activity actually originated with me when I developed this collaborative assignment sequence and (to some extent) set its sequence, scope, and limitations as it was presented to students. And it was bounded by my evaluation of the final essay package. I, as instructor and representative of TCWP, set the composing dynamic in motion, participated actively in it, and finally judged the success of its outcome.

But the human agents do not exhaust the components of the collaborative writing assignment. The ecology of this composing situation also included the physical environment and, in particular, the technologies by which the writing was constructed. It is evident from the tapes that two of the writers considered the computer integral to the composing process. During their first meeting on the writing assignment, the group discussed how the composing would be done.

Dana: You guys can write the paper and I'll go home.
Annie: Yeah, right.
Dana: I'll type it, OK? That's fair, isn't it?
Annie: No, because we're typing it on the computer—you, your
    computer—
Dana: I don't have a computer!
Annie: I know, that's what I said, you don't have one. If you don't
    have one, how can you type it up? If you have a computer you can
    check for spelling mistakes—
Rick: Yeah, it's fun when you have a computer—
Dana: Well I can check for that, my typewriter has that little—
Annie: Oh that's right, it has the—
Dana: . . . thing on it.

As it turned out, the first two drafts of the essay were composed as the collaborative group gathered around a single computer, either in Rick's dorm room or in Annie's, with one person inputting or changing text or reading back what had been written as the others made suggestions. While the group was composing and revising, the extent to which the computer had become embedded in the composing process was evident.

> Dana: That's a leadin for the next paragraph where we talk about what kinds of illnesses you can get . . .
>
> Rick: Well, we can list a whole bunch, too . . .
>
> Dana: Can we make a page out of it? Just kidding! Just kidding!
>
> Annie: We can always use a bigger type size and triple space, and narrow the margins. . . .
>
> Rick: Well it doesn't have a uh, the conclusion on it because we didn't come up with one.
>
> Annie: One, two, three, four. [sound of pages turning] That is very depressing. It was longer than this before.
>
> Rick: Yeah, it . . . shrunk, by, uh . . . point eight k. . . .
>
> Annie: We will definitely have to do a spellcheck on this.

The final draft was revised on the computer printout of the second draft; one person read aloud and recorded the suggestions for revisions. Then the final copy was keyed in by Rick, working alone the night before it was due. The question of whether the essay might have been stronger if it had been produced via a more traditional method (for instance, handwritten drafts followed by a typed final version) is a moot one; this particular writing situation, like any other, was distributed across a specific set of technologies for writing. The technologies themselves may vary (from papyrus or clay tablet to quill pen and parchment, from typewriters and onionskin to computers and their monitors), but the distribution of composing across some set of technologies is undeniable. And where they are able to, writers will continue to adopt new technologies for composing; in return, these technologies fundamentally constrain and enable not merely the form but the structure and content of the writing as well. In this case, the computers and software used by the writers functionally altered the writing environment and the production of text; it might be argued that they became part of the collaborative writing ensemble—unacknowledged participants in the writing group.

Less central, but still significant, were the copy machines that made it possible for multiple copies of drafts to be shared in the workshop. Here the influence of the technology was less on the form or content of the writing itself than on its distribution to and reception by readers, who were thus able to provide feedback that could inform revisions. For this reason, we should include copy machines in our ecology of composing as part of the dynamic process of text production, even where they have a relatively minor direct impact on the actual product. When there is only a single original draft, it is much more difficult and time-consuming to get feedback from multiple sources, and there is a much greater possibility for confusion; multiple copies allow writers to distribute drafts and coordinate responses.

What we observe, in this case, is a distributed system for composing that includes three writers, an instructor, six student readers, a textbook, three computers with their software, and a photocopier, situated in a set of physical environments and institutional structures that include the TCWP, the Third College dormitories, and the larger university as well.

Embodiment and the Writers

The embodiment of writers is impossible to overlook in this study. The writers chose as a topic a problem that was grounded in their physical experience: the noise that disturbed them in the dorms. They opened and closed the essay with parallel vignettes of physical description: "Imagine lying in bed on your back as your face gets covered with white specks of what used to be the ceiling. . . ." "Imagine you are sitting at your desk on a Tuesday night. . . ." Further, they invoked physical distress as evidence of the seriousness of the problem of noise in the dorms.

> Annie: OK we'll talk about lack of sleep, sickness, missing classes and then conflict between students . . .
> Dana: OK, lack of sleep is one, two is sickness, three is—
> Rick: So, lack of sleep first, huh . . .
> Annie: Yeah, lack of sleep first.
> Dana: OK.
> Annie: We don't have a paragraph on this, though.
> Rick: Well now we need an intro into this . . .
> Dana: So, the high level of noise in the dorm—
> Annie: Is nearly impossible—
> Rick: Nearly impossible. . . . We gotta make it sound real . . . bad . . . though.
> Annie: *Real* bad.
> Rick: I'm about ready to hang myself! [laughs] Just do something!
> Dana: OK, we're all into drugs—
> Annie: We're using sleeping pills . . .

They were determined to write the essay while in close physical proximity (when one member of the group had to be out of town, no one suggested that the group discuss the work by phone; instead they waited until they could all get together). The work itself seemed to be physically tiring; fatigue played a role in the drafting and revising process, even though the group's meetings generally occurred fairly early in the evening, especially by student standards.

> Rick: How about "various." I can spell it.
> Dana: "Various noises"?
> Annie: "Various . . . sounds."
> Dana: Well this can still be a rough draft, as long as we get this down on paper—
> Annie: "Interruptions . . . distractions"?
> Rick: Oooh! That sounds nice. [types]
> Annie: "various disruptions"—
> Dana: As long as we get, um . . .
> Rick: How about "a cacophony." [laughs]
> Annie: No, thank you!
> Dana: Do you have a thesaurus in there [the computer]?
> Rick: Yeah.
> Dana: Whoa . . .
> Annie: I do too.
> Dana: Let's leave these for when we do the revision; we just have to get . . . an essay out.
> Rick: Oh, you're no fun!
> Dana: I just want to go to sleep tonight.

In her week-nine journal, Annie responded to the following question: "What obstacles and problems did you experience working within the group situation?"

> Our schedules seemed to be our worst obstacle. It usually worked out that we could only meet once between each draft. This probably made our paper more rushed—therefore not as in depth as it maybe could have been. The only other obstacle or problem I can think of would be that of edgyness after we had spent some time together. When one of us would get tired or bored it affected the overall moral of the group.

Beyond causing fatigue, however, the composing process was grounded in the physical experiences of the writers in other ways ("Anyways, let's get back to this. I've got a really bad headache. I don't know why you keep distracting me."). For example, the discussion in which the seriousness of noise in the dorms was being established turned into a lengthy digression on illness, disease, treatment, and prevention. The diversion reveals some typical features of folk models of illness, such as conflating the treatment for a disease with its cause, but it also ties together the physical and the textual.

Dana: Read it, I'm going to be taking it and putting it in the package, so read it.

Annie: "On the basis that students are already living in close quarters, many contagious elements are" . . . "with the additional disadvantages being lack of sleep, many students have, are that, are that, are open to becoming sick. Many students are open to becoming sick" . . .

Dana: "Are susceptible"?

Rick: Yeah.

Dana: OK, "one very um, extremely, bad, one"—

Annie: "one good example of this is mononucleosis. Mononucleosis—

Rick: How about "one . . .

Annie: —comes from overexhaustion and—

Rick: Something about—

Annie: —the breakdown of the immune system."

Rick: OK, OK, go on home, we'll use that! We should say something about what's going around now.

Annie: OK, such as the cold that you get over and over again, and over and over and over—

Dana: You never have a chance to fully recover, because you never get enough sleep to actually . . . recover.

A bit later, there is another merging of physical embodiment and text construction:

Dana: We're doing great on time . . . [laughs at sound of stomach growling]

Annie: Want to take a break?

Dana: No, it's just all night we sit and we just hear our stomachs going . . .

Rick: That doesn't say much about our noise problem if you can sit there and listen to your own stomach!

Dana: It just does this . . .

Rick: Well, it's really the highlight of my night! [laughs]

And then the physical simply takes over entirely:

Rick: OK, "mononucleosis, period."

Dana: "Once gotten, that" . . .

Rick: [laughs] once gotten?

Annie: Once you buy it . . .

Dana: You do not have to get this . . . from kissing.

Annie: Really, no, just, seriously, when you have mononucleosis you're pretty much out of it for about two months!

Dana: The only cure for it is—

Annie: And the only cure for it is much sleep.

Rick: Much sleep? [laughs]

Annie: A lot of sleep, I mean with mononucleosis you can't do any-thing, you can't read, you can't study, cause you get headaches, you're too tired.

Dana: We were very scared that I had it, I had to get a stupid blood test—

Annie: I had it two years ago—

Dana: They found out I was fine; I had every symptom in the book. I slept all day long, I had the worst swollen glands, I had—what's it called—cause I had been with someone that had it, I just had the visible effects, I went to the doctor, I had a dentist's appointment and he looked at my throat too, and he said, you'd better go get yourself checked out—

Rick: Is it a virus?

Dana: Yes it is, it's a disease.

Annie: Period.

Dana: And then we went to the doctor and I had my stupid blood test, I hated it.

Annie: I've had my blood taken, like, four times—

Dana: Oh, I hate it when they prick your finger, that's the worst thing.

Annie: Oh, I didn't have that.

Dana: You know what they do? On top of just pricking your finger, that hurts like hell—

Annie: That hurts worse than the arm—

Dana: I know, so he pricks my finger and I'm like, and then, on top of it being, all sore and it's like bleeding, they put a little tube on it and they push so that all the blood transfers to a little vial, and she took four vials full, and it—

Rick: [laughs] your finger's all deflated . . .

Annie: Why didn't you ask him to do it in the arm?

Dana: I asked him and he goes, "No, you can either get, like, a prick in the finger . . ." I'm like, "Can't I just do this in the arm?" and he's like, "Or a ten-inch needle in the neck." I'm like, "OK, finger[.]" . . . He took this little like, I swear to god it was like this little plastic tube thingy and he pushed so hard in order to get the blood getting up there and I'm like sitting there, like, God, this hurts so much! It was like, "I'm almost done," and I'm like, "How many bottles do you need to test for one little thing?" Might as well test for everything else in the book, he took so much blood.

Annie: I can't even think about it.

Dana: How many pages have we done?

Rick: We're on page two.

Writers have physical interactions with the technologies for writing, but not always in the ways we might predict, as these two brief excerpts from the transcripts demonstrate:

Annie: Do you want me to type? Are you doing OK? You want me to type?

Rick: Naa . . .

Annie: OK.

Rick: Why, don't I type fast enough for you?

Annie: No, I probably type slower than you, but I'm just saying, some people get sick of typing. . . . Just want to be sure to do my equal share on this paper you know!

Rick: [Laughs] It is pretty difficult.

Annie: My feet are so cold . . .

Dana: Then you shouldn't wear sandals!

Annie: I'm freezing if I'm not wearing socks.

Dana: Really.

Annie: I dropped a computer—

Rick: What????

Annie: I dropped the keyboard of Erica's computer on my foot, and I bruised this whole—

Rick: But what'd you do to the keyboard?

Annie: Oh, the keyboard's fine, it landed on the floor, and I bruised my foot up and I couldn't wear shoes for a while, cause it was like, right *there*. . . .

Dana: Can you see it [the computer screen] from here?

Annie: Uh huh.

Rick: [Keyboarding] Great! I can't see it from here. [laughs]

Dana: You know that, I can't even see it from there when I was wearing my glasses.

Annie: I can.

Dana: Right now, all I see is a green speck.

Rick: Well thanks!

Dana: With my glasses on?

Annie: I can't see it completely clearly, but enough where I can make it out what it says.

Dana: You can make it out? I can't even make it out what it says

Annie: What are you doing?

Rick: I'm saving it.

Annie: Oh.

Rick: Paranoid! "What are you doing to the paper!"

Writers are not only physical beings, they are also inhabitants of physical environments. The two most significant environments for this group were the dorm rooms, in which much of the composing was accomplished, and the classroom, in which they interacted with other students and with me. In each of the dorm rooms in which they met (Rick's room and Annie's room), the group worked with one computer, so typically one person was keyboarding the text and the changes while the other two gathered around the computer so that they could see the text as it was being produced or revised. Alternatively, one person would read aloud from the draft, and suggested revisions would be handwritten on the page. At first, Rick did the typing (probably because it was his computer), although the group switched typists so that everyone eventually took a turn. It was a pretty loose arrangement: it is clear from the tapes that the two people who were not actively keyboarding could (and did) move around the room looking at objects, interact with other people who occasionally came into or left the room, and sit on chairs or on the bed. It was evident from the construction of this space, its furnishings and personal belongings, that it was a personal space, in contrast to the public space of the classroom. The two women remarked on how neat it was, and Annie commented on the house plans Rick had put up on his walls.

> Annie: What are those plans of?
> Rick: My house.
> Annie: Your house? Did you draw them up?
> Rick: Yeah.
> Annie: Did you design the house and they used those?
> Dana: Or did you do those after . . .
> Rick: We had to design the most buildable house and mine passed out of the class. What a deal!
> Dana: [reads] "the tenants above you"—
> Annie: Is that what you want to do? Be an architect?
> Rick: No, actually, I'm just going to be a molecular biologist.

The physical environment of the classroom was typical of college classrooms in modern concrete and glass buildings: it was roomy, well lit, and minimally furnished, with several large tables and contemporary upholstered chrome chairs, which could be arranged freely about the room. The layout made it easy for students to meet together in their small groups or to gather around the table for a general discussion, and it also moved the instructor from the traditionally authoritative position at the head of the class to the large seminar table along with the students. The room was modern, bright, and cheerful. But it was far from an environment I would consider typical for writers, an environment usually rich in resources such as reference books, notes on other topics, and files of articles; computers; telephones; supplies such as scissors, tape, paper, and pens; a comfortable chair, sofa, or bed for reading; bulletin boards with calendars and notes about current projects; shelves with baskets for ongoing work; easy access to food and drinks; and so on. Naturally, the environments for composing vary widely, but few writers would choose to work in such a spartan environment as the typical college classroom. Even for writers in government or corporate settings, many resources for composing are ready-to-hand.

Emergence and the Writers

Coordination and adaptation are emergent properties of self-organizing systems. In ecological systems of readers, writers, and texts, we can observe emerging coordination at different levels of scale. At the level of the individual in this group, writers attempted to coordinate their internal structures—such as prior experiences with, knowledge of, skills and strategies for, and beliefs about writing—with external structures, including my expectations, the other writers in the group, the emerging text, the structured task, the technologies for composing, and the demands of other course work. Coordination at this level, where most research in composition studies has focused, primarily concentrates on an individual's interactions with the immediate environment. However, at another level of scale, the group itself was co-evolving with a larger environment, that of the TCWP 1A class. In workshops, conferences, and class discussions with other students and with me, as well as in well-defined "instructional" settings, there was a constant process of mutual adaptation: student readers responded to the writing group's drafts; the group made revisions and provided a new draft to be read by me; I responded with further suggestions and advice, all intended to bring the members of the writing class into coordination with each other. Even the final grade was intended to help in this coordination effort by providing feedback about the instructor's view of the relative success of its achievement. In turn, the weekly meetings to discuss program design and implementation by program instructors and coordinators were informed by my and other instructors' experiences with students.

But it is also possible to continue to enlarge the scale of observation and examine how the entire writing class emerged in coordination with its institutional environment, the TCWP at UCSD, and how, in turn, the institution attempted (with greater or lesser effect) some coordination with the larger cultural and physical environment in which it was situated. In 1993, for example, the TCWP was replaced with a large-scale required core humanities course, Dimensions of Culture, based on topical readings in the social sciences and cultural studies, broadly conceived around themes of diversity, justice, and imagination. Where the TCWP had focused on preparing students for academic forms of writing, the Dimensions of Culture course reflects new trends in higher education and old economies of scale: large lectures on fashionable topics, such as cultural diversity and race, gender, and class; interdisciplinary faculty teaching teams; section meetings taught by graduate students; and an emphasis on "writing across the curriculum." The effects of such institutional efforts at coordination are necessarily reflected in changes at the other levels of scale: writing programs, individual classrooms, and the particular writing situations in which instructors and student writers find themselves.

While we are primarily concerned here with the students' emerging understanding of themselves as writers, the development of this writing group as a complex adaptive system, and the group's situatedness in an ecology of composing, we must also be aware of the ongoing effects of the mutual attempts at coordination (what Varela, Thompson, and Rosch call "codependent arising") at different levels of scale as well. For this collaborative group, coordination seems to emerge as a function of

- shared language
- bounded physical proximity
- humor
- shared experiences
- a perceived need to unite against a threat
- the common task with its goals and requirements over time

Undoubtedly any one of these could serve as the basis of a major study; however, I am only able to briefly touch on each of these functions and its role in the emerging coordination of the collaborative writing group.

Shared language. Probably the most effective means of coordination between humans is language. Even complete strangers with little in common can find a basis for communication through the common structure, vocabulary, grammar, and syntax of a shared language.

Where there is no shared language, people generally attempt to construct one through a pastiche of gestures, facial expressions, sounds, and body movements. But those who have grown up and been acculturated in the same geographical region, who are close in age, and who are also sharing similar life experiences have a very rich linguistic palette indeed, from idiomatic expressions and specialized vocabulary to large-scale patterns of coordinated communication such as "class discussion," "reviewing a movie," and "telling a joke." The extent to which language serves to coordinate this group is evident on the audiotapes, where the students are commonly heard finishing each other's sentences. They used language about writing drawn from prior experience, as well as language from the class discussions, workshops, conferences, and also from the textbook to coordinate their understanding of the composing situation. In the following conversation, for instance, Rick reveals an assumption about paragraph length, although the subject of the paragraph as a unit of text had never come up in class discussions or in the textbook:

> Annie: Um, are we going to have anything else to say about that? . . . to make a paragraph?
> Rick: [laughing] We've got a one sentence paragraph here . . . let's see, what other direct effect would it have on me?

This assumption, that one sentence alone cannot make a paragraph, is confirmed in other conversations, where writers in the group make it clear that they share from prior experience the default definition of a "paragraph" as a unit of three to five sentences introduced by a "topic sentence."

> Dana: We gotta make it at least three sentences long, to make a paragraph. . . .
> Rick: . . . And then we could list some of the rules in this paragraph and then go on with that . . .
> Dana: How many sentences do we have in this paragraph?
> Annie: Two.
> [laughter]
> Annie: Well one of them is a long sentence.
> Rick: One of them's a runon but hey, we're lookin' good! [laughs] . . .
> Annie: Period. And then on with the next paragraph . . .
> Dana: "would be set"?
> Annie: Yeah.
> Dana: It's a very short paragraph.
> Rick and Annie [in unison]: I know!

Dana: It's just that the topic sentence is in it, we don't have to begin with it.

The use of the textbook—another source of language about writing—to coordinate the group's composing efforts is more marked at the beginning of the assignment, during the invention phase of the work:

Dana: So you know what? Cause here [in the textbook's invention activities] it says now, "analyze your problem," and they ask you all these questions. Let's analyze both of them [the two potential topic choices] and then we can choose.
Annie: Which one's better?
Dana: Yeah, so one of them is enforcement of quiet hours?
Rick: What's our solution to it?
Dana: We'll think of it in a sec.

The awareness that the language in the textbook might actually inform the composing process is an emerging discovery:

Annie: We only pick one . . . thing?
Dana: No, one problem.
Rick: She's going hairball on us, writing down everything! [laughing]
Dana: I have to. This is the way invention works, that's the whole complete sense of it.
Rick: I wish you could do all my invention work . . .
Annie: I'm so excited, the last essay I actually did my invention first; the first essay I did it later, because it wasn't helping me, it wasn't getting anywhere—
Dana: Oh it helped me sooo much.
Annie: —and on my evaluation—I didn't get through the invention, so I skipped to the paper, because I wasn't getting anywhere—so I did bad on the paper.
Dana: See, part of the reason she wants you to do the work, and correct me if I'm wrong—
Annie: Did you do all the invention though?
Dana: Yeah, at first I was like, this is not helping me, but then—
Annie: The only part of the invention I did before was like, maybe, went through and brainstormed and did that kind of thing, but I didn't do, like, the freewriting, because when I freewrite I freewrite about a lot of stuff, and I usually don't even end up writing about my topic.

The writers also depend on the language of the text they are constructing to scaffold new text:

Dana: Wait, we've got, like a whole page saying why this is good, like
. . .

Rick: Well, we'll take that out and say the rest of that.

Dana: So, um, "another failed attempt to not"—maybe we should just say, "Many people believe that," um, well, cause how would we change the wording here, "The one and only reasonable solution to this problem is to direct our complaints to the resident dean and her assistants"? Do you believe the resident staff has the full authority to reinforce the resident advisors' duties regarding this concern?

Bounded physical proximity. The members of the group decided to work on the collaborative essay when they could all meet together, generally in one of the dorm rooms. The physical proximity gave them a much wider and more intimate range of communication with each other, through gesture, movement, facial expression, and so on, than they could have had working at a distance, and the room bounded them in a way that separated them from the activities of other students.[3] The audiotapes, unfortunately, cannot capture these effects; we can only speculate about the degree to which they contributed to the emergence of coordination in the group. But a brief exchange in the middle of the meeting to prepare the final revision suggests the importance of creating and maintaining a bounded space.

Annie: [from outside the room] Gotten anything new, like Sam's present?

Other voice: Yeah, I've actually gone shopping.

Annie: [entering the room] What are you doing in here?

Other voice: I'm lounging.

Annie: You do *not* lounge in my room!

Other voice: Too late!

Annie: *Nobody* lounges in my room.

In the classroom, the collaborative groups often came together for discussion of the readings, journals, or writing assignments. At these times, students in each group would draw their chairs together and move away from the other groups, often deliberately turning their backs to them and creating, even in an open classroom, a shared yet bounded space that defined their group. This arrangement is, of course, a very practical one for students to be able to communicate with other members of their group without confusion, but it nevertheless represents a physical restructuring of space to enable the group's coordination—both among group members and between the group and the environment. Finally, the task itself established a bounded space, both socially and temporally, by grouping students and sequencing tasks to be completed by specific deadlines.

Humor. In the early stages of composing, and even later, when the challenges of the task became more apparent, humor was an important means of coordination for the collaborative group. The work started out in high spirits, with a great deal of kidding and laughter. On the tapes, Rick can often be heard laughing affably, or making a self-deprecating comment accompanied by a chuckle; when making an objection, typically he would repeat the offending word or phrase as a question, with a gentle laugh.

> Dana: We said, "with the many responsibilities of the dean . . ."
> Annie: "presently have"?
> Dana: "with the presently"
> Rick: [laughs] "with the presently"? What are you talkin' about?

This gentleness and self-deprecation in his humor seemed to offer assurance that he had no intention of asserting some kind of dominance in the group. The two women, who were also friends outside of class, used humor to include him in their joking about dorm life, the project, and school in general. The good-natured talk ranged widely. When their discussions threatened to divert the group too far from its task, Rick created the "tangent alert":

> Dana: Okay, what was that solution you were rambling about?
> Annie: You should have seen me Friday night when I rambled—
> Rick: Uh-oh, we're hitting a tangent. [makes alarm sound] Tangent
>   alert! Tangent alert!
> [general laughter]

The "tangent alert" became a kind of running joke that later served not only to reconnect the group to the task but also to recall the members' shared history and reconfirm their shared conventions for working together. Here are two slightly different interpretations of this device. Rick wrote, in his journal for week seven,

> Our major problem is really a minor one in the overall group work. We will often hit tangents and start talking about other things. Our solution is a "Tangent Alert." Usually two out of the three group members will start talking about something else. When this happens, the odd one out

will give a Tangent Alert, usually accompanied with a siren sound (which in itself is good for a laugh) and we'll get back to the subject.

Annie wrote,

Our main distractions are Dana and I. We are friends outside of class and therefore we go on tangents and start talking about other things. You will find lots of evidence of this on our tapes. To handle this, Rick yells "Tangent alert" because he doesn't care to join in on our conversations.

Shared experiences. In searching for a topic during the invention process, the writers discussed some of their common experiences as students at UCSD—from the writing requirements of Third College to the construction flaws in the dorm to the lack of information about college sporting events—but they did not pursue any of the problems associated with these experiences as topics for the essay. Still, like the use of humor, these shared experiences served as brief touchstones that enabled them to affirm their common ground. They also briefly enlarged the scope of their inquiry into experiences they had in common:

> Rick: So we either alter the dorms or we—
> Dana: Should we try something that doesn't relate to school?
> Annie: Something that we can all three talk about and know about.
> Dana: We're all 18 and we know about . . . we're in the age of AIDS and all that sexual stuff.
> Annie: We're in the age of, like . . . well that's not what I found . . . I was going to say something like, we could go on about some kind of law, but we can't . . .
> Dana: Drinking?
> Annie: I don't think we've got a whole lot of arguments for changing it, so. . . .

A perceived need to unite against a threat. At two crucial moments, the collaborative group's emerging coordination was threatened by challenges to its "worldview" of the composing situation. The group prepared the first draft internally; no one outside the group had yet read it. The workshop in class the following day provided the first feedback from readers outside the group, and it was clear from the workshop responses, noted above, that one reader, Steve, was very critical of the draft. His critique raised some important points: (1) the proposal would result in more conflicts between students; (2) security guards were needed in the parking lots to deter thefts; (3) "I don't want another babysitter watching me"; (4) quiet hours were already too restrictive; (5) the dorms lacked insulation to contain noise; (6) when people move into the dorms, they give up some of their privacy rights; (7) people who needed more quiet could move off campus; and (8) these dorms were actually conservative compared to those at other universities. While other readers' responses were, for the most part, both more general and more favorable toward the proposal, the proposed solution to the problem was overwhelmingly criticized by readers as obvious, unenforceable, and vague.

This response represented a serious challenge to the very foundations of the collaborative group's text and to the group's sense of its emerging coordination. As noted above, the writers responded to these challenges primarily by agreeing to ignore them. This decision brought them more closely into coordination with one another but signaled a disjunction in the coordination between the group and at least some of its readers. The marked degree of this disjunction was revealed in Rick's response to one of the final journal questions: How might the instructor provide more support for collaborative writers?

> The instructor should provide two group conferences [with the instructor] through the duration of the assignment because the conference enables the group to hear another viewpoint. By hearing another viewpoint, the group then might realize a new approach to a problem they were never experiencing before.

In fact, the purpose of the workshop was precisely to provide the writers with other viewpoints: in this case, six other viewpoints. And, of course, within the group itself there were three different viewpoints from the individuals who were involved in the collaboration.

Actually, the conference with the instructor confronted writers with new difficulties, representing the second crucial challenge to the group's emerging coordination. In particular, I argued that the proposed solution was superficial and obvious; to interest readers or mount an engaging argument, they would have needed to present a surprising or innovative solution to the problem of noise in the dorms and argue convincingly for it. I also pointed out that the assignment required writers to present a range of solutions that have been tried or suggested or that might be proposed by others and show why the proposal's solution is superior to these other possibilities.

Following the conference, the group apparently drew on the workshop responses for help with the revisions. The solution of creating quiet dorms was suggested by TW (see above, workshop responses), for example. At this point, the group became more responsive to the critical questions posed by their workshop readers.

Dana: Um, did you guys think of solutions?

Annie: I've just been thinking . . .

Dana: I think the quiet dorms is a good idea.

Annie: That's what I was thinking.

Dana: I think we should pursue that. . . . It's more original, you know, it's not just like, "tell them to enforce it," you know.

Annie: So then, um, "the one and only reasonable solution to this problem is," . . . that should be ours?

Rick: Well now we'll just turn that into another, ah, solution that didn't work.

Annie: Yeah, well, we can turn it into . . . Because it's obvious that some people object to this because they feel like they are adults now, and [laughs] . . . like Steve . . .

A little later, Annie said, "It has to be agreed upon by the students who are paying this much money and feel that they should be treated as adults."

Through these efforts, the group worked to bring itself into coordination with both the outside readers' and my own expectations as they understood them from the conference. The vehicle for accomplishing this coordination was the modification of the text along the lines suggested by workshop readers. However, the necessity for accomplishing closer coordination with readers' points of view and expectations was not addressed by the group until the conference with the instructor.

The common task. The shared task structured the system's emerging coordination and also determined the need for coordination. In this course, students completed a sequence of developmental activities in preparing an essay—invention work, rough drafts, revisions, and final draft with its self-evaluation—and needed to provide evidence that they had actually engaged the activities at various stages of the assignment. They also included this evidence in the final package, which they submitted for my response at the end of each essay sequence and at the end of the quarter for the final evaluation. The sequence of tasks was both constraining and enabling. Students often struggled against doing the invention work or multiple drafts with revisions, convinced it was time-wasting busy work; once they had seriously engaged it, however, most students found it enormously helpful. The goal was to introduce students to one way of structuring the composing process and to ensure that they understand it thoroughly by seriously engaging it. The developmental evidence students produced (several pages of invention work, two or more rough drafts, journals, workshop comments on other students' drafts, final revisions, and self-evaluations) helped me see whether we were, together, achieving some coordination in our mutual efforts.

It is clear that as the collaborative writing group became more internally coordinated, however, it grew more resistant to challenges to its views about the writing. Fleck suggests that in emerging "thought collectives" such as this group, there exists a "harmony of illusions" marked by the shared assumptions, methods, beliefs, and "facts" of its members. Consequently, when a conception becomes strongly enough established, contradictions appear "unthinkable and unimaginable." In the beginning, the group only recognizes those facts that conform to their shared beliefs (*Genesis* 28). For the collaborative writing group, this stage corresponds to the invention and drafting stage. Fleck continues, "Then comes a stage with complications, when the exceptions begin to come forward" (29), as when the group received critical feedback during the workshop on the draft. Finally, Fleck concludes, "In the end there are often more exceptions than normal instances" (29), the situation faced by the group following the conference with me. It is at this stage, according to Fleck, that the thought collective is poised in readiness for a shift in its thought-style, the kind of shift described by Kuhn as a "scientific revolution." There is a slight sense of this readiness following their conference with me. It is likely that, for the collaborative writing group, however, a real shift in the thought-style of the group did not emerge until much later, perhaps even after they had received my final comments on their essay. The specific practices and activities of the writers as they struggled for coordination are discussed in the following section.

Enaction and the Writers

Coordination can only be developed, or demonstrated, for that matter, in the context of some activity or practice, or set of activities or practices. *Practice* is an activity that recurs at different times in similar situations: walking is an activity, but Reznikoff's long daily walks in New York were a practice. Further, practice implies a kind of intentionality that is not necessarily a feature of activity: laughing at a joke is an activity; telling a joke is a practice. In practical terms, there are three types of activities and practices that engage both individuals and the composing system: those that define the composing situation, those that affect the situation, and those that are peripheral to it. These distinctions are not rigid categories, but functional ones. An activity, such as talking to one's parents, may migrate from a position peripheral to the composing situation to one affecting it. The collaborative writing group, for example, felt some pressure to come up with a first draft quickly.

> Rick: Yeah, but we've got to come up with it first.
> Annie: Yeah, let's do it.
> Dana: We still got problems. I haven't talked to my parents, and I
>   want to talk to them.
> Rick: Yeah, mine are going to call tonight, too.
> Dana: OK, let's be calm.

The activities and practices that defined the composing situation in TCWP 1A were structured as a way of enabling students to manage the demands of the writing situations they were likely to encounter in college and beyond. They were carefully designed and sequenced to guide students through a well-defined process of constructing a text. Below are some of the typical activities student writers engaged in while working through one essay assignment:

- Students read example essays that shared salient features with the type of writing they would be asked to produce.
- They responded (either in writing or in class discussion and presentations) to questions that asked them to analyze or reflect on the essays from the perspective of a writer.
- They spoke and listened in class discussions.
- They wrote responses to journal questions provided by the instructor.
- They prepared written invention work following heuristics in the textbook section on invention.
- They planned and prepared a first draft.
- They participated in a workshop in which they shared drafts with other students, both reading and writing focused responses to the writing.

- They revised the first draft, producing a second.
- They met with the instructor for a conference to discuss the second draft.
- They revised the second draft.
- They prepared the final draft for submission to the instructor by typing or word processing it according to guidelines provided by the instructor.
- They wrote a brief memo to the instructor reflecting on the writing experience: what went well, what problems they encountered, how they dealt with problems, what specific issues they would like the instructor to address in reading the essay, and so on.

Obviously, each of these activities incorporated other activities, from speaking and listening to operating a copy machine. These activities ranged from microscale (keyboarding, reading drafts, spelling a word, brainstorming topics, and constructing sentences) to metacognitive comments on the process of composing, to larger-scale class activities, such as workshops, conferences, and discussions, and beyond that to activities involved in "doing school"—midterm exams, other course work, dorm life, and so on.

At another level, we attempted in the TCWP 1A course to introduce students to certain activities and practices that transcended the specific writing assignments and that were also common features of academic environments, including reading carefully and analytically, understanding certain forms of argumentation, researching a topic and incorporating outside source material in written texts, recognizing and accounting for different perspectives on an issue, critiquing their own or others' writing. The tapes of the conference reflect some of these attempts:

> Me: You have a really classic conflict between personal freedom and the social good here, you know, in the dorms, and, ah, it's really a question but . . . it's hard to determine whether it is a serious enough problem to address this way. You know, the average person reading this is going to think—even the dean reading this is going to say, "why didn't they call me?" "Why didn't they pick up the phone and give me a call and say, 'This is a continuing problem, what can we do to solve it?'"
>
> Annie: So we're saying, instead of calling we're writing this paper. [laughs]
>
> Me: What I'm saying is you can do it in two sentences on the phone, that's what makes it hard to make an interesting essay out of it,

you know what I mean? It's, um, it seems not very substantial, as an essay.

And a bit later,

Rick: Well, there's a lot of people living in a real small area [in the other dorms on campus, in high-rise buildings], closer . . . so why do we have so much noise when we're so spread out? [laughs] Maybe we can bring that into it.
Me: You might talk to the RAs in both places, you might talk to some students in both places, um, be sure you credit those as interviews. Say, "interview with so and so, UCSD student," you know, and the date as part of your citations. . . .

Again,

Me: The thing you want to do is develop some weight to it, and the reason I want you to do this is not for my benefit, but because when you write this type of an essay, later, you need to have a good sense of how to make a persuasive and interesting argument for a solution that isn't obvious and wouldn't instantly leap to mind the minute you think of the problem. That's, I think, sort of the heart of what you have here being problematic.
Dana: It was kind of hard to think of a solution that nobody can really think of—

The collaborative writing assignment introduced another level of activity, which students interpreted much differently than I had anticipated. It never occurred to me that the writers would attempt to construct the texts "by committee," trying to jointly decide word by word, sentence by sentence, concept by concept just what went down on paper (or on the computer screen, in this case). This was collaboration with a vengeance.

Dana: One of the biggest problems I found was that it was very hard to get the essay down on paper. When three people are working together and all three have different ideas, than it is very hard to get 3 words down on paper. We overcame this problem, but it took us a long time to finish the paper.

Even though this recognition came very early in the composing process (this journal response was written following the preparation of the first draft), the writers never really discussed any alternative method of constructing the text (e.g., taking turns working on the draft, breaking it into sections to work on individually and then discussing revisions, each writer taking primary responsibility for a different stage of the work, and so on). In their last journal, students wrote, in response to a question asking how they would compare the amount of work that was done individually to the amount of work done communally:

> Rick: Almost the entire paper was comunal work. The only time there was any individual work was the basic typing up of the paper.
> Annie: The majority of our work was accomplished together. For some reason, the idea of splitting up the work did not come up.

Following is an example of the partial construction of a single sentence of text according to this method (the transcript for the construction of the entire sentence fills six pages):

> Dana: Um "these dormitories would remain the same. Those students who feel that"—
> Annie: Ow!
> Dana: [laughs] "those students who feel that they are mature, that they are"—
> Annie: "Mature adults, and who"—
> [loud laughter in background]
> Dana: Well you're not, you don't feel that you're a mature adult you just feel like you're becoming an adult. You're mature adults and can handle. Wait, wait, wait, "Those students who feel that they are mature adults and can handle themselves in a"—
> Rick: "Civilized manner"? [laughs]
> Dana: [types] "in a civilized manner," um . . .
> Annie: Isn't it "o-r"?
> Dana: "Can live there."
> Rick: [Laughs]
> Dana: "Would live there." How do you say that in a better way?
> Rick: "Would remain in these dorms."
> Dana: Well no, we just said, "will remain . . ."
> Rick: "Would be here." "Would be there." Wherever they are!
> Annie: "Would live" . . . "These students . . ."
> Dana: "These students who feel that they are mature adults and can handle themselves in a civilized manner"—
> Annie: "Would live . . . in these dorms"?
> Rick: Note: eleven twenty, Annie's losing it.
> [laughter]
> Rick: The stress of the group work has taken its toll.

Dana: "In a civilized manner would live in these dorms," um . . .
　　Something about the noise, um, "Although quiet hours"—
Annie: "Would still exist" . . .
Dana: "Quiet"—
Rick: "They would not be as stringent as those of the quiet dorms"
Dana: —"hours would"
Annie: What a word!
Rick: Yeah, what a word!
Annie: "This," comma, "they would not" . . . "they would not be
　　as"—what did you say?
Dana: Um, "as stringent"
[laughter]
Annie: What?
Dana: "As stringent as the quiet hours in the," "as the—
Rick: "As the," uh . . .
Dana: "As the ones in the quiet dorms."
Annie: "The quiet dorms."
Rick: "As those in the quiet dorms."
Dana: "In the" . . . "as those in the quiet"—
Rick: "those in" or "of"?
Dana: "of" I mean.
Rick: Dickering over two-letter words. [laughs]
Dana: Loud music, sports—
[other voice, calling]: Annie! What are you making?
Annie: Noodles.
Dana: "Loud music would still," "loud music would still" . . .
Rick: How about—
Dana: "Would still continue."
Annie: Am I off track?
Rick: Ah "would still . . ."
Dana: —"in the quiet dorms. Loud music would still be played" . . .
　　"And heard by everybody."
[laughter]
Rick: "And enjoyed by the masses."
Dana: I mean "would still be played"—
Annie: "Loud music would still be played" . . .
Rick: Oh my god!
Dana: "Loud music would still be played, and sports" . . .
Rick: "Outdoor sports would still be played in the dorms."

These examples make it clear that it is a bit misleading to say that
we plan or design activities for students, and we should remember
that these are shorthand expressions for a much more complex and
interdependent reality. Our course structures exist only in the context

of the unfolding activity of agents—students, instructors, program administrators, and so on—interacting with each other and their environment. We have certain expectations of student writers based on our experiences, and we attempt to anticipate students' needs and plan experiences that we hope will coordinate our expectations and their needs. While we can plan some aspects of their experience (the writing tasks we will set, the reading we will assign, the sequence of assignments), the activity unfolds as a kind of jazz improvisation, interactively constructed by independent musicians. In Lucy Suchman's view, "The stability of the social world . . . is not due to an eternal structure, but to situated actions that create and sustain shared understanding on specific occasions of interaction" (66). Some of our plans for students turn out harmoniously, others inexplicably falter; since students and instructors are always codependently creating the activities in "real time," every class, no matter how carefully planned, is an entirely different experience.

However, the activities and practices planned for the course represent only part of the composing picture; as we see from the examples in this chapter, sometimes other activities overlapped, competed with, or even interfered in the process. During the preparation of the final draft, for example, Annie was preoccupied for a considerable time with T-reg, UCSD's system of telephone registration. As the system was then organized, students were assigned a "window" of time during which they could dial into the university and register for their next quarter's classes via a menu-driven electronic system. If students did not register during the assigned time, they had to wait and register at the start of the quarter. Those who registered late often had difficulty getting into the classes they wanted or needed to take, so there was some urgency about getting the registration accomplished. Further, the large numbers of students phoning in during a given time ensured that the lines were nearly always busy. The composing process was temporarily derailed to discuss this phenomenon.

Annie: I sat here for forty minutes, redial, redial . . .
Dana: The last time I tried getting in it took five hours.
Rick: Five hours-straight?
Dana: Getting in, right, I would redial, redial—not like I'm sitting there for five hours, but I mean, the whole day through, like from like three to eight, I finally got in. I tried redial, redial, redial, wait a while, go back and redial, redial, redial . . .
Rick: I spent twenty minutes this morning and then I looked my thing over and I goofed up so I called up again and got right on.

Annie: I know that all of them are going to be closed; I'm just going to take whatever I can get.

The composing process was compressed by one writer's visit home and another writer's trip out of town, so that the first and second drafts had to be completed in very short time frames—one evening meeting of about an hour and a half for the invention, planning, and first draft, one meeting of about two hours for the second draft. The group clearly felt the strain caused by the time pressure, which undoubtedly played a part both in their unwillingness to entertain alternative topics as a serious possibility and in their lack of any kind of supporting research—even an informal survey of other students living in the dorms. Other "peripheral" activities also intruded, creating distractions at other times, as students noted in their journals:

Dana: Many distractions occur like people coming in and bothering us, telephone calls and just going off on tangents. Our distractions usually did not last long enough to hinder our work so we just continued working.

Rick: So far the only distraction the group has had are those usually experienced in a dorm. For example of such distractions are people playing their music loud, people asking group members about classes, grades, weekends, and other such interesting topics. The group will always go back to work when the person has left.

Writing environments, even in carefully planned programs, are enacted through practices and activities by which agents in the system are attempting to come into coordination. This does not mean that there is some optimal "goal" whereupon coordination is fully realized; rather, there is a continuing dynamic process in which instructors, students, program administrators, the institution, and the environment act and interact to co-construct an ecology for composing. However, it also does not imply that "everything is relative" and "anybody's opinion is as good as anybody else's." Writing instructors generally have a little more experience than students with what does and doesn't work well in certain composing situations, some useful theories about how to think about such situations, and some strategies to help less experienced writers develop their coordination with these environments. While it is true that both the naive tourist and the forester can walk in the woods, the forester has much greater potential for surviving there.

Conclusion

The concept of *coordination* gives us a new perspective on composing situations, particularly in educational settings. In composition studies, we tend to think of our mission as helping students adapt their writing to the demands of the academy, the marketplace, or the professions or disciplines toward which they are moving, without reflecting on the inescapable fact that all of these situations are complex dynamic ecologies that are themselves always changing. The concept of socialization suffers from many of the same assumptions: the need to mold the student as writer—the raw clay—into a suitable form for the presumed target discourse community.

The concept of *coordination* helps us see the mutual effects—on the part of the individual or a particular system and its environment—as they "co-adapt." While students are actively trying to develop new strategies for reading, writing, and thinking, the culture of the academy is actively trying, not merely to assist them in their efforts, but also to adapt to them as well. So when students stumble and produce a disappointing text in response to an assignment, reflective students and instructors look for causes. In the same spirit that investigators review the events that led to an oil spill, a nuclear accident, or an operating room mishap, we consider the composing situation to try to understand what caused the difficulty. The purpose of this inquiry is not to assign blame or liability but to gain a better understanding of how to improve the coordination between students and the writing environments we construct. Borrowing a concept from accident investigators, should we attribute the disappointing outcome of the student essay to "human error"? And if so, where does the error lie?

Did the group of UCSD students writing collaboratively commit a serious error (or complex of errors) in composing their essay on noise in the dorms? Did their emphasis on internal coordination somehow blind the writers to the group's discoordination with the composing environment? It is true that the writers decided to ignore the fact that at least some faction among their readers felt that the problem was not a serious one, that resolving the problem might involve conflicting rights, and that the proposed solution might create even greater problems. They attempted to allay the instructor's doubts about the topic with verbal persuasion rather than recognizing those doubts as rhetorical challenges that needed to be resolved on the page. They did not make thoughtful use of the textbook to think critically about the essay. But most damning of all, they produced an unsatisfying essay based on a trivial topic, an essay marked by a predictable structure, thin reasoning, a lack of any supporting evidence beyond subjective assertions, and general confusion about its purpose and audience.

On the other hand, perhaps the error lay with me. As the instructor, I could have been clearer about the expectations for this essay and stronger about what kinds of topics would be acceptable; or I might have rejected the topic of noise in the dorms out of hand in the beginning, as soon as I heard about it during the first-draft workshop. It has not been my practice to reject topics except where they involve illegal activities, invasion of privacy, or physical danger; I prefer to point out the rhetorical difficulties with problematic topics so that writers can make informed decisions. Since student writers have occasionally surprised me with delightful writing about unpromising topics, I am reluctant to reject topics outright. Still, I might have worked more closely with the writers on strengthening their arguments, on acknowledging readers' potential objections, or on developing a sense of the problem's significance in readers. The conference might have been more sharply focused and better managed. Sometimes it seems as if teaching is a continuing process of finding out too late exactly how you have failed your students.

Or perhaps the error lay in the textbook upon which so much of the teaching and learning in TCWP depended; perhaps a different mix of activities, a different set of readings, or an entirely different conceptual structure for the text would have resulted in a more successful outcome for this piece of writing. It may be that the extensive scaffolding for student writing was actually overwhelming, like an overprotective parent running alongside a child on a new bike, providing so many suggestions, comments, warnings, and assists that the child becomes distracted and fearful about her own capabilities and ultimately must ignore much of the "assistance" that is offered in order to be able to move at all. Yet the *St. Martin's Guide to Writing* has been enormously popular with instructors and students; through my own experience with a wide range of students, I can testify to its effectiveness.

And we should not forget the institutional structure of TCWP itself. Perhaps four essays per quarter was too many to expect of students already burdened with other course work; in fact, within a year, the program reduced the number of required essays to three per quarter. Perhaps classes should have met more often for shorter periods or less often for longer periods. Or students may have needed more frequent feedback on their writing in terms of actual grades—rather than narrative comments—to better understand how they were being evaluated while they could still adapt to the demands of the course.

It may be the activities themselves that were in error: maybe a different mix of assignments would have improved the outcome for these writers. Students often expressed a longing for more "creative" writing in the course, for example. Perhaps the conference with the instructor should have preceded the workshop to provide earlier guidance for the writers. Or perhaps the collaborative writing task was an ill-conceived assignment, too far removed from typical collaborative situations in non-classroom settings. In such situations, writers who voluntarily collaborate (such as scholars, researchers, professionals, or irate citizens) usually have a shared purpose and a strong motivation to work together to accomplish the composition of a well-defined text for a clearly understood audience.

We are somehow always convinced that we can locate the single cause of an unexpected outcome, such as the unfortunate essay about noise in the dorms. Recently, however, researchers in the field of human error have argued that our judgments of a process that produces an unwanted outcome are subject to hindsight bias, that such judgments assume (often erroneously) that process and outcome are tightly coupled, that they oversimplify the situations in which people actually operate, that they assume that a "single cause" (or a very few causes) of an unwanted outcome can be identified, and that they tend to place artificial boundaries on the "beginning" and "end" of an incident (Woods et al.). Even if there is such a single cause, we may be constrained from providing the silver bullet to eliminate it: in complex ecologies, a single change can have unpredictable results—if we had somehow altered the course of events to prevent this mishap, perhaps these writers would have fared better, while others foundered instead.

When things go wrong, when writers produce disappointing work in response to an assignment, for example, we assume that the cause can be found in what might be termed *human error,* either on the part of the students or on the part of the instructor, depending on one's ideology. In looking back at the composing experience, we assume that there must have been some causal flaw in the process and that either the writers or the instructor ought to have anticipated or detected the problem and prevented or remedied it. We are quick to judge and slow to understand the complexities of the composing situation both for writers and for instructors: the competing demands for production under serious time constraints ("Dana: We can go on and make it longer, but I just want to get it out."), the difficult balancing of priorities ("Annie: My calculus class right now is so hard, I don't know what in the hell we're doing."), the possibilities for confusion in the process of communicating expectations ("Annie: One way to provide more support for the collaborative writers would be to give more specific instructions on what is expected from this essay."), the existence of competing attentional demands ("Dana: Hey, is this calculator the kind that does graphing on it and stuff?"), and the lack or inadequacy of relevant experience to lend expertise ("Rick: We have to analyze our readers . . . oh, I hate analyzing our readers. I always do it wrong."). And interruptions are common:

> [Knocking sound]
> Annie: [Calls out] Come in!
> Dana: And then the next paragraph we could talk about—
> [Other voice, whispering] Can I ask you just one thing? Are you in
>   math 2b?
> Rick: No, 2a.
> [Other voice, whispering] Never mind.
> [General laughter]

It is common for participants in simulation studies that examine the causes of human error to marvel at the gaps in their own knowledge, remarking during debriefing: "I never knew that I did not know this. I just never thought about this situation" (Woods et al. 46). This is not only the predicament of the student writers, it is also our own predicament as instructors and researchers. To put it plainly, we don't do a very good job of helping students see what we see when we look at texts, or of arming them with real strategies for adapting to the demands of more sophisticated writing tasks they will encounter in the academy and beyond.

While I was disappointed in the quality of the final product of this collaborative writing assignment, I have also come to realize that it represents only one text in a much larger landscape of texts these writers will be engaged with. Although my chief goal was to provide students with the experience of writing collaboratively, I did recognize the possibility that the unfamiliar composing situation could affect the quality of their final product, and I am not alarmed at the outcome. Woods, Johannesen, Cook, and Sarter point out that variability in behavior and performance is crucial for learning and adaptation:

Error, as part of a continuing feedback and improvement process, is information to shape future behavior. However, in certain contexts this variability can have negative consequences. As Rasmussen (1985) puts it, in "unkind work environments" variability becomes an "unsuccessful experiment with unacceptable consequences." (17)

They argue, further, "Errors are not some mysterious product of the fallibility or unpredictability of people; rather errors are regular and predictable consequences of a variety of factors" (17). Whereas real-world writing situations often occur in "unkind work environments," with high-stakes consequences for readers and writers, we ought to recognize that the role of educational systems is to provide "kind" work environments, where writers and readers can experiment widely, make errors with less dire consequences, and in this way learn and adapt to the larger discourse environments in which they will need to survive. Jens Rasmussen, writing about the impact of information technology on errors, maintains, "The ultimate error frequency largely depends upon the features of the work interface which support immediate error recovery, which in turn depends on *the observability and reversibility of the emerging unacceptable effects*" [emphasis mine].

The Third College Writing Program was structured to provide extremely "kind" work environments, with a high degree of observability via peer workshops and conferences with instructors, as well as considerable reversibility via the multiple opportunities for revising drafts (in fact, I gave students the option of continuing to revise any essay right up until the time to submit their final package at the end of the quarter) and the opportunity to drop an unsuccessful essay from the final evaluation. While observability and reversibility obviously do not guarantee a successful outcome, they do prevent an unsuccessful outcome from assuming the proportions of a catastrophe; thus they can greatly assist the coordination efforts of participants in the system. In fact, the unsuccessful essay of the collaborative group gave all of us, writers and readers alike, some important insights into the ecology of composing, a point argued by Woods et al.:

When error is seen as the starting point for study, when the heterogeneity of errors (their external mode of appearance) is appreciated, and the difference between outcome and process is kept in mind, then it becomes clear that one cannot separate the study of error from the study of normal human behavior. We quickly find that we are not studying error, but rather, human behavior itself, embedded in meaningful contexts. (14)

It would be a pity if we construct composing situations for students as unkind environments with a high penalty for variability simply because the environments our students will encounter beyond our classrooms are so constructed. Like flight simulators used in the training of aircraft crews, our composing environments should be engineered so that it is safe for students to attempt different approaches—even to "crash and burn" and "crash and burn" again until they are competent, confident pilots of their own texts.

The next chapter looks at the dynamics of a real-world textual ecology in which a system composed of academic readers and writers (experienced, capable pilots) narrowly escapes a catastrophe.

4
Desert Storm on the Network: Ecology of Readers

In the fall the war was always there, but
we did not go to it any more.

—Ernest Hemingway,
"In Another Country"

Introduction

In the last two chapters, we saw how ecologies of writers, readers, and texts evolve through interdependent activities as agents work to coordinate their internal structures with external structures in their environment and with each other. Though not without its difficulties, this process of emergent self-organization seems generally benevolent. So we might wonder how such a complex adaptive system manages conflict. In particular, we might raise some specific questions about conflict in an ecological system of writers, readers, and texts:

- How is conflict perceived and framed in the system? That is, in what ways does the conflict reflect the distributed, embodied, emergent, and enactive properties of the system?
- What "meaning" does the conflict have for the system?
- What changes influence the system, and what changes are originated by the system to respond to conflict?
- What effect does conflict have on the ongoing processes of the system?
- What mechanisms does the system evolve to contain, mediate, displace, reduce, or banish the conflict?
- If the conflict is resolved, how is the resolution effected? If it is not resolved, what effect does it have on the structure of the system?
- How does the conflict serve or stress the self-organizing properties of the system?
- How does the system incorporate the history of the conflict into its dynamic structure?

This chapter helps clarify how conflict can affect ecologies of composing by analyzing a situation in which genuine conflict, rather than mere controversy or disagreement, stressed one such ecosystem to the breaking point. The conflict is all the more surprising because it occurred in a collegial forum of academics and researchers who share an interest in learning, and because its basis was not scholarly argumentation or differences of theory but war—not war in the abstract but war in the Persian Gulf. The conflict drove this forum from its comfortable niche of ordered complexity right to the edge of chaos.

Chapter 2 focused on the role of texts in ecologies of composing; and chapter 3 examined the role of writers. This chapter will direct our attention to the role of readers in these complex adaptive systems; and once again, it will become apparent that we cannot separate out the readers from the system's network of structures, relations, and processes. It will demolish the folk model of readers as standing outside of the system of text production, merely the passive consumers or judges of its "products." Instead, it situates the readers as integral and active components of the ecology of composing at every stage. The particular ecological system considered here is a computer forum, xlchc, and the conversations in this forum during the time of the Persian Gulf War.

Conflict as Perturbation

How is the "historical war" in the Persian Gulf related to the conversation on that topic in the xlchc arena? The answer, I think, depends on our understanding of the concept of *perturbation* as it applies to complex systems. One such complex system that has been extensively studied is the nervous system. Although it may seem that nervous systems and scholarly computer forums have little in common, as complex systems they share many striking similarities.

In *Autopoiesis and Cognition,* Maturana and Varela use research on vision in frogs to support their argument that the nervous system is a closed network of interacting neurons. The optic fibers in a frog's eye are sensitive to a dark spot surrounded by light. When light strikes the frog's retina, it triggers chemical changes in the nervous system, leading to changes in patterns of activity. The pattern of light is a perturbation, but it would obviously be overstating the case to imply from this that the frog's mind has a "representation" of a fly. A *perturbation* is a change in the state of relative activity of a group of neurons that leads to a change in the state of the relative activity of other neurons or the same set of neurons. It would not be accurate, they argue, to say that some phenomenon outside the system effects these changes, or that the nervous system has "inputs" and "outputs." Rather, the system can only be perturbed by structural changes in the network itself; these changes affect its activity.

In *Understanding Computers and Cognition,* Winograd and Flores apply this concept to human cognition, arguing that we should focus on the interactions within the system as a whole, not on the structure of the perturbations, because perturbations do not determine what happens in the nervous system, but rather trigger changes of state. Therefore, it is the structure of the perturbed system that specifies what structural configurations of the medium (environment) can perturb it. They point out that, from this perspective, there is no difference between perception and hallucination:

> Of course an observer of the nervous system within its medium can make statements about the nature of the perturbation and its effect on patterns of activity. For this observer it makes sense to distinguish the situation of an injected irritant from one of heat. But from the standpoint of the nervous system it is not a relevant, or even possible distinction. (43)

These observations seem to fly in the face of our commonsense understanding about the world and our perception of it. Winograd and Flores neatly summarize Maturana's extensive explication:

> Along with this new understanding of perception, Maturana argues against what he calls the "fallacy of instructive interaction." "Instructive interaction" is his term for the commonsense belief that in our interactions with our environment we acquire a direct representation of it—that properties of the medium are mapped onto (specify the states of) structures in the nervous system. He argues that because our interaction is always through the activity of the entire nervous system, the changes are not in the nature of a mapping. They are the results of patterns of activity which, although triggered by changes in the physical medium, are not representations of it. The correspondences between the structural changes and the pattern of events that caused them are historical, not structural. They cannot be explained as a kind of reference relation between neural structures and an external world.
>
> The structure of the organism at any moment determines a domain of perturbations—a space of possible effects the medium could have on the sequence of structural states that it could follow. The medium selects among these patterns, but does not generate the set of possibilities. (44)

In a different kind of system, such as a complex ecology of readers, writers, and texts in a particular environment, similar effects can be observed. That is, some factor outside the system can trigger a perturbation that propagates, in which a change in the state of the relative activity of the components of the system leads to further changes of state either in the same components or in other components. But we cannot say that the perturbation "causes" these changes, and it is quite impossible to predict which perturbations will trigger significant changes of state in the system, or how these changes will manifest themselves: perturbations that appear quite minor to an observer may trigger changes that propagate on an enormous scale and result in global changes to the system, while perturbations that seem enormous by contrast may trigger little or no change in the system. From the standpoint of the system a perturbation is perceived as minor when it results in minimal change of state; it is major if it results in large or widespread changes in state, regardless of the size of the "disturbance" from the observer's point of view. This phenomenon is very familiar to anyone who has participated in a computer forum over time.

Per Bak and Kan Chen have studied catastrophic events such as earthquakes, stock market crashes, and dinosaur extinction in large interactive systems. They maintain that investigators have traditionally analyzed large interactive systems in the same way as they have analyzed small orderly systems, believing that they could predict the behavior of a large system by studying its elements separately and by analyzing its mechanisms on a microscopic scale. As they explain, "For lack of a better theory, investigators assumed that the response of a large interactive system was proportional to the disturbance. It was believed that the dynamics of large interactive systems could be described in terms of an equilibrium state that is disturbed now and then by an external force" (46). However, it turns out that many chaotic and complex systems cannot be adequately explained via the traditional analysis.

Bak and Chen propose a different model, which they call the *theory of self-organized criticality,* arguing that "many composite systems naturally evolve to a critical state in which a minor event starts a chain reaction that can affect any number of elements in the system" (46). "According to the theory, the mechanism that leads to minor events is the same one that leads to major events. Furthermore," they point out, "composite systems never reach equilibrium, but instead evolve from one metastable state to the next" (46). While Bak and Chen demonstrate their model using physical systems such as sandpiles, earthquake simulators, and dominoes, the model has been extended to biological and social systems as well, via Stuart Kauffman's model of evolution and Philip W. Anderson's and Benoit Mandelbrot's economic models. Such a model is holistic, note Bak and Chen, in that global features of the system, including the relative number of large and small events, do not depend on the microscopic mechanisms. For this reason, such features do not yield to a traditional approach of analyzing the parts separately.

Similarly, the size or nature of the disturbance to an ecological system of readers, writers, and texts, such as a computer forum, cannot be predicted from analysis of a single writer or a single message— its textual features, timing, author, length, or register. It is a global property of the system, based on the dynamic interaction of texts, readers, and writers situated in a particular environment that both constrains and enables interactions. It is dependent on technological structures that support and complicate both text construction and communication, a complex web of intersecting technologies (for example, messages can be forwarded, redirected, or distributed out of order, so that readers might receive a response before they have received the message to which it is responding).

To understand the context of the analysis of the Gulf War conflict on xlchc, it is helpful to have some background about the group and its origins.

Context of XLCHC

XLCHC is one of many thousands of computer-mediated discussion groups (sometimes called *forums* or *lists*) in operation today. Anyone with computer access to the Internet may subscribe to the group. These groups function like electronic mailing lists: a person sends a message to xlchc, and it is automatically sent to everyone on the mailing list. Anyone on the list who reads the message may respond, either by sending an email message directly to the individual writer or by posting a response to xlchc, where it is then distributed to the list. In this way, people are able to read, write, or respond to messages at their convenience, wherever they are. The more than three hundred subscribers to xlchc came from various academic disciplines and from countries all over the world, yet via this interactive medium they were able to carry on conversations with colleagues they had never even met. These ongoing conversations represented the ecodynamics of xlchc as a complex system.

Although social structures in computer forums vary, often one person takes a more active role, acting as a sort of "host" or hub for the conversation. On xlchc, the person I identify as Matt Connors served as this kind of electronic host, introducing topics, commenting on responses, asking provocative questions, drawing out a speaker, recalling previous points or conversations, welcoming new members, and so on.[1]

A new subscriber usually received a brief introduction to the discussion group, which explained the group's focus and provided information about how to send and receive messages; the introduction sometimes also included background about the beginnings of the group, its norms and conventions, and suggestions about etiquette and ethics. The introduction to xlchc, in this case, offered an "origin myth":[2]

xlchc came into being in 1984 as a medium for discussion of research on learning and development with a general concern for issues of education in modern technological societies and a special concern about the ways in which educational systems are a source of socially engendered social inequality. The "call letters" of this discussion group (to borrow terminology from another medium) indicate its initial goals. LCHC is the Laboratory of Comparative Human Cognition, a research unit founded at the Rockefeller University in the early 1970's which moved to the University of California, San Diego in 1978. Until 1984, LCHC had an ethnically diverse faculty that conducted an active post-doctoral program in the use of comparative methods for studying culture and cognition with special interest in problems of learning and development in school and non-school settings. By 1984, two years into the Reagan–Bush era, we had lost virtually all of our minority group faculty, our research concerns were explicitly rejected by federal funding agencies, and we were denied post-doctoral funds on the grounds that there was insufficient minority group faculty. :-)

xlchc was one response to this non-benign neglect. The "X" in the title had a dual significance: First, it was meant to provide a medium for continued interaction and cooperation by the many visitors and post-doctoral fellows with whom we had interacted in the past, that is, for "ex-LCHCers." Second, it was meant to provide a broadened constituency for discussion of the issues traditionally associated with the Laboratory by including scholars and graduate students from around the world who wished to participate.

> The technical organization of xlchc is designed to be minimally
> constraining. xlchc and its sub-conferences exist as lists of addresses in
> the social science computer facility at UCSD. A message sent to an X-
> address is simply re-routed to all addressees with no filtering. A file
> containing all such mail traffic is stored at LCHC as a form of collective
> memory, but it is rarely consulted (which means that xlchc is a sort of
> "decorticate" entity entity!). (LCHC staff)

It is evident from this interpretation of xlchc's origins that the "special concern about the ways in which educational systems are a source
of socially engendered inequality" is more than a case of ivory-tower
liberal-minded idealism but springs from the direct experience of institutional threats to a program with a dedicated cross-cultural em-
phasis on learning and development. In an earlier conversation, on
May 19, 1990, Connors elaborated on the difficulties LCHC confronted:

> There was a time, long long ago, when a major function of LCHC was to
> conduct doctoral and post-doctoral training. During a 13 year period we
> worked with about 30 young scholars, almost 20 of whom were American
> minorities. When Reagan came to power, the kind of work our lab does,
> including the training, were explicitly ruled inappropriate. When it came
> time to renew our training program, we were told, using guidelines of
> which I thoroughly approved, that unless minority group professionals
> occupied senior positions in the training program (as they had earlier,
> when Bill Hall, A. J. Franklin, and others participated) it would be can-
> celled. (Note the irony of a Carter regulating system being used by
> Reagan to further reduce training monies!). The following year, when two
> senior minority group UCSD faculty joined the training program, the
> reviewers took me aside and asked me why I was involving inferior
> scholars in the program. The training grant was terminated.
>   In parallel with these events, my university hired no minority group
> scholars in either of the departments with which I am associated. The
> consequences of these events have been simultaneously to delegitimate
> our comparative research and to deprive us of badly needed ethnic and
> cultural representation on our faculty.
>   The reason that there were minority group people to work with in the
> 1970's is that the civil rights movement and earlier riots galvanized the
> country temporarily into action. And this time around?

The introduction to xlchc also offers some guidelines about norms
and conventions for this discussion group. These guidelines are brief
and sketchy, which may reflect a desire to avoid creating a formal

atmosphere oppressive to a free and lively exchange of ideas and opinions:

> During the past 6–7 years xlchc has grown from a dozen or so participants to over 300. Very naturally, the topics under discussion have expanded to fit the interests of new members. A few weeks of observation will give you a feel for how things work. Any member of the discussion group is welcome to send messages to xlchc or its subconferences on a topic (or topics) they feel will be of interest to the group addressed, or because they are seeking information that the members of xlchc might be able to provide. Everyone is welcome to respond to any message and participate in any discussion. . . .
>
> If the past is any guide to the future, some messages will generate considerable discussion, some will be met by silence. Silence is not a reliable indicator of the message's value to the group: it may be that no one is interested in the topic; it may be that there is general agreement, but nothing to add, or it may be that people do not feel competent to add to the discussion and do not know how to ask a good question about it. In such cases one can try again or simply wait to see what develops.
>
> A general norm for the system is that messages are informal communications, what have sometimes been referred to on xlchc as "half baked" messages, which, it is hoped, will be baked up into fine food for thought as a consequence of the interactions that occur subsequently. From time to time, xlchc messages appear in articles or books, with some form of acknowledgment of their source. The norm in this case, as in daily use of the system is to be considerate of one's colleagues. (LCHC staff)

The XLCHC Conversation on the Gulf War

The most basic description of the Gulf War conversational episode on xlchc is confounded by the medium. For example, a simple way to begin would be to tell how many messages were posted on this topic, and how many different people posted them. However, in this episode we have messages embedded in other messages, gaps in the message archives, and the emergence of a subgroup called *xwar*, intended to deal with this topic exclusively. Consequently, there follow messages posted to xlchc in which the writer asks to subscribe to xwar, messages posted to xwar that refer to messages posted on xlchc and vice versa, and a message sent to xwar in which the writer asks how he came to be subscribed to xwar at all. There are several messages that attempt to summarize a thread of argument involving some messages posted to xlchc intertwined with messages posted privately, or to un-tangle a thread of messages that were posted or received out of order, confusing readers about who was answering whom. There is a mes-sage forwarding several messages from people having some technical trouble connecting with the list; and there are two postings in which one writer forwards messages from another person who wants to re-main anonymous. These complications defeat a simple count, although I can say with some confidence that over seventy-five messages were involved and somewhere between thirty-five and forty people. (For a map of correlations between the historical events in the Gulf and the numbers of messages posted to xlchc and to xwar, see the timetable in appendix D.)

A count of subscribers reveals that 264 people were on the xlchc mailing list during this period. However, this number does not fairly represent the number of readers of this particular conversation: people often delete messages unread, whether because they are simply over-whelmed or because they do not want to follow a certain topic. So we might argue that the number of readers would be significantly fewer than the number of subscribers. On the other hand, messages are eas-ily forwarded or saved and printed to be shared with people who are not on the list. Such is the case with a message written by George Lakoff, posted to a different forum, and forwarded to xlchc by one of its subscribers. Because of the ease of forwarding messages, not only to individuals but to entire lists, it is quite impossible to say how many people might have read some or all of the messages posted to xlchc during the Gulf War episode. The only way to determine for certain if a reader has read a post is if he or she makes some response to it, whether posting to the list or to the writer privately or forwarding the message to someone else, thus becoming a writer, as well as a reader. And there is no writing, in this episode at least, that is not based on or responding to something the writer has read. However, writing that was forwarded to the list is not the result of reading postings to the list: thus these writers are responding to other texts, outside of the list. Question: Can we really distinguish between readers and writers, or even between reading and writing? We should note that this question is not confined to electronic environments but is also significant for conventional media as well.

Perhaps we should concentrate on dating this episode, a task that seems simple enough; but here, too, a simple task turns complex. Shall we date the episode from the first mention of the Middle East in Sep-tember 1990, or at the point where it began to emerge as a significant topic in January 1991? When shall we say it ended (if we decide to say it ended at all)? In my opinion, the logical bounds of the episode are from September 1990 to the following April, the last direct reference to the conflict in the Middle East.

The real issue for analysis, though, is not how to quantify the messages or boundaries of this episode; the issue is not how the conversation on xlchc "represents" the war in the Gulf, or how "accurate" individual members' views might be in relation to historical events outside the group. The real goal is to better understand how conflict is distributed, embodied, emergent, and enacted in the ecological system of readers, writers, and texts situated in this environment.

The Gulf War on XLCHC: Part One

On September 13, 1990, the first reference to the Middle East occurs in this message forwarded to xlchc by Richard Sessions.

Date: Thu, 13 Sep 90 19:51 EDT
From: Richard Sessions
Subject: Culturally sensitive material for the forces
To: xlchc@ucsd

I forward the following message to xlchc as much to stimulate discussion about its ethical-political underpinnings as anything else. Are others as confused as I feel when reflecting on whether and why such a course might be worth offering ?

Richard

<rex@albny.bitnet>
Date: Thu, 13 Sep 90 11:49:00 LCL
From: Charles Livingston
Subject: Materials needed
To: 'Richard Sessions'

For a course that's being prepared on very short notice that will deal with psychological issues in a sensitive way for American servicemen who are likely to be present for some time in the Middle East, we need good material with Middle Eastern content. All references that you might suggest would be welcome. Materials that could be reproduced are of particular interest to us as we are preparing a set of materials to be used in a correspondence course format. Unpublished material is also welcome as are general suggestions and comments. We are working under time pressure. Please respond as soon as possible. Thanks.

Charles Livingston

Notice that Sessions is writing as a reader who is responding to and relaying some text he has read elsewhere, text that had been posted by Charles Livingston. There were three responses to this message, and these responses are to some extent representative of the various positions the later conversation would take. Jake Olson responds to Sessions's request for a discussion of the "ethical-political underpinnings" of Livingston's message by addressing the request in Livingston's message. Notice that his response does not, however, directly address Livingston's request for material with "Middle Eastern content."

> I'm not too familiar with specifics, but for psychological issues to be presented to U.S. servicemen in the Middle East, one might start with discussions of service in Afghanistan by returning Soviet soldiers and discussions of service in Vietnam from the perspective of returning American soldiers, especially now that Iran seems inclined to keep us busy and unlikely to make things easy for a U.S.-supported post-Hussein government.

The second response, from Matt Connors, appears to overlook or ignore Sessions's invitation to discuss the ethical-political issues and directly addresses Charles Livingston (who is not a subscriber to the xlchc list) and his request, with a specific reference for further reading.

> Charles—In response to your call for work on the middle east see Punamaki, R. (1987) Psychological stress responses of Palestinian mothers and their children in conditions of military occupation and political violence. Quarterly Newsletter of LCHC, 9, 76–84. The article deals with life on the West Bank, but it is generalizable to a much broader range of conditions that war imposes on indigenous populations who are nominally non-combatants and might help people better understand the hatred they engender in the name of defending democracy.

The third message, from Martha Bunker, was forwarded by Jake Olson:

> pLEASE FORGIVE THE CAPS...MY MACHINE DEVELOPED THIS DISEASE SUDDENLY...THE ISSUE BEFORE THE SERVICEMEN IS FOR THEM TO COME HOME...THE USA IS SPENDING SOME 30 MILLION DOLLARS A DAY ON KEEPING THOSE TROOPS THERE...I BELIEVE THEY ARE THERE BECAUSE BUSH DOES NOT KNOW WHAT TO DO ABOUT OUR UNEMPLOYMENT PROBLEM AND THE FACT THAT HE CANNOT MAINTAIN A MILITARY MACHINE WITHOUT SUCH ADVENTURES AS THOSE I N THE ARAB LANDS...I DON'T KNOW IF THIS WILL GET TO MORE THAN YOU BUT I DO NOT KNOW HOW TO GET IT TO EVERYONE WHO MIGHT HAVE READ YOUR MOST RECENT NOTE. SINCERELY MARTHA

Following this message, there was silence on the topic for four months, while discussion on xlchc continued on other topics: the possibility of perfect communication, models and metaphors, culture and ontogeny, scientific methods and psychology, microgenesis, cross-cultural psychology, literacy. On January 9, Roger Forrest forwarded a long essay (seventy-three hundred words) on war and metaphor by George Lakoff, in which Lakoff presented a critical analysis of the metaphors by which the Bush administration was marshaling support for war in the Persian Gulf, metaphors such as "politics is business" and "war is politics pursued by other means." Lakoff posted his essay originally to Internet newsgroups, with the following explanation and its unusual request:

> January 15 is getting very close. As things now stand, President Bush seems to have convinced most of the country that war in the gulf is morally justified, and that it makes sense to think of "winning" such a war.
>
> I have just completed a study of the way the war has been justified. I have found that the justification is based very largely on a metaphorical system of thought in general use for understanding foreign policy. I have analyzed the system, checked it to see what the metaphors hide, and have checked to the best of my ability to see whether the metaphors fit the situation in the gulf, even if one accepts them. So far as I can see, the justification for war, point by point, is anything but clear.
>
> The paper I have written is relatively short—7,000 words. Yet it is far too long for the op-ed pages, and January 15 is too close for journal or magazine publication. The only alternative I have for getting these ideas out is via the various computer networks.
>
> While there is still time, it is vital that debate over the justification for war be seriously revived. I am therefore asking your help. Please look over the enclosed paper. If you find it of value, please send it on to members of your newsgroup, to friends, and to other newsgroups. Feel free to distribute it to anyone interested.
>
> More importantly, if you feel strongly about this issue, start talking and writing about it yourself.
>
> Computer networks have never before played an important role in a matter of vital public importance. The time has come. The media have failed to question what should be questioned. It is up to us to do so. There are a lot of us connected by these networks, and together we have enormous influence. Just imagine the media value of a major computerized debate over the impending war!

> We have a chance to participate in the greatest experiment ever conducted in vital, widespread, instantaneous democratic communication.
>
> Tens of thousands of lives are at stake. During the next two weeks there is nothing more important that we can send over these networks than a fully open and informed exchange of views about the war.
>
> Here is the first contribution. Pass it on!

Immediately, Nora Sanders and Sarah Emerson replied, using terminology from prior ongoing discussions of internalization, appropriation, and activity theory on xlchc:

> We applaud Lakoff for interjecting into this rather esoteric discussion a note of reality.
>
> We would like great minds, such as those of the members of this network to internalize his message, appropriate his thoughts and externalize them through ACTIONS regarding the crisis in the Middle East. We urge our colleagues to take time out from your scholarly endeavors to contact your congressional representatives, as well as Speaker of the House, Tom Foley and President Bush at the White House and to march locally to express your concerns. War is not the solution to the complex problems of the Middle East.
>
> Let's hope that at this time next week our actions will have made a difference!

Although Lakoff's essay was a massive post for this forum, and in spite of its openly provocative perspective, this was the only immediate response to it, further evidence that effects of a perturbation in a system do not necessarily reflect the size or scope of the "disturbance." Five days later, on the eve of the January 15 deadline set by Bush and the United Nations for the use of force to expel Iraq from Kuwait, Matt Connors posted a message musing on the coincidence between that date and the celebration of Martin Luther King's birthday. He also noted the coincidence that he had recently been reading the founding documents of the United Nations and UNESCO. And he reflected on the coordination resulting from the use of technology.

> We are all experiencing new forms of coincidence as a consequence to the technological innovations that have allowed us to interact in near real time for little expense in various media, despite vast differences in space. The downside of course, is that access, and forms of use of, new means of interaction are not under our control: the denser the layer of technology needed for interaction, the more vulnerable it is.

So, coincidentally, it will not be weeks before I hear about parades in Hamburg, Baghdad, Tel Aviv, Vilnius, Moscow, as well as San Diego and San Francisco, my "homes." We will all be highly coordinated over the next 24–48 hours, even if none of us signs onto this medium or even talks to another soul. That is a new mode of communication; It is very highly mediated. Is it a mode of thought? And how is that thought related to action?

There followed another week of silence on the topic, and then Gene Saltzman posted a wrenching message forwarded from Sam Trautman, a colleague in Tel Aviv.

Dear friens,

I hhhhad sent a letter to many of you when the war broke out, but we have been completely out of bitynet contact and I'm not certain if and when the letter was sent. I'll assume it was sent and will tell you what has been happening in our lives these past several days. And, as I wrote in the last letter, I won't be able to make personal comments because this letter will go to many people and I don't have the possibility of adding something personla to a letter of this nature. Bitnet constraints.

We have been attacked, as you have almost surely read in the papers and seen on CNN. You probably saw it on live TV, on-line, real time. Very weird! The sirens have been sounding off fairly often and we've taken refuge in our sealed room in our home. Several of the Scud missles came fairly close to our home: around a 10 minute walk from where we live. The sickening thud of the missle exploding along with the wails of the sirens is a sound we can all do without. It's pretty frightening. When we went in thhe room for the first time and donned our gas masks, sealed the door with masking tape, put a wet towel under the door, and turned on the radio to hear what's hhappening and to get instructiuons about what to do, we were all sitting on thhe couch in that small room; I looked at my two kids (Joshua is ironically in the army in a place safer thhhhan where we are) and Jessica and felt scared for all of us, angry and frustrated. Yael, who is now almost 13, said that she didn't want to die, and Uri, who is almost 17, said that hhe wanted to have a chance to beat the shit out of Sadam. I told Yael that nothing would happen to her because I was thhere and would protect her, and told Uri that I'd help him. But in my heart, I wanted to cry that we were there, sitting like hhelpless individuals, about to get bombed. The amount of time we have between the siren and the bomb is around 1 minute, so getting into thew room and doing all thhat has to be done has to be quick and efficient. By the second time we had to do all of this, we were much more re;axed and in charge of things and by the third time, we sort of mosied in because we knew how to time things. I am amazed at how we, and everyone else I spoke to, got so accustomed to it with such little practice.

Now there hhave been two days since we've had an attack, and the assumption is t thhat Sadam iswaiting for us to get lulled into thinking all is OK, and then he's going to try to hhit us again. That shhould send everyone into a deep depression, somthing he'd like since all of this is psychological warfare, anyway. And most believe that he'll try chemical warfare against us the next time around. He is a collosal piece of shit, and anyone who is participating in demonstrations against the war cannot fathom who this man is, and hhow far he is willing to go to force hhis will on others.

Our part of the country is on the border of where people are now allowed to leave their homes (with gas masks, of course) and can travel to and fro, but not into the places that are designated as "hot spots". The university at Tel Aviv is one of those places, hhhot spots, that is because it's in Tel Aviv, one of Sadam's targets.

I'm afraid the compuetr will go down soon, so I'll sign off here and will send missive #3 soon.

My best to all of you, and love from Jess and me to all of our friends.

Two days later, another message from Sam Trautman was forwarded by Saltzman.

Subject: missive #3
January 23rd, 1991

Dear all,

Here's another communal letter. Your e-mail letters have been wonderful and I have shown them to family and colleagues. Thanks for the thoughts and encouragement!

As you know, the inevitable happened last night: Sadam sent another missile to the Tel Aviv area and succeeded hitting a residential area, causing 99 casualties. Thius happened around 8:30pm, and we were in our selaed room for around 30–45 minutes until we got the all-clear sign. We heard the Patriot missile taking off (there's a battery not far from our house) so that gave an added dimension to the location of the incoming Scud missile. The Patriot hits a Scud at around a distance of 10 miles. You can imagine what was going on in our minds and hearts. We then heard the explosion of the Scud and knew immediately that it was far enough away that we wouldn't be hurt. We waited for more, but there weren't any. Until now, he has sent volleys of 3 or 4 at a time.

Uri remains pissed at the situation we all find ourselves in. Yesterday he ranted about sitting in a room, waiting for a Scud missile to fall on our heads, not being able to do anything about it, and when it falls on our neighbors, you feel relieved that it weasn't on you, and you feel awful that that's what you feel. He summed it up in his one minute tirade. Yet his almost-17-year-old fantasies (very healthy ones) came out, too, so he still wants to have Sadam alone for 5 minutes to beat the shit out of him, and he talsk about being a pilot, flying to Iraq witgh the country behind you, taking out the missile sites and Sadam, too.

Yael has been a real trooper, too. She, too, feels the helplessness (who couldn't?) of being like a sitting duck wondering if the next Scud is going to hit you. She spends alot of time on the phone with her friends when we're in the room with the gas masks, talking with them and feeling in touch with them while with her family.

It doesn't matter much, of course, but I'll never forgive Sadam for making my kids (any kids!) feel that way, and for making them face adult realities at such an early age. I'll never forgive him for having them feel that he can kill them in a moment and that their lives are on a slender line. I'll never forgive him for killing their childhood.

Shit, huh?

Some of you asked about the dailies when these things happen. So here goes. The siren goes off and we have about a minute to be secure. I unplug the TV and wheel it into the sealed room where we've added an antenna so that we can see TV and get news about what';s up. Everyone puts on their gas masks, and last minute pees are taken, if there's time. (Yesterday I heard the Patriot take off as I was peeing, so I knew that didn't leave an awful lot of time). Yael puts a wet rag on the door's bottom and Jessica seals the door's frame with masking tape. We then just sit there and wait.

The room is around 9 feet by feet, zand has a sofa for three. The other person sits on a chair. The room is equipped with a radio plugged into the wall, a transistor radio in the event of a power shoratge; 4 bottles of a powder to rub on us if the attack is a chemical attack; and syringes which we use to inject ourselves if it's a nerve gas (signs, in ascending order: salivation and eye-tearing; loss of focus in eyesight; dizziness; difficulty in breathing); a large bucket with water for peeing and crapping and a powder to cover the odors (we've already used it on the first night when we were in the room for 4 hours); flashlights; candles; spare batteries; water (not Perrier but we wouldn't mind that); canned foods; eating utensils; and lots more. You get the idea.

Everyone calls everyone else to make sure that all's OK and that our friends are handling the situation well. (So it's not just a 12-year-old daughter who talskj alot).

Yesterday I took the kids to see the Patriot missiles near our house to give them a sense of security. God knows what they're thinking now after last night's attack.

We remain hopeful that things will be over without chemical missiles and without suicide planes dropping them onto us but the truth is that most of us believe that this, too, may wel;l happen. Sadam is a cruel and ruthless tyrant who has little regard for others' lives. Although there aren't many (perhaps no) just wars, I believe that this one is about as close as tyou can come to one.

I'll sign off now and will do my best to remain in contact.

Despite the chilling details, know that we here have the feeling that we can weather the storm and that life will go on. Not as usual, but as close to that as one can get in the present circunstances. The reaction here is one of resolute steadfastness along with a realistic sense of being in danger. So, despite the problems, we're going to tough it out.

God bless and love to all of you from me and my family.

Sam

A set of notes from the physician and poet Robert Werman, giving further details of daily life in Israel, was also forwarded to Gene Saltzman, who passed it along to xlchc on January 29. This set of messages bore a copyright notice; following the Gulf War, Werman published *Notes from a Sealed Room,* a collection of email messages he sent and received during the war.

Distribution and Readers

It is easy to see that the conversation is distributed, both in the sense of "divided" and in the sense of "shared," among writers and readers who are separated in space and time. They post email from seven countries: the United States, Argentina, Denmark, Canada, Germany, Austria, and Israel. These writers and readers are also diverse in their disciplinary specialization, including ten scholars in education, nine in psychology, five in communications, four in cognitive science, and one each in linguistics, physics, anthropology, and applied math. (See table of distribution in appendix E.) We can safely infer, as well, that the conversation is also distributed across physical structures in the environment—computers, display terminals, keyboards, telephone lines, and networking software, for example.

However, it is not as easy to see how a perturbation spreads through such a distributed system, creating a conflict. In a large sense, every message posted in a computer forum such as this represents a perturbation: the conversation consists of a network of perturbations surrounded by vast reaches of silent space. Consistent with the power law discovered by Bak and Chen as a property of "self-organized criticality," the vast majority of messages generate a fairly small disturbance in the overall system, with only a few messages responding to the initial proposal of a topic; a much smaller number propagate more widely, affecting more people over more time and generating a higher volume of messages on the topic. This is a function of distribution, and it represents one of the most fascinating areas for study in research on computer-mediated discourse. For a rough illustration of a power curve, we can look at the distribution of messages by participant (see fig. 10). Note that the vast majority of participants posted only one or at most two messages, and only three participants posted more than five messages. This is a somewhat surprising finding, considering the "high affect" associated with this topic. But it also demonstrates just how distributed the conflict in this episode really is. Further, there is no way to strictly divide the participants or their messages into two "sides," even on the topic of whether the United States was responsible for precipitating the war.

The interactive system of any computer forum is constituted by its messages; the elementary fact is that without messages there is no system. Thousands of discussion groups have been created, enjoyed a brief life, and then disintegrated and died as, under whatever influence, messages became sparse and eventually stopped. Others have been choked to death by excess: participants appalled at receiving several hundred messages in a day from a single group rush to un-subscribe. In general, to survive, computer discussion groups must generate enough controversy to engage a significant number of their readers as writers: the conversation must be distributed over more than two or three chief voices, no matter how eloquent they may be. However, when controversies propagate too widely, or emerge into bitter conflicts, the results can be catastrophic for the group.

Consequently, we can observe a dynamic process as we watch a typical group over time: there is a drive toward controversy when the group becomes too equable and a corresponding drive toward stability when destructive conflicts threaten chaos.[3] This process is demonstrated quite markedly in the xlchc conversation on the Gulf War. The first message, inviting comment on the "political-ethical underpinnings" of Charles Livingston's forwarded message, is provocative, posted during a period of collegial discussion of "perfect communication." But the Gulf War topic never quite takes off at this point; it generates a few messages in response but does not develop the "critical mass" of distribution to become a substantial conversation. On the eve of the January 15 deadline, Matt Connors sent two separate messages, which appear as musing reflections but also might be ex-

Name	Number of messages	Total
Armand Endicott	✈	1
Anne Brice	✈	1
Nora Sanders	✈	1
Martin Taylor	✈	1
Dave Covey	✈	1
Jim Barrett	✈	1
Bob Reasoner	✈	1
Frank Simpson	✈	1
Art Lopetsky	✈	1
Michael Schwartz	✈	1
George Lakoff	✈	1
Donna Jensen	✈	1
Sarah Emerson	✈	1
Mark Green	✈	1
Lisa Moffett	✈	1
Elena Juarez	✈	1
Robert Werman	✈	1
Amy Wood	✈	1
Lars Nilsson	✈✈	2
Sam Trautman	✈✈	2
Pat Benson	✈✈	2
Ana Milano	✈✈	2
Roger Forrest	✈✈	2
Penny Grolier	✈✈	2
Ethan Morse	✈✈	2
Steven Schnell	✈✈	2
Gene Saltzman	✈✈✈	3
Lauren Lane	✈✈✈	3
Larry Goldman	✈✈✈	3
Hans Rausch	✈✈✈	3
Richard Sessions	✈✈✈	3
Gerald Parsons	✈✈✈✈	4
Martha Bunker	✈✈✈✈✈	5
Katherine Grayson	✈✈✈✈✈✈	6
Matt Connors	✈✈✈✈✈✈✈✈	8
Jake Olson	✈✈✈✈✈✈✈✈✈✈✈	11

Fig. 10. Distribution of messages on the topic of the Gulf War, by writer

pected to provoke response on the topic. Then the topic gradually began to acquire some momentum as more readers and writers engaged it, and response times began to shorten. (The visual map in appendix D shows how the messages on the Gulf War are both distributed and connected in time.) Sam Trautman's letter, forwarded from Tel Aviv, had the effect of a seed crystal in qualitatively changing the global state of the system. As we shall see, at this point, rather than focus on events outside the system, participants began to turn on each other, using the Gulf War as an ostensible topic while establishing conflicting positions on a wider range of subjects. Almost from this exact moment, a parallel set of messages struggled to prevent disintegration into catastrophic hostilities: a message suggesting the creation of an xwar subgroup, a proposal to "shut down xlchc for a while," the forwarding of a conciliatory speech by the Finnish philosopher Georg Henrik von Wright, and a heartfelt plea, "Somewhere, somehow we have to give peace a chance and what a better medium than a communication system that puts so many of us from such diverse backgrounds at earshot." Even as the conflict was propagating itself through the escalation of inflammatory rhetoric, these parallel peacemaking efforts were emerging through expanding distribution across readers, writers, and texts.

The Gulf War on XLCHC: Part Two

Returning to the Gulf War and xlchc, on January 29, Lars Nilsson responded to Saltzman's original post from Sam Trautman.

> Subject: Re: message from Israel
>
> While Sam writes about his feelings about the 'just war', I wonder does he consider what American missiles and bombs are doing to the people of Iraq. Sam's 'chilling details' may be rather mild compared to what is happening to families in Baghdad and other places. His 'resolute stead-fastness' sounds exactly like the attitudes that generated this idiotic and criminal war in the first place.

Amy Wood posted this reaction to Lars's message:

> Lars, you have got to be kidding! A man is sitting in a sealed room listening to sirens, waiting for a bomb to fall on his head, and YOU are LECTURING HIM about a bad attitude? And you call it MILD conditions? Does he actually need to get killed before you allow him the luxury of feeling angry at those who started this war, who I might point out are neither Israel NOR the USA?!

But Hans Rausch had a different reading of Lars's post. In a message that reflects on his own memories of Allied bomb raids in Munich during World War II, he draws a parallel with the victims of the Gulf War; he also recalls Lakoff's essay.

> Through our media we also get more and more reports on how other people in war zone try to find their way. I guess that Lars tried to make the point that we should try to de-center, to disengage from terror and overwhelming emotion, in order to be able to see clearly the still existing possibility to stop the killing, and go on with every possible effort of developing a new regional order in this "near-east" part of our world.
>
> At Hamburg University, I have distributed the Lakoff analysis from New Year's Eve. It has proved to be very helpful in disentangling ourselves from the information whirlpool after Jan 16.
>
> Frankly, I do not understand why the Lakoff note has not been taken up seriously in this network. I had some side exchanges, though, with several listeners.
>
> Closing with hope, in spite of it all

At this point, the exchange of messages began to take a different shape. The next four messages were posted within two days and set the terms of the basic conflict:

> Date: Mon, 3 Feb 91 00:39:20 +0100
> From: Jake Olson
> To: xlchc@ucsd.EDU
> Subject: Re: message from Israel
>
> I suppose the silence on this topic, apart from the thoughtful comments of Lars and Hans, is due to general embarrassment at the discussions from Israel, which obviously and understandably arise from fear and are incapable of addressing the points that Lakoff, Chomsky and others have raised in recent days. I assume that 95% of xlchc is in general agreement with Lakoff and Nilsson and the other 5% is not too interested in reflection at the moment. Still, it is sad to see vitriolic attacks on the anti-war movement going unanswered.
>
> I've found this war intensely depressing, bringing to an end an illusion of a different future that I had almost consciously, wilfully constructed out of the events of the last couple years.
>
> The situation faced by Iraqi civilians is much worse than that faced by the Israelis. The difference in magnitude is perhaps metaphorically exemplified by the Israeli concern that electricity might be lost for a period of time contrasted with over a week without electricity in Baghdad. And in truth,

the citizens of "democratic" Israel have been more active in bringing this horror upon themselves and in inflicting it on others. Their government was widely reported to have pushed the United States into attacking from the outset.

I have not lived through the fear of death by bombing but saw trhe destruction in Managua not long after Somoza's air force rained bombs and bullets on the citizens. Israel was a particularly close ally of Somoza, as of course was the U.S. until near the end; when I visited, both were supporting the contras. Without hashing through the issues of the West Bank, ties to South Africa, and so forth, it can be noted that because Israel's rather fascistic government is openly supported by large numbers of its people, blessed with relative freedom of expression, its citizens are relatively accountable for its actions. With no trace of irony, Amy denies that the U.S. started this war. I beg to differ. Certainly Hussein did not. When Indonesia invaded Timor and murdered hundreds of thousands of people, there was no war because the U.S. did not start one. When our present ally Turkey invaded Cyprus (half of which it sits on to this day), there was no war because the U.S. did not start one. When South Africa grabbed Namibia, there was no war because the U.S. did not start one. When Israel grabbed territory and held it in the face of U.N. resolutions, there was no war. For that matter, when Iraq grabbed a chunk of Iran, not only did the U.S. not go to war with Iraq, it supported Iraq.

For one who went through the Vietnam era as a student it is amazing to see how different it looks at age 40. As criminal as the perpetrators of that war seemed at the time, it looks far worse to me now, the exercise of power to rain suffering and death on so many young people who have no chance even to understand their situations, both on their side and ours. It was stunning to sit through the apparently popular movie Dances With Wolves and try to fathom how every viewer could not be thinking "What if the army then had B-52s with 2000 pound bombs and cluster bombs to "soften up" the Sioux?" Or to listen to CNN reporters comparing the bombing to the finale at the fourth of July, apparently in ignorance of similar poetry by Mussolini's pilots as they bombed the Ethiopians. Of course it is terrible to read about frightened Israeli kids who may be turned into a new generation of ruthless killers, but that is just one small part of the horror.

— Jake

Date: Sun, 3 Feb 91 17:31:01 PST
From: Katherine Grayson
To: xlchc@weber.ucsd.edu
Subject: re: message from Israel

I agree, Amy, that Lars was far too harsh in his condemnation of Sam Saltzman. One of the reasons I have been silent so far is that I cannot imagine the constant psychological wearing that he and everyone else in Israel is enduring. And I cannot imagine (not being Jewish) how Saddam's threat to "turn Israel into a crematorium" rings in the collective memories of a people who so narrowly escaped absolute genocide.

On the other hand, I disagree, entirely, with Sam's and Amy's analysis of this war. There is ample proof that the US in fact did start this war, and I would hope the Israelis would begin to direct some of their anger toward a US foreign policy that begets this kind of violence. The double-speak out of Washington is that the war began on August 2 when Saddam invaded Kuwait. Thinking people have to reject that attempt to rewrite history. Come on, Bush. The war might have started last year when, according to an article in last week's New Yorker magazine (author???) the CIA met with Kuwaitis to talk about destabilizing the economy of Iraq. Or, it might have started with the wink and nod the US ambassador gave to Saddam on July 30 when she claimed that the US had no opinion about Arab-Arab conflicts and simply asked (was this an invitation) that they "resolve it quickly."

I think the best starting point for the war was Bush's post-election (November) escalation of troop force from a defensive to an offensive number. Up until then, the world could afford to wait out the months of sanctions, which would have worked, according to a model tested against 101 historic cases of the use of sanctions (authors Gary C. Hufbauer, Kimberly A. Elliott, Jeffrey J. Schott, "Economic Sanctions Reconsidered" excerpted in the New York Times, January 14).

The US could not afford the huge buildup of troops, however, and that placed a timeline on the beginning of war. (Another good candidate, though, is the Congressional vote that essentially gave Bush a free reign.)

My 12 and 14 year olds believe they will be drafted into this war when they reach 18. They watch with horror every escalation and wonder where they can turn for sanctuary. They feel themselves at odds with a country that has accepted this manipulation from an administration hot for war, from an administration of old, white men who have no vision of a "new world order" where world consensus can impose economic sanctions to stop a murderous bully.

What is "new" about war? My sons have marched with my husband and I, before and after the first bombs began to fall. My infant son rides on our backs and sometimes sleeps, sometimes raises his arms to the strangers who flank us, the men and women who come nearer to hug a baby, feeling the urge to shelter children, even if they have none of their own.

The cost, to my children, is their at-homeness in this culture. Like their parents, they have begun to feel marginalized, alienated. The story is that there are few who appose this war. We, too, do not sleep well at night, though I cannot compare our distress with that of Sam's family. Ours is a frustration and anger, a rage and a sense of powerlessness against a war machinery and mentality that seems dedicated to its own survival, above all. At a conference of military contractors in Milwaukee last October, a speaker opened his remarks with the obscene, "Thank you, Saddam Hussein." Even more obscene was the standing ovation this remark received.

Sam, the peace marches aren't obscene. The war is, the thinking that allows such a remark to be celebrated is, the bombs dropping on civilians in Iraq and Israel are.

And yes, Saddam is. Death would be too good for such a monster. (Not all peace marchers are pacifists.) But Saddam was a monster when he gassed the Kurds. There are monsters in China who kill children for daring to speak out for democratic reform. There are monsters in the Soviet Union who fire on demonstrations in the Baltics. There are monsters in South Africa, in Korea, in El Salvador, and yes, in Israel. And the US government supports them all.

This is not a just or moral war; Saddam's outrageous behavior simply allows the US to make that excuse for it. And here is the thing—Saddam threatened to bomb Israel, to burn the Kuwaiti oil fields, and to pour oil into the Gulf if he was provoked by the US.

Having made those threats, he has carried them out when provoked by the US.

Who is to blame here? Yes, Saddam is a monster; yes, he is to blame. But isn't the US's bullying posture also to blame for the bombs that drop on innocents in Israel? For the ecological disasters of oil fires and oil slicks? For the deaths of civilians and soldiers in Israel and Iraq and Saudi Arabia?

Matt Connors reminded us of a song, the refrain, "When will they ever learn?" Like juveniles, Bush and Hussein have carried out threat, counter-threat, posture, counter-posture. And at such cost to the world, including Sam's children and my children. The sad thing is that the maturity needed to bring in a "new world order" seems out of the reach of the old leadership.

Sam, I'm trying to shelter you from those bombs by telling my government to stop this nonsense. My family will continue this cry.

Shalom,

Kathy Grayson

Date: Mon, 4 Feb 91 11:17 CDT
From: Ethan Morse
Subject: Israel
To: xlchc@UCSD.BITNET

I simply cannot let stand Jake Olson's assumption that 95% of xlchc is in general agreement with Lakoff and Nilsson and the other 5% is not too interested in reflection at the moment. I do not know what the views of other people in this network are—and I don't presume to speak for anyone other than myself—but personally I found the comments by Nilsson—and later Jake and Kathy Grayson—repulsive in the extreme. Lakoff did in fact thoughtfully lay out the metaphors being used—quite consciously I assume—by Bush and others to justify "starting the war" with Iraq. The trick is that I'm sure that he could do the same—if he were politically driven to—with the mindless propaganddistic crap laid out by Lars, Jake, and Ms. Grayson. These texts are precisely the counterpart of the shallowest of administration propoganda—and as such do nothing more than extend the discourse at that level.
....
I began to look through the texts here to engage in argument, but one cannot make any real sense out of Jake's "argument" via implication that Israeli civilians deserve to be attacked because they hve a democratic government—and they're ruthless killers—or Kathy's "arguments" than its somehow ALL our fault—or the silly statement that "sanctions would of worked" because some "model" said they would ("silly" not because she's wrong but because her apparent certitude is ridiculous). Discourse oriented toward tryig to understand what is going on in this mess does not connect with propoganda of this or Bush's kind—or perhaps I just lack the intellect or heart to do it.

A lot of people have been quoting someone lately with the line that "The first causalty of war is truth." Certainly that is true to the extent it fosters—maybe even demands of people who care enough to get involved—this kind of (often purposely) mindless exchange.
>>

And a footnote directed to Kathy Grayson—for public consumption. Would not the line "from an administration...who have no vision of a "new world order"" worked as well without the insertion of OLD, WHITE MEN in the descriptive clause? I know it is impolitic in the contemporary university environment to object to racism and sexism when directed at "white males," but frankly I've had just about enough of that as well. I can take the assualt personally, but as I was listening to a discussion of finding ways of "narrowing the stream" of qualified white males in academics and business at a Spencer Foundation dinner the other night, it suddenly struck me that this was not only me under discussion but my sons. So I guess this is my first public expression of distast for that as well, in saying that you can take that attitude and shove it up your ass.

Ethan Morse

Embodiment and Readers

This is a good point to stop and consider the second attribute of an ecology of composing: embodiment. Are computer forums, such as xlchc, a kind of academic utopia of disembodied discourse, a perfect community of shared ideas, information, and opinion? This utopian view has propelled a great deal of activity, commercial and political plans for the information "superhighway," a push by hardware and software manufacturers to create standards that will facilitate collaboration, and overheated rhetoric in the popular media about "virtual communities." There have been many claims that computer-mediated communication masks physical and social differences, including race, age, physical disability, status, and gender, allowing participants to interact more democratically.

However, as Cynthia Selfe and Paul R. Meyer point out in their study of the computer discussion group Megabyte University, some early claims for the egalitarian nature of computer-based communication may not hold up. Selfe and Meyer analyzed discourse in this group for gender and status differences based on amount of discourse, verbal assertiveness (as demonstrated by introduction of new topics and disagreements with other participants), and politeness (as demonstrated by agreement, apology, and question asking, marks of politeness that have been identified with female talk).

Their findings, while not definitive, indicate that patterns of interaction in the Megabyte discussion group were not markedly different from those of other groups in society: "The amount of discourse and verbal assertiveness both seemed linked to male gender and high profile in the Megabyte conference; however, no corresponding connection between politeness and low profile or female gender was apparent" (179). They also presented statistics for the number of times a participant was referred to by others as an indication of individual influence. These statistics yielded the surprising finding that there were no significant differences across the conference—an indication that "members of the conference paid the same amount of attention to low-profile and female contributors as they did to high-profile and male contributors—as measured by the number of times the authors of messages were referred to directly by others" (180). Results were similar during the period in which participants were identified by name, as well as during the period when pseudonyms were used. Selfe and Meyer conclude,

It seems that Megabyte University offered fairly equal access to participants but at the same time tended to be dominated by men and higher-status members of the academic community. This paradox may be partly explained by differences in linguistic style and behavior that remained constant in the conference regardless of the use or nonuse of pseudonyms. Consistently, though in some cases only with marginal significance, men and higher-profile individuals tended to engage in more assertive behavior than women and lower-profile participants. These behaviors included contributing more messages, introducing more new topics, and disagreeing more frequently with others. (187)

Mark Johnson and George Lakoff would argue that it is not possible for writers and readers to escape the fact of their embodiment because it is embedded in language and the schemas by which we understand the world. In fact, the physical experience of being in/of a body is a recurring theme in the Gulf War conversation. In the essay forwarded to xlchc on metaphor and war, Lakoff argued,

> Metaphors can kill. . . . The use of a metaphor with a set of definitions becomes pernicious when it hides realities in a harmful way. It is important to distinguish what is metaphorical from what is not. Pain, dismemberment, death, starvation, and the death and injury of loved ones are not metaphorical. They are real and in a war, they could afflict tens, perhaps hundreds of thousands, of real human beings, whether Iraqi, Kuwaiti, or American.

On January 12, Hans Rausch wrote, at the end of a long message on another topic,

> We had 40,000 today in Hamburg, demanding "No War on the Gulf. No Oil for Blood"

And of course, the fact of physical embodiment is palpable in Sam Trautman's forwarded message from Tel Aviv, describing his family's experiences while Israel is being attacked. Amy Wood reiterated this physical threat in response to Lars's message.

> A man is sitting in a sealed room listening to sirens, waiting for a bomb to fall on his head, and YOU are LECTURING HIM about a bad attitude? And you call it MILD conditions? Does he actually need to get killed before you allow him the luxury of feeling angry at those who started this war . . . ?

On February 3, Hans Rausch posted a message recalling a parallel physical experience during World War II and raised the specter of chemical warfare:

First: a remembrance from Munich, Germany, 1944
During an allied bomb raid I remember to have been in a cellar room,
asking huge adults for an apple, saying "Apf?". My father was upstairs on
the attic of the four stories house, looking for posphor bombs that could
be in most cases thrown out and down to the street before igniting. I do
not remember being frighted, and know of no symptoms that many other
persons of my generation still show. I was lucky.

Even doubly so, because neither of my parents was involved with the
Nazi terror against Jews, Sinti, other Germans, other Europeans...

Second: German chemistry again
Both my parents were/are chemists, though. Beginning in the mid
seventies, around their retirement, they had to cope with the still
growing avalanche of facts showing the environmental destruction (first),
and the nearly unbelievable news about chemical warfare against the
people of forme Kurdistan. Now they feel very old and helpless against
this recurrence of the threat of a gas war. The terrors of this they know
from their youth (both were one year olds when the first world war
started).

Kathy Grayson linked the fears of her sons with her own physical
experiences marching against the war, connecting the threat of physical danger to one's "at-homeness" in a culture. Using a term generally
applied to physical behaviors and their representations, she calls the
war "obscene" and summons up other global examples of physical
oppression in the form of torture and murder:

And yes, Saddam is. Death would be too good for such a monster. (Not
all peace marchers are pacifists.) But Saddam was a monster when he
gassed the Kurds. There are monsters in China who kill children for daring
to speak out for democratic reform. There are monsters in the Soviet
Union who fire on demonstrations in the Baltics. There are monsters in
South Africa, in Korea, in El Salvador, and yes, in Israel. And the US
government supports them all.

Finally, she represents her antiwar protests in metaphorical terms
as a kind of physical protection.

Sam, I'm trying to shelter you from those bombs by telling my government to stop this nonsense.

But Ethan Morse's furious reply to another section of Kathy's message—"OLD, WHITE MEN"—makes a blunt physical suggestion in
marked conflict with her peacemaking rhetoric. Jake Olson also responded, with an apologia for the facts of embodiment:

This does not mean there is anything intrinsically wrong with any of these conditions. I don't feel bad about being a white male and would be delighted were someone to make me wealthy. Being old is something that happens to some of the best of us and does not appear to be necessarily damaging, although we do of course see an unfortunate correlation with senility and incontinence.

Later the same day, he recounted his physical reaction to Morse's message:

I spent an almost entirely sleepless night as a result of Ethan's message.

Matt Connors compared the growing conflict in the group to a terrifying bodily experience:

As a professor of communication interested in the affordances and shortcomings of this medium I find the current behavior fascinating, like a cobra sitting 12 inches in front of my nose!

Donna Jensen at first argued for keeping the conversation on xlchc rather than forming a subgroup. She contrasted the turmoil in her thoughts with her everyday physical routine:

I was dismayed with the anger unleashed, but to use that as an excuse to halt talk would be unfortunate. I think there's a real reason why the war has generated so much transmission—I know I'm just going through the motions each day, preparing for classes, dealing with household chores, etc. This xlchc conversation has provided an avenue to think about the issue that is uppermost in my mind; everything else seems trivial right now.

On February 7, however, she took extreme measures in reaction to the conflict; she physically removed herself from the xlchc group by having her name removed from the subscription list:

I can't stay on xlchc, xclass (which seems dormant in any case) for a discussion of academic trivia when my life has been so profoundly altered by this war. Please take my name off the xlchc, xclass lists and add it to the xwar list.

Jim Barrett addressed the connections between the physical and the metaphorical in discourse, pointing out that the physical situated-ness of the "speaker" is reflected in discursive conventions:

Wars do that to you. You come down off of mountains, get scared or disgusted, or get holed up in a room while somebody is trying to kill you. Or notice "who" is constructing this horror for you. You deal with the problem of peeing. These are EARTHLY positions—with REAL SELVES—and identitites at stake. These conditions lead us to connect with deep committments and fundamental searches for models to generate meta-phors from (a somewhat neglected point in Lakoff's piece—the meta-phors come from a position and a modeling—they as much reflect that position as construct it in language). This is grounded activity folks.

These examples show the pervasive influence of physical embodi-ment, even in a supposedly "disembodied" discourse arena. But em-bodiment is not merely the grounding of conceptual and discursive structures in physical experience. In this episode, we see how embodi-ment is employed as a means of structuring relationships—strength-ening alliances or creating distance or barriers, even sundering a rela-tionship, as Donna Jensen does with her withdrawal from xlchc. Just as face-to-face relationships are structured through shared physical experiences and interactions such as eating, making love, fighting, sleeping, holding hands, talking, and writing, these texts invoke physi-cal experience to structure the dynamics of relationships in this eco-logical system. It is not a simple case of tit for tat in such relationships, however; Kathy's maternal and nurturing response to Sam, in which she denounces a government of "old, white men," draws a punishing rejoinder from Morse, which Kathy characterizes as a "full frontal assault," a phrase echoed by Morse in a later response.

The Gulf War on XLCHC: Part Three

Ethan Morse's bitter message drew these immediate responses:

Date: Mon, 4 Feb 91 20:10:01 +0100
From: Jake Olson
Subject: Re: Israel

It is unfortunate to see such emotionalism as that expressed by Ethan Morse, which certainly can't coexist with intellectual discussion of the issues. This kind of emotion-laden discussion is just what email is terrible for, so after attempting to clear the record about what I said, I will try to refrain from contributing further to this sad situation. Here are my words and Morse's characterization of them:

I wrote:
... the citizens of "democratic" Israel have been more active in bringing this horror upon themselves and in inflicting it on others. Their govern-ment was widely reported to have pushed the United States into attack-ing from the outset.

...
Of course it is terrible to read about frightened Israeli kids who may be turned into a new generation of ruthless killers, but that is just one small part of the horror.

Morse wrote:
One cannot make any real sense out of Jake's "argument" via implication that Israeli civilians deserve to be attacked because they hve a democratic government—and they're ruthless killers . . .

Please consider:
At no point did I say that Israeli citizens deserve to be attacked. As far as this thing goes, I'm a pacifist and am incredibly depressed that anyone is being attacked. The facts as credibly reported are these: Hussein said that if Iraq were attacked, he would respond by attacking Israel. Israel was repeatedly reported to be exhorting the U.S. to attack Iraq. The U.S. attacked Iraq. Iraq responded by attacking Israel. I think it takes no great logician to see the logic to my statement, given the power of Israelis to influence their government and the relative lack of such power in Iraqi civilians. But completely apart from the accuracy of my statement, in no way did I make the charge that Ethan Morse ungenerously attributed to me. Nor did I describe Israeli civilians as ruthless killers. There are, unfortunately, such people in the world. Environment undoubtedly plays a role in creating them and it does not seem a wild hypothesis that the kind of frightful situation now being experienced by Iraqi and Israeli children MIGHT be such an environment. The more extensive U.S. bombing MAY produce more such sociopathic adult behavior amongst the present generation of Iraqi children than the Scuds will produce among Israeli, and that is a consequence that we all will have to live with. Certainly I doubt living through Scud attacks is a recipe for turning out well-balanced adults, although Morse may have other views of child development.

This debate happens to be uncannily similar to one in my own family, where this war is the first issue that my parents cannot discuss. My father is so emotionally tied to Israel that he cannot discuss the matter without becoming enraged, whereas my mother goes about reading carefully on the topic and discussing it with those who can do so calmly. Although it is all interesting, I guess I wish Gene had spared us the letters from Israel.

— Jake

Date: Mon, 4 Feb 91 15:42:20 PST
From: Katherine Grayson
To: Ethan Morse
xlchc%UCSD.BITNET@lilac.berkeley.edu
Subject: Re: Israel

Ethan,

It's funny that I once thought of you as a (distant, perhaps) ally, given a similar perspective on language and learning, as far as I can tell from your writing and speaking.

Now I think of you as someone given to emotional ventings and particularly vicious and public verbal attacks. Funny how this war keeps making the world worse.

Katherine Grayson

Date: Mon, 4 Feb 91 20:41:00 PST
From: Katherine Grayson
To: xlchc@weber.ucsd.edu
Subject: the war, cont.

Having regained balance after Ethan's frontal attack, I'd like to respond to Gerald Parson's message, which I appreciated very much. [This message had been sent to her privately but was later posted to the list.] In fact, I meant to convey, by my reference to the "old, white men," the dangerous insularity that Gerald described so well. If my phrasing offended anyone, I'm terribly sorry. My own sons, like Ethan's, are white, as is my husband, and I certainly did not intend to attribute anything in particular to men, in general, of any age or color. My apologies.

(I'm not sure what Gerald meant by the Diversity Mafia, however...)

I'm surprised, frankly, at Ethan's response, particularly at the charges of "mindlessness" and "silliness." While I was careful to include references to the information I drew on in my analysis of the situation, Ethan's tirade offered no back-up in the way of citations or informative sources, and therefore no access for the independent review of others. Argument ad hominum can't substitute for the kind of support a counter-argument demands.

If more people were willing to grant intelligence and reasonableness to others, even, and perhaps especially, when they disagreed, there would doubtless be less war in the world.

By this point, the topic of war in the Gulf had taken off, and it now dominated the discussion on xlchc. As we have seen, within the discussions on this topic, other recurring topics were embedded: sexism, racism, rules of argumentation and evidence, distrust of the government and the media, the role of the academic in public life. On February 5, Matt Connors first suggested that a subgroup, xwar, be set up, writing,

Without anyone intending it so, the great divergence of opinion and the necessarily high affect associated with this topic (to name only two factors) have brought people to forms of verbal assault that it is difficult to interpret as constructive.

However, according to our cultural conventions, if any three people want to discuss a topic they deem relevant to xlchc, in which everybody is considered a member with rights and responsibilities equal to everyone else—should they choose to exercise them—I would ask that those interested in setting up a discussion on "xwar" to send a message to pbenson and such a discussion group will be set up.

The same day, Hans Rausch proposed a "psychological and sociological" link between gender and violence control, reconnecting the topic of war in the Gulf with xlchc's established focus on psychology and culture. And there began to be some confusion between messages that had been sent privately and those that had been posted to xlchc. This situation was compounded by readers who responded publicly to messages received privately and vice versa. As Connors put it:

> Jake— I think in both the cases you are talking about the difficulty is on the sending end. There was a mixup over an important message of Martha's on appropriation that somehow got lost between Martha and me. I had been meaning to follow up, thanks for the reminder. And I too did not see the diversity mafia message, and suspect it did not get posted to a conference.
>
> The discoordinations in xlchc are of many kinds, some technical, some resulting from level of sophistication in posting, some from very different points of view.... at least the medium keeps one on one's fingertips, so to speak.
>
> Perhaps Martha and Gerald would re-post for those of us who missed their contributions.

And Jake Olson also attempts to set the record straight:

> Some of you may be confused by Gene's latest message, notably what it is in response to.
>
> The history of the exchange is this:
>
> I sent my msg to xlchc. Gene replied in a message that was addressed only to me. I replied to Gene in a message that was addressed only to him. He has now chosen to escalate this private exchange into a public one. I am very sorry he has chosen to do this.
>
> I will of course reply to his message once I've calmed down.
>
> (My assumption is that Gene is confused about the use of email, and either believes that his original message to me and my reply to him were public, or else he believes that this message was sent privately. Of course, he would probably object to my "assuming" anything about his confusion regarding email, just as he admonishes me for making assumptions about confusions over the war.)

At this point, Mark Green sends a message making an unprecedented proposal:

From: Mark Green
Date: 5 February 1991 1540-PST (Tuesday)
To: xlchc@ucsd.edu
Subject: Let's shut down xlchc for a while

As Matt Connors' suggestion for a new xwar seems to have fallen, I have a stronger suggestion: Turn off the alias for a week or two, to let people settle their battles on their own, or perhaps to let the vitriol die down.

The current traffic, with no connection to xlchc "business" is increasing in volume and ugliness. No good will come of it, and it might lead to the self-destruction of xlchc.

I would think that xlchc subscribers would be familiar with the phenomenon that there is rarely such thing as "truth" or "correctness." As we see this in well-controlled research, I would hope we'd realize its prevalence in world events—especially during a war.

No one's going to get convinced. Give xlchc a rest for a week or two and hope that things get worked out. The sooner the better.

Obviously, this suggestion could not be implemented: in order to find out whether there is support for such a proposal, it is necessary to keep the list open. And it is hard to imagine how things could possibly "get worked out" if the list were to be shut down, for whatever length of time. In any event, this suggestion was not implemented. And, in the last message of this stormy day, Connors wrote,

What a sorry sight, sorry plight. Those interested in debating their views about the war are so intent on what they are doing that they seem completely oblivious of the damage they are doing-to themselves, their colleagues individually, and this discussion group collectively.

Each person who has contributed to this discussion has the e-mail addresses of everyone else who has contributed. Several messages sent to the staff at LCHC have exhorted us to put an end to this discussion. One long time member of xlchc who is active in the discussion has resigned from xlchc on this account.

As a professor of communication interested in the affordances and shortcomings of this medium I find the current behavior fascinating, like a cobra sitting 12 inches in front of my nose! As a friend and colleague to several of the participants in the debate I am very distressed.

Communication must rest on a foundation of sufficiently common presuppositions to allow "reduction of uncertainty." the topic of war in the middle east is not a topic with such a shared foundation in this collectivity. Mutual assumption of good will having been shattered, e-mail is a LOUSY medium for re-establishing it. Instead of a medium for creating increased misunderstanding, it is a fabulous medium for tying every more elaborate doubled-binded knots.

Please move this discussion to a private correspondence or to a subconference. So far only one xlchc members, one who has NOT contributed to the discussion, has asked to join.

The messages that followed argued either in favor of moving the discussion to a subgroup (on the grounds that it was disrupting the regular discourse on xlchc) or against such a move (on the grounds that the Gulf War was—or should be—foremost in people's thoughts). This view was expressed eloquently by Elena Juarez on February 6:

In spite of all the finger pointing and remarks close to I thought I knew you better, I think the discussion should continue. Somewhere somehow we have to give peace a chance and what a better medium than a communication system that puts so many of us from such diverse background at earshot. I honor all those of you who have taken the risk of voicing an opinion no matter how private and different from the others. And, yes, I know it has hurt you because of the backlash but you brave souls know the alternative to discussion—Bush has proven that. Somehow we have to learn from this how to deal with differences—if we don't learn at least this, then all your pain and ours would have been in vain.

Emergence and Readers

What are the emergent properties of the Gulf War discussion on xlchc? How is this episode different from a set of unrelated messages in which individuals simply voice their opinions about the Gulf War (as a chaotic system), and how is it different from a formal scholarly debate (as an ordered system)? That is, how does this conversation emerge into a coherent episode that brings readers and writers and texts into conflict with each other? And what is the central role of readers in this process?

As we observed in chapter 3, emergence is a process of coordination. We have already seen how emergence operates in collaborative writing situations as writers attempt to coordinate themselves and their texts with each other and with the expectations of their readers. Clark and Brennan have also studied how coordination, which they call *grounding,* occurs in conversational episodes. But how is coordination accomplished in this new medium? How do readers, writers, and texts operating autonomously and distributed across space and time gradually acquire coherence around a topic? There are a number of ways that participants in these systems structure coordination, including references in the subject line of the message, direct references to a writer's name, and references to message contents.

Subject-line reference. The subject line of an email message is often used to help readers connect the message to previous posts on the same topic. Sometimes the subject line simply repeats the previous subject line, often prefaced with "re:" Or there may be a rephrasing of the original subject line, to give a slightly different twist to the topic; the subject line may also pick up a phrase or concept from the body of the original message as a way of framing the response. In all such cases, the subject line is an important navigational aid for readers trying to sort out and follow an often bewildering array of email messages on various topics. But readers must also make inferential leaps when subject lines are not explicitly linked. Sessions's original message forwarding Charles Livingston's request for materials dealing with psychological issues for servicemen stationed in the Gulf carries the following subject line: "Culturally sensitive material for the forces." The subject lines of the three messages in response are "psychological issues for servicemen in Saudi Arabia/Iraq," "middle east," and "From Martha Bunker on U.S. in Middle East." Roger Forrest's forward of Lakoff's essay has the subject line "George Lakoff: Metaphor and War," while the subject line of the first response, from Nora Sanders and Sarah Emerson, is "Crisis in the Middle East." Other seemingly unrelated subject lines follow, for example: "Coincidences," "Intervals of Civilization," "a message from Sam Trautman at Tel-Aviv," "Re: message from Israel," and "When and how is metaphorical analysis useful?" In such cases, the links are not obvious, and readers make connections with support from the content of each message. However, as the conflict emerges and becomes more defined, the subject lines begin to be repeated more often: "Re: message from Israel," twice; "Israel," four times; "our political debate," three times, and so on. By this point, writers may assume that readers will find the topic familiar. Finally, some subject lines begin to counter the Gulf War topic: "racism, sexism, ageism (but not the war)," "my last message on war," and "peace."

Direct references to a previous writer's name or other identifier. In responding to Richard Sessions's first message forwarding the request from Charles Livingston, Matt Connors writes, "Charles, in response to your call for work on the middle east," which allows readers to connect with Sessions's message both by addressing the original writer (who is, however, not a subscriber to xlchc) and by summarizing the content of the message. Direct reference is used again when Nora Sanders and Sarah Emerson respond to the forward of the Lakoff essay, "We applaud Lakoff for interjecting into this rather esoteric discussion a note of reality." And Lars writes, "While Sam writes about his feelings about the 'just war', I wonder does he consider what American missiles and bombs are doing to the people of Iraq?" In all of these cases, readers are responding to a writer as if the writer were in fact part of the forum, which is not the case. However, following Lars's message, Amy Wood directly addresses him: "Lars, you have got to be kidding!" This is the first expression of conflict within the forum itself. Three days later, following Hans's message recalling his experiences during the Allied bombing of Germany, Sessions writes, "Hans Rausch's message strikes 2 responsive chords in me," an opening that moves toward resisting open conflict and restoring harmonious relationships. The message from Olson that follows opens with a similar gesture of support, "I suppose the silence on this topic, apart from the thoughtful comments of Lars and Hans, is due to general embarrassment at the discussions from Israel."

References to message content. Another connection provided for emerging topics is some kind of reference to the content of previous texts. Usually the reference takes the form of quotation, paraphrase, summary, or retort. In email messages, quotation from another message is often signaled by the character > preceding the quoted material. But this convention is not universally applied. Morse writes,

> Would not the line "from an administration who have no vision of a 'new world order'" worked as well without the insertion of OLD, WHITE MEN in the descriptive clause?

Other directly quoted messages, such as Lakoff's essay and the speech of von Wright, are forwarded with only a brief introduction by the person forwarding them, to make the topic connection for readers. Morse paraphrases Olson's and Grayson's messages ("Jake's 'argument' via implication that Israeli civilians deserve to be attacked because they hve a democratic government . . . or Kathy's 'arguments' than it's somehow ALL our fault . . ."), paraphrases that Olson and Grayson insist represent Morse's deliberate misreading. Amy's "Lars you have got to be kidding!" combines direct address and retort, but she also goes on to paraphrase both Sam's and Lars's messages in her refutation: "A man is sitting in a sealed room listening to sirens, waiting for a bomb to fall on his head, and YOU are LECTURING HIM about a bad attitude?"

In the early stages of discussion, messages often make use of two or more of these means to help ground readers, but once the topic is well established, such cues are often highly abbreviated or even dropped, a fact that can create confusion for someone joining the group in mid episode (of course, this is also true of other media, from print to conversation to television). For example, in the midst of the most heated exchange on the topic of the Gulf War, at a time when the conflict dominated the traffic on xlchc, a new subscriber posted this message:

> Date: Thu, 7 Feb 91 09:51:44 pst
> From: Sven Larson
> To: xlchc@ucsd.edu
> Subject: Childrens play
>
> Hello ! I (Sven Larson) am visitor researcher at LCHC for three months. I am going to carry through a cross/cultural study of the psychological development of Danish and American 6 year old children in the light of early academic education. My project description and a paper "From Play to Learning Activities". On request I will send a copy of my project description and a paper "From play to learning activity. I would appreciate any communication.
>
> Sven Larson

Notice, also, that the emergence of the conflict is a function of reading and is dependent upon how readers engage the topic. Lars reads the forwarded messages from Sam Trautman and in his response reminds xlchc readers that the "chilling details" Sam describes may be far exceeded by the devastation in Iraq; he links Sam's "resolute steadfastness" with the attitudes that generated the war. Amy's reading interprets Lars's message as "calling conditions in Israel mild" and "lecturing Sam for having a bad attitude." However, Hans's reading of Lars's message, framed as a kind of defense of Lars, and thus also a response to his reading of Amy's post, is more charitable.

I guess that Lars tried to make the point that we should try to de-center, to disengage from terror and overwhelming emotion, in order to be able to see clearly the still existing possibility to stop the killing.

In the next sentence, he recalls his response to reading the Lakoff essay, which he distributed at his university: "It has proved to be very helpful in disentangling ourselves from the information whirlpool after Jan 16." Sessions's post later the same day responding to Hans's message focuses on the reading experience, and it reveals his uncertainty about the power and limitations of language:

Hans Rausch's message strikes 2 responsive chords in me:

- the importance of decentering (surely one of ideological themes linking all of us on this wonderfully far-flung network)
- the puzzle of why George Lakoff's masterful analysis elicited so little discussion here among us.

For me reading the Lakoff piece was a distinctly ambivalent experience. I was impressed by the depth and thoroughness of it, learned more than I expected about alternative perceptions of the issues at stake from people raised in and addressing their representations toward the Arab world, yet frustrated as I searched for a clue to how I might act.

I wonder now whether the timing was not a critical aspect of this. During those last few days before war was officially declared, there was a seductive dream in the air:

"this can't really happen, it's just too ridiculous" some people said "it's all a game of bluff, eventually someone will stand down" "how the *** could modern-day politicians allow themselves to get their backs up against the wall in this way, nobody really wants this war"

etc.

But as the hours and minutes ticked by, it began to dawn on us all, some sooner than others, that there was in fact a powerful group of people who had decided to have the war. In that context, it suddenly seemed to me futile to try and argue with the politicians that they had formulated the problem all wrong, that their understanding was clouded by a set of seductive metaphors. I even hesitated to share the essay with some of my colleagues, realising that some of them would already be bracing themselves to endure the conflict and might regard a semantic analysis as trivialising a matter of life and death for people close to them. Mesmerized by the illusory goal of DOING something concrete at that last minute to avert the tragedy of the outbreak of war, I could not use the wisdom of Lakoff's analysis in any practical way. Talk seemed to be too late and too weak a resource to bring to bear.

Now that the war has set in and become part of our way of life (however remote its influence on our daily lives), I find myself drawing on Lakoff's analysis more and more to remind myself of what are the real issues, as against the monstrous propaganda with which we are bombarded every hour over the news media. Maybe the contributors who urged us to "externalise" the message and get down on the streets to protest can explain to me what I missed. Doubtless part of my paralysis arose from my marginal position as a visitor in the US, with no inside knowledge of, nor personal commitment to, any of the nationalities of the middle east. But as I talk it through with my children and their American friends, I find myself more and more convinced that I would have felt a similar power-lessness during those last few days even if I were an American, an Iraqi, an Israeli, a Kuwaiti, a Saudi, or a Brit (which I once was).

Jake Olson's reading of the messages from Lars and Hans is solidly supportive; he also claims that 95 percent of the readers on xlchc are "in general agreement with Lakoff and Nilsson," while he expresses open disagreement with Amy's assertion that the United States did not start the war. However, it is not clear that either Lars or Hans would agree with Olson's position on the war. Katherine Grayson, on the other hand, supports Amy's criticism of Lars's post, yet disagrees with both Sam and Amy about the role of the United States in starting the war. She offers some evidence, based on her reading of articles in the *New Yorker* and the *New York Times,* in support of her argument that the United States did start the war.

Meanwhile, Morse challenges Olson's claim that 95 percent of xlchc is in agreement with Lakoff and Nilsson. Claiming to speak only for himself as a reader, he takes a more combative tone: "personally I found the comments by Nilsson—and later Jake and Kathy Grayson—repulsive in the extreme." He raises the level of conflict by referring to the posts of Nilsson, Olson, and Grayson as "mindless propaganddistic crap." And he reports that his reading of their texts is unsatisfying:

I began to look through the texts here to engage in argument, but one cannot make any real sense out of Jake's 'argument' via implication that Israeli civilians deserve to be attacked because they have a democratic government—and they're ruthless killers—or Kathy's 'arguments' than its somehow ALL our fault—or the silly statement that 'sanctions would of worked' because some 'model' said they would ('silly' not because she's wrong but because her apparent certitude is ridiculous). Discourse oriented toward trying to understand what is going on in this mess does not connect with propaganda of this or Bush's kind—or perhaps I just lack the intellect or heart to do it.

This message, with its bitter footnote about Kathy's use of the phrase "old, white men," ratchets the conflict to a globally different level of discourse. The messages that follow show the attempt of readers both to exploit this passionate energy and to control it. Writers begin to try to correct what they see as others' misreading of their texts. Olson first laments the "emotionalism" of Morse and then tries to set the record straight:

> Here are my words and Morse's characterization of them. . . . Please consider: At no point did I say that Israeli citizens deserve to be attacked. . . . Nor did I describe Israeli civilians as ruthless killers.

He is the first person to suggest that the conflict in xlchc was a direct consequence of reading and might have been prevented altogether if readers had less information: "Although it is all interesting, I guess I wish Gene had spared us the letters from Israel." Thus Gene's forwarding the letters from Israel is viewed as a form of assault, and reading is one of the key links between embodiment and emergence, as when Olson writes, "I spent an almost entirely sleepless night as a result of Ethan's message."

The conflict over the Gulf War (and other issues) emerges as a global phenomenon for xlchc, even though only a handful of subscribers participate actively by taking a position relative to the issues raised by writers/readers. Readers and writers responding to individual messages on the basis of their quite localized experiences, without a governing set of rules or formally specified procedures, nevertheless generate a conflict that dominates discourse in the group and qualitatively changes the properties of the entire system. More than one xlchc member has expressed to me privately the opinion that this conflict fundamentally altered the way the group evolved. In fact, the same might be said for any number of topics that have engaged the group; since the conversation is itself an emergent phenomenon, the forum continued to evolve on the basis and history of its interactions.

I think the striking point about the Gulf War episode, however, is the way the system struggled against disintegration, even as it provided a forum for powerful disagreements that threatened its continued existence. While some onlookers wavered between scolding the combatants—

> What a sorry sight, sorry plight. Those interested in debating their views about the war are so intent on what they are doing that they seem completely oblivious of the damage they are doing to themselves, their colleagues individually, and this discussion group collectively.

—and comforting them: "I honor all those of you who have taken the risk of voicing an opinion no matter how private and different from the others"; others tried to displace the conflict into a subgroup (xwar or xpeace) or refocus it either along more conventional academic lines (as in Rausch's reflection on Lakoff's essay) or to match other agendas (as we shall see in messages forwarded from an "unknown gay").

These struggles reflect, in more limited way, the current theoretical debate over control of the "master narrative" by which cultures at every level of scale attempt to define themselves. Obviously, the real battle depends upon and is causally motivated by attempts to gain the support and commitment of the group's readers and to draw them from a passive or uncommitted state into an active one. There can be no other grounds for a conflict such as this to emerge in a public forum like xlchc: private email or other private communication would suffice for expressing individual disagreement with a writer (and in fact, there was obviously a great deal of such communication even in the midst of the public conflict). Ultimately, some readers expressed themselves through a rash of messages (fourteen) asking to subscribe to xwar (or xpeace), although once subscribed, they did not generate a substantive discussion of the issues related to the Gulf War or of any other topic.

The Gulf War on XLCHC: Part Four

The discussion on xlchc continued, taking some unpredictable shifts. On February 6, it was linked to the question of the influence of the political left in the academy. Ethan Morse wrote that he had received email privately from various people who had written, "I am in total agreement with you but I'm a [try: secretary, graduate student, assistant professor, dean] so to state this [publicly] would cause me trouble." Morse argued,

> It is not simply that political flag-waving is offered up in place of analyses of complex and difficult situations (e.g., racism, sexism, and affirmative action), but that those of us who fall to the left of center politically feel tremendous pressure to overlook the political motivations and one-sidedness of the analyses presented. The result is the retardation of intelligent discussion of important social issues by people with liberal leanings and a corresponding serious insult—or flanking attack—on the university as a social institution.

Jake Olson replied:

If this question is controversial, by all means let's not discuss it. But perhaps there has been research on the topic.

Ethan Morse seems to say that holding the views reportedly shared by 80% or so of the American public endangers a [secretary, graduate student, assistant professor, dean] due to the left's "attempts to impose thought and value control through manipulation of a generous-hearted intelligentsia."

My question, which is not rhetorical, is: Is there evidence that the left has this kind of influence in academia? When I was around in the 60s and 70s it seemed that faculty on the left were being driven out of a lot of places (including my relatively liberal undergrad institution), and I don't recall comparable actions against the right, although they may have occurred. Most of the people on the left seemed to be ACLU types whereas many on the right seemed rather more interested in imposing values. It would be interesting to discover that things shifted in the 80s.

An alternative explanation that seemed to hold back then was that people who consider themelves liberals are sometimes more uncomfortable being criticized from the left than from the right, because it undermines their self-image of being "on the left""(of mainstream). They feel an emotional pressure to respond to such criticism by accepting it. This may not be what is going on, but if even partially true, then the "pressure" Morse reports is at least in part self-generated (and not balanced in response to criticism across the spectrum) and one feeling the pressure should be careful about attributing blame.

But I don't really know what goes on in U.S. academia, except that not much of it would probably pass as very "left" by standards found in parts of Europe.

Jim Barrett argued for the role of critical theory in considering the Gulf War discourse, claiming that the Lakoff essay was an example of "Olympian" discourse—discourse that sees over the heads or through the language of others. We have already seen a brief selection from this message in the section on embodiment. What follows is the larger context for it:

Olympian like "academic". The all-seeing eye seeing all.

But olympian discourse comes from a position on earth—on the ground—and not a mountain. We generally want to defend its olympian status. Our own identity is at stake.

Perhaps that is why there was such a hoo-ha (with discussions of soiled identity and the like) about Ethan Morse's "shove it up your ass" commentary (a great example of backchanneling?). It wasn't just that he was being impolite—or accurate—or whatever—he just broke the discursive rule of olympian-ness.

Wars do that to you. You come down off of mountains, get scared or disgusted, or get holed up in a room while somebody is trying to kill you. Or notice "who" is constructing this horror for you. You deal with the problem of peeing. These are EARTHLY positions—with REAL SELVES—and identitites at stake. These conditions lead us to connect with deep committments and fundamental searches for models to generate metaphors from (a somewhat neglected point in Lakoff's piece—the metaphors come from a position and a modeling—they as much reflect that position as construct it in language). This is grounded activity folks.

- There is usually a knower in the known. Most often the knower is hidden beneath olympian and objective forms of talk. Sometimes he/she emerges. Good!

- We should, could, might—at some point, I hope, discuss the discursive issues involved—and examine our great sensivity to breaking of discourse rules. Content aside, I found the break disturbing but refreshing. Finally there was an "agent" inside of talk—not speaking from the mountain but speaking from a self as white, male or whatever it may be.

- Back to appropriation—If the critical perspective is let in the door we have a couple of choices. You can go for an olympian "eye" that sees—and this would mean some sort of un-conditioned possibility for mind (e.g. transcendent rational processes) or you can go for a discursive—"difference in perspective" approach. Or some other model. At some point the problem of "voice" in perspectives—or even in transcendent mind—will get addressed non-polemically.

And on February 8, another shift occurred when Penny Grolier forwarded a message from a writer who wanted to remain anonymous. The message first argued that psychologists should not be acting like experts on war and then went on to make a connection with gay activism:

Maybe you don't like it, and maybe it disgusts you, but no psychologist has done a systematic study of the decisions/actions leading to war and the eventual long term outcomes (and if somebody has, we are not discussing that). Many clinicians have done work on the effects of battle exposure, and I think some people have studied the effects on children's school performance and you have done things on people's political beliefs. I think this is the kind of thing psychologists are qualified to comment on, AS PSYCHOLOGISTS.

My opinions about what is appropriate political activist behavior from psychologists come from my own experience and ongoing participation in gay activism and how I reconcile it with my participation in my profession. I am committed to improving the lives of gays because this is an issue I care about, but I don't feel qualified to comment as a pychological expert on various gay issues. I don't think there is such an expert, and there may never be.

The forwarded message continues to discuss the same writer's background as a researcher who is gay but who does not feel that research on gays is useful if it is politically motivated. The writer continues,

So, as you might imagine, the one thing that I find the most jarring is a psychologist who had done no research pontificating about gays, as a psychologist. I am familiar with all the research, and I know nobody knows anything for sure, that there are no facts relevant to psychology. (The only compelling gay related findings that I know about were discovered serendipitously by some neuropsychologists. Lesbians's brains are more lateralized than straight women's and they are more likely to be left handed.)

I feel the same way about some of the stuff that is coming about the war. We are unqualified to comment as researchers, but we are certainly qualified to object as thinking human beings. However, xlchc is not the place to do it as it is now defined. Anyway, the point of all this might be that I take activism seriously but I see it as separate from research, and from being a psychologist/researcher.

One night there was a meeting for psychologists who wanted to get involved in stopping the war. I couldn't go because I had to attend something on gay bashing. Somebody gave me shit about my priorties, and I remember thinking that the day straight psychologists get involved in stopping the murder and psychological terrorism of lesbians and gays, I will accept guilt about not getting behind other causes. The war most real to me is ongoing and right here in the US and the physical and psychological casualties are members of my extended family.

Another long message, this one from Steven Schnell, objected to the "unnamed gay's" suggestion that psychologists refrain from discussing war, asking,

Isn't it ironic to ask for such behavior on lchc (comparative human cognition) of all academic territories? Isn't it the typical researcher's behavior to hide behind scientific data which have been purified from all emotional stuff that gets in the way, that would make it more difficult to look at things with a more real or realistic perspective?
The ethnopsychoanalysts M. Nadig and M. Erdheim have written a nice paper showing how scientific experience is usually destroyed through the academic milieu. They argue that when doing empirical research, emo-

tional parts are suppressed into subconsciousness, from where they destroy the liveliness of research in an uncontrolled and destructive way. What would we do as psychologists cutting out all the emotions concerning things happening right now which are far more relevant for human communication than empirical or other data on our research projects. Can we work towards a global community disregarding everything that seems to destroy this (utopian?) thought? This takes me to the most important point of what I want to feed into the discussion (incidentally for the first time on this network, although I have been a silent participant on xlchc for some time, which again seems to support the force of emotional involvement in motivating people doing things including research!): Aren't there issues which affect every (not only social) scientist? If science is to help people gaining better conditions for their existence in this world, everybody has to contribute to this aim, making use of all his or her capacities. Or do you want to split this up into academic and personal achievements? Economic or political etc.?

Considering all this, does the unknown discussant really mean to leave expertise on war to the political scientists or philosophers if it is economists, politicians etc. who take the decisions on starting, continuing or finishing a war? Does he really want to wait for somebody doing "a systematic study of the decisions/actions leading to war and the eventual long term outcomes" before he or or she can discuss the topic of a present war on an academic network? I strongly believe that human relations on such a large scale as warfare, its consequences etc. across cultures we are hardly familiar with (and yet dare to interfere with them) cannot be systematically studied. How would you like to study into the possible behavior of somebody like Saddam Hussein to find out about his real intentions? Not even a psychoanalyst would do, I guess.

There is another point I have to make as somebody involved in education, training teachers on different levels. Do I have to do all the research necessary before I can bring in my own feelings, thoughts and worries about war and its consequences? Don't I support politicians who care less about human beings than economical interests if I shut up in an academic environment? And here I cannot differenciate between being an individual as anybody

2

else and being an educational researcher dealing with pedagogical issues academically. This affects me right now as Austria has been asked by the US to allow them to take about 100 tanks (supposedly used for repair work in the desert) across Austria, which, through its neutral status, is not a member of NATO, and it would probably be too inconvenient for the US Forces to take those tanks across France or elsewhere. Our teachers have to tell the kids about Austria's status of neutrality in class and at the same time our government does not object those tanks to be taken through our country. I think we have to take a (political) stand here even as scientists if we want to support teachers at the "chalk front" educating young people for a global citizenship. The more so as Quaile has already mentioned that the US would also think about using atomic

weaponry if everything else does not help in "ending" the war. Do we
really want to argue "systematically", "objectively" as scientists any
more if we are confronted with a hostile environment as that. I'd better
close here otherwise I get carried away. I want to bring in the issue of
global responsibility which should not be sent into a subsection of a
network. If we try to set up a global scientific community on xlchc, we
should also make use of it as a forum on how to "act" human communication, not just talk or write about it from an ivory tower - sorry, computer
I meant.

Peaceful wishes from Innsbruck in Austria, where American tanks may
shortly pass through on the way to Italy and on to the Gulf. I have just
heard in the news, however, that, because of a bomb threat the train
system has come to a halt. Thousands of school kids cannot get on their
skiing holidays, for whom about 80 extra trains had been arranged to get
to the ski resorts. I hope they will learn their real lesson from that,
although I doubt it ...

On February 13, Pat Benson announced that the subgroup xwar
was officially established. There followed a flurry of requests to be
added to the group. However, aside from one very long posting, which
forwarded the full text of a speech by Jordan's King Hussein and an
article by Noam Chomsky, there was very little substantive activity on
xwar. Most of the messages sent to the list were requests to be added
to the group. The exception was a disclaimer by Jake Olson, who
wrote, on February 14:

I never actually signed up to join xwar. I probably got on the list by
forwarding a msg from Martha Bunker expressing her interest in getting
on.

I'm not sure what the purpose(s) of this list might be. The comment that
xlchc was probably 95% in general agreement on the war drew a strong
response, and perhaps now I would lower the estimate to 80%, but it
seems possible that over 95% of the people on xwar are in general
agreement. Is the purpose to share factual information and analysis? To
discuss avenues for expressing opinions and bring about change? To
intellectualize anxiety? To engage in cultural or linguistic analysis of
aspects of the events and discussions? To feel more numerous than polls
might suggest?

He then continued the argument he had been engaged in on xlchc.

I will pass along a news item reported in Agence France-Presse because it
addresses some of the "balance" issues that precipitated this and might
not have been covered in the U.S. It describes comments by Israeli
General Nachman Shai praising the "patience and sangfroid" of Iraqis on
Voice of Israel radio. He said "They are showing great endurance given

the fact that they are sustaining very severe strikes and that tens of thousands of bombs are being dropped on them. Unlike the inhabitants of Tel Aviv, the people of Baghdad are without water, electricity and food."

This directly echoes things that some of us said to balance the letters from Israel. I felt sorry for the people in Israel, driven to what seemed to be an irrational frenzy by their helpless situation. But the balance was missing. Before the hostilities there were some transcribed interviews with Iraqis and never did I see one reporting anything other than a hope for peace. Many Israelis were described as wanting the U.S. to attack. The dilemma is similar to one that is currently sugar-coated regarding the Vietnam period. Through about 1968, it seemed reasonable to be sympathetic to returning vets. But after that, soldiers who went over had had ample exposure to arguments for not going and if they came back expecting sympathy it was hard to muster. One can be more angry with the leaders but at some point the fiction of individual accountability has to be adopted or things lose their point.

Back to the General. It seems reasonable to assume he made the statement to build Israel's increasingly positive image amongst the Arabs in the "alliance" and thus widen the Arab schism but the statement stands nonetheless.

By February 22, the Gulf War was no longer dominating discourse on xlchc, although there were several responses to Jim Barrett's message on appropriation and war. Iraq, on February 28, agreed to Bush's terms for a cease-fire, but there continued to be an occasional post mentioning the Gulf War, more and more infrequently, until August 1991. On April 1, Armand Endicott posted this message to xwar:

This is the translation of an editorial written by a Brazilian writer about the recently past war. The translation is mine.

RIDICULOUS (Luis Fernando Verissimo)

Most of the rockets missed the target. Atomic weapons, there weren't any. Chemical weapons, didn't show up. The soldiers that would put the infidels to run, ran to surrender themselves. How ridiculous the Third World is, ain't it? Even its most terrible tyrants, in the end, are bluffs. Small dictators. Generals of operetta. One gets drunk and decides to conquer a piece of England. Of England of all places, there is no respect! Another, just because his country industrialized a bit, thought it was something and that it could play the superpower like the great. Now, there he is mooning the world, making a fool of himself. Clowning. How the Third World is a circus, ain't it?

Not the First World, no sir! Great people. What class! What fangs! What intelligent weapons! They only kill after assuring themselves that they have the moral authority to do it. They give it themselves, but who else

could? Some inferior with the GNP down in the dumps? THey are elegant!
You'll never see them being condescending with the childish ways of the
Third World. On the contrary, they lend money to it and teach it to pay
high interest which is the adult way. They tolerate its monkeying, they
show how it must behave to become similar to them and socially accepted, as long as no one wants to be equal. Ambition, no! But they only
intervene when a monkey gets out of the cage or a clown offends the
ladies.   ˎ

How the Third World is primitive and gauche, ain't it? Not the slightest
tact, the slightest skill. It lacks that elegant humor, that sensitivity, those
calories, not to mention those inertial systems of balistic orientation. To
put it bluntly, it lacks pedigree!

The First World, what grandeur! They just destroyed, already they are
talking about reconstructing. As a matter of fact with the same compa-
nies in both cases. Civilization, is like that.

I think we should surrender, all of us...

And on April 2, one final note from Martha Bunker sent to xwar
gave the academic coup de grâce to the topic:

In connection with a talk I am giving on the aftermath and racism and
sexism, if anybody has any information, papers, etc. that might bear on
this topic, I would appreciate having a line on it. Thanks. Glad the network
still exists.

At this point, the Gulf War became the topic that was rather than
the topic that is. Still, even as recently as 1994, there were several
messages referring to the conflict and the "flame war" it provoked on
xlchc.

Enaction and Readers

I am concerned in general with how ecologies of composition are
enactive, and in particular, I am interested in how readers engaged in
enacting the Gulf War episode on xlchc. How do readers participate
in activities that "bring forth" the world of composing and establish
their existence in it? What kinds of activities does such enaction en-
tail? Obviously, the conflict on xlchc could not have been distributed,
embodied, or emergent except through the activities of its participants,
and even, to some extent, its nonparticipants. The discourse on xlchc
was enacted not only through the familiar-seeming practices of reading and writing, academic (and not so academic) argumentation, political debate, and scholarly communication, but also through a very

different ensemble of practices—from switching on a computer to launching a program that could connect to an email server, retrieving and replying to messages, scrolling through text, deleting or saving email to a disk, and so on.

The practices associated with using a computer vary widely from person to person and developmentally, so that at one stage a person can barely turn the computer on without assistance, while later, with more experience, the same person may end up writing elaborate scripts to control a high-speed modem, configuring a network of computers, programming a new application, or serving as an ad hoc consultant to less experienced users. But at every stage and through every practice, the person will depend upon a spatially and temporally distributed system of material, psychological, and social structures in the environment, from computer manuals and software technical-support teams to the casual acquaintance who uses the same type of computer. Further, computer-mediated communication is itself situated in a nexus of practices associated with specific institutions and disciplines, with academic research and scholarly study, and with interpersonal relationships. And it is obvious from the conversation about the Gulf War that these practices are embedded within a larger cultural and historical environment.

At the most basic material level, readers and writers in this forum without exception interacted with a computer both to read and to compose texts. Further, they distributed and received these texts using a modem and connecting phone lines or direct-access cables. Some kind of software was also necessary, as well as a network connection, generally via the Internet or Bitnet. These "metanetworks" are a loose, anarchic aggregation of smaller networks operating locally and regionally.

Problems with the material level of equipment and connections contributed to some confusion during this episode, as when Matt Connors remarked,

> I think in both cases you are talking about the difficulty is on the sending end. There was a mixup over an important message of Martha's on appropriation that somehow got lost between Martha and me. . . . The discoordinations in xlchc are of many kinds, some technical.

And later, Olson wrote, "Apologies if this is repeated for you—I sent it hours ago and never received it myself. I had not then read Parsons' message." Martha Bunker writes, "pLEASE FORGIVE THE

CAPS...MY MACHINE DEVELOPED THIS DISEASE SUDDENLY."
The apology refers to a common criticism of messages that appear in
all capital letters: in the early days of computer-mediated communication, the text display was always all caps, much like a telegram, because that was the only format supported by the technology. Once it
became possible to send text in mixed case (both capital and lower-
case characters), sending messages in all caps was frowned on. Readers and writers were socialized into this new convention through observing or experiencing responses to such texts in computer forums
and newsgroups: "Why are you shouting?" was a typical reply to a
message in all caps.

More important, the interactions that evolved into the Gulf War
conflict on xlchc depended on the underlying technologies that supported it. In another, materially different discourse arena, whether a
radio call-in show or a series of exchanges in an academic journal, the
episode would have emerged in a different form, probably with entirely different participants as both "readers" and "writers." The conversation itself continued to raise material and technological issues as
part of its content as well: from Livingston's first request for "material
with Middle Eastern content" and Bunker's response that "THE USA
IS SPENDING SOME 30 MILLION DOLLARS A DAY ON KEEP-
ING THOSE TROOPS THERE" to Matt Connors's xwar post on
February 14 (note the date of the article mentioned):

> I was reading an article I published in Science in 1973 this morning when
> the story following it caught my eye. It was entitled "Military R&D: Hard
> Lessons of an Electronic war." It discusses the fact that Missles and wire
> guided anti-tank missles had given the Israeli forces a hard time (75
> planes lost in a hurry and many tanks), provoking "a number of military
> analysts to begin to extract some technological lessons that will influence
> the course of tactical weapons R&D. Look how far humanity has pro-
> gressed in the intervening years! :-(

And, of course, much of the debate in this episode focused on the
relative physical and material devastation experienced by both Israelis
and Iraqis, although, with the exception of the messages forwarded
by Saltzman, the participants in the discussion were well removed from
actual physical danger from the Gulf War conflict itself. Nor did the
participants refer to the relatively privileged material circumstances
that provided them access to computers, networks, and the time to
engage in discussions such as these.

There is a vast literature on psychological effects of human-
computer interaction, but such a discussion is not my focus here. In-

stead, I am concerned with the psychological dimensions of the practices that enacted this episode. Among some of the challenges for readers were navigation among and through the messages, maintaining coherence and following the reasoning as the topic unfolded, linking the discussion within the group to experiences and events outside the group, and recalling what had been said and who had said it. Typically, readers and writers use both internal and external structures to manage these cognitive challenges.

As noted earlier, navigation among email messages is aided by information in the message headers, which typically include information about the sender, the recipient, and the date and offer a brief description of its subject. Most email programs allow users to display a collapsed list that shows only the header information, so that the reader can quickly select messages that need prompt attention or delete messages the user does not want to read. There are more sophisticated programs that allow filtering and sorting of email, so that readers can manage it more easily. Once the message has been read, the reader has several alternatives: write a reply to the message, delete it, save it on a disk, or print it out. The whole message or part of it can also be forwarded to another reader.

These structures serve readers as a kind of external navigation and memory resource. Further, a forum itself can serve much the same function, as when Connors writes on xlchc, "Perhaps Martha and Gerald would re-post for those of us who missed their contributions." An additional "external memory" is the xlchc archive of messages and the memory storage of forum members. When I discovered that the xlchc archive was missing several key messages from this episode, I posted an inquiry in the forum and soon recovered them from a participant who had saved the messages to a disk. In contrast, most of the people who were involved in this episode had only a partial or hazy memory of exactly what happened: one participant said he vaguely recalled "an unpleasant young man from Denmark who thought the war was all Israel's fault"; another confided, "I think I sent a message that was rather inflammatory"; and still another expressed the general opinion that some people who participated in this episode "never raised their voices on xlchc again," but few could remember specific details of either the participants or the messages.

Maintaining coherence in lines of reasoning and "who said what" is much more difficult, as we see in Olson's attempt at connecting a thread.

> Some of you may be confused by Gene's latest message, notably what it
> is in response to. The history of the exchange is this: I sent my msg to
> xlchc. Gene replied in a message that was addressed only to me. I replied
> to Gene in a message that was addressed only to him. He has now
> chosen to escalate this private exchange into a public one.

Among the threats to coherence for readers was the confusion between email sent privately and that sent to xlchc and, later, the confusion between mail sent to xwar and xlchc. Part of the confusion may have been the result of intentional shifts in audience, as Olson believed Gene had intended, but others were probably the result of the idiosyncratic way the "reply" function worked for xlchc and its subgroups. In most computer forums, when a reader wishes to reply to a message posted in the forum, it is only necessary to choose the command *reply* (often a single keystroke, *r*), and the reply is directed to the forum. However, for xlchc and its subgroups, the command *reply* generated a reply sent only to the individual who sent the original message. To reply to xlchc, it was necessary to generate a "new" message addressed to xlchc specifically. For this reason, there were more accidental "private" posts in replying to xlchc than accidental "public" posts that were intended to be private messages; the reverse is true in most other forums. More important, this episode gives us some interesting insights into the ways readers use external structures to accomplish what we have conventionally thought of as "internal" psychological processes.

It should be obvious that the psychological dimension cannot be separated from either the physical dimension or the social dimension of the enaction of this episode. The intersection of many social structures and practices—including cultures, political structures, religions, popular media, academic disciplines and institutions, constructions of gender and sexual practice, and conventions of written discourse—are evident in the messages containing the unfolding conflict over the Gulf War. While most of these social structures pre-exist the conversations in this forum, the social structure of the forum itself was constantly under construction.

Because we do not have well-established models for this form of discourse, as we have in other arenas (such as academic journal articles, face-to-face conversations with store clerks, letters to the editors of newspapers, and so on), participants are always enacting the social structure of a group based on their differing expectations and interpretations. In the Gulf conflict, their concepts about social interactions in the forum were often borrowed from other cultural models.

In Sessions's opening message, he suggested that the forum might reflect on ethical and political issues raised by a request from a colleague. Connors's response, directed toward the request rather than Sessions's proposal, reframed the issue by providing bibliographic references, shifting the structure to one of scholarly inquiry. On the other hand, Bunker's response picked up Sessions's suggestion with an impassioned polemic, shifting the focus to personal opinion. The forwarded message from George Lakoff provided a lengthy academic argument in the scholarly essay tradition, yet it was also a call for political activism based on his analysis of semantic features of the Gulf War conflict. Responses to this message did not adopt the form of the academic essay, however. The letters from Israel moved the discussion in a different direction with their detailed accounts of lived experience under the threat of war. This move was then echoed by Rausch, who recalled his experiences as a child in Munich during World War II; by Olson, who mentioned his visits to Managua while it was bombed by Anastasio Somoza's air force; and by Grayson, who described her experiences as an antiwar protester.

Other messages, however, resisted this move toward accounts of immediate, personal experience. Olson wrote,

> It is unfortunate to see such emotionalism as that expressed by Ethan Morse, which certainly can't coexist with intellectual discussion of the issues. This kind of emotion-laden discussion is just what email is terrible for.

Connors's suggestion that the topic be moved to a subgroup—

> Without anyone intending it so, the great divergence of opinion and the necessarily high affect associated with this topic (to name only two factors) have brought people to forms of verbal assault that it is difficult to interpret as constructive

—and Green's later suggestion to shut down the group for a week or two—"to let people settle their battles on their own, or perhaps to let the vitriol die down"—were stronger moves to take control of the conflict. However, both of these moves were resisted as various readers/writers struggled to determine exactly what the bounds of such discussion ought to be.

An Ecology of Readers

During the period prior to the Gulf War discussion on xlchc, there was no shortage of significant historical events, including Armenia's declaration of independence from the Soviet Union; the intervention of five West African nations in Liberia's civil war; the reunification of East and West Germany; the ending of the segregation of libraries, trains, buses, toilets, swimming pools, and other facilities in South Africa; and Gorbachev's proposal for a radical restructuring of the Soviet government. None of these events appeared as a topic or even a mention in messages posted to xlchc; thus they are inconsequential, indeed nonexistent, perturbations for this ecological system, even though they may have had major consequences for individuals situated in the system. On the other hand, the question of how Lev Vygotsky or Jean Piaget might define *internalization* or *appropriation* set off a blizzard of messages and generated a great deal of controversy in the group. And to pick up Maturana and Varela's argument in *Autopoiesis,* although the Gulf War topic triggered a great deal of discourse activity on xlchc, we can hardly say that the episode constructed a "representation" or "mapping" of the war itself.

In terms of ecological systems, we might say that a conflict occurs when a perturbation triggers changes that set one component of the system against another; the conflict is a history of those structural changes. It may seem that a conflict represents a failure of coordination between components of the system, but that is not necessarily the case. In natural ecologies we often see the predator-prey relationship as a conflict, yet it may be highly coordinated, as well, resulting in fairly stable patterns within the ecological system as a whole. In interpersonal relationships, we have all witnessed the phenomenon of enduring stable relationships (such as between a husband and wife or an employee and supervisor) that are grounded in perpetual conflict. In social systems, conflicts—such as those we see in Northern Ireland, in Bosnia, and in the Middle East—seem intractable precisely because the components of the system, from street fighters and grieving mothers to political and economic systems, have achieved a high degree of coordination. To those who are embedded within such systems, peacemaking efforts may actually represent a threat of destabilizing the well-defined coordination among the components, rather than a welcome advance in restoring "order." The dynamical responses of readers/writers to the unfolding conflict on xlchc represent efforts both to reshape the ecosystem of the forum and to adapt to its changes. The texts of the messages as we now read them are what Hutchins in *Cognition* calls "residua," traces of the system's response to this episode's perturbations. But the real structural changes to the ecosystem itself are found in altered social structures that are instantiated by historical activity. As Maturana and Varela point out, the consequences of a perturbation, such as the Gulf War perturbation to xlchc, are determined from among a space of possibilities constructed within the system itself; they are not a direct result of the perturbation's invasion of the system.

It should be apparent, however, that any attempt to represent the conflict via conventional rhetorical models of argumentation does violence to the phenomena, which cannot be reduced to well-defined oppositions between individuals, oppositions that proceed in a chain of reasoning towards any logical conclusion.

The final chapter suggests some implications of an ecological approach for composition research, instruction, and assessment. It will present a current model of an ecological approach to composing and offer some conclusions about the need for conceptual and institutional changes emerging from this research.

5

Conclusion: Implications and Proposals for an Ecology of Composition

We would rather be ruined than changed,
We would rather die in our dread
Than climb the cross of the moment
And let our illusions die.
                              —W. H. Auden

In presenting case studies of three very different writing situations, I have attempted to show how a theory of composing situations as ecological systems might be productively applied in composition studies. Such a perspective obviously refutes the reductionism of theoretical approaches that depend on individualist assumptions about readers, writers, and texts. But it also refutes the opposite form of reductionism, which implies that writing situations are so culturally, historically, and socially contingent that each is unique and incomparable. A more sophisticated, "postmodern" version of this approach might argue that researchers construct the realities they presume to observe and interpret and that their understandings are therefore fragmentary, ephemeral, compromised by bias, and in some fundamental sense, fictional. I disagree with all three of these positions. By selecting four attributes of complex systems—distribution, emergence, embodiment, and enaction—and examining their characteristics in particular composing situations, I believe I have demonstrated the irreducibly interdependent, dynamic, and adaptive properties of ecological systems of readers, writers, and texts, and I have also demonstrated that there are indeed some regularities across a range of quite different writing situations. In the process, I hope I have shown not only how new research in cognitive science and complex systems can inform composition studies but, in turn, how composing situations can be fruitful sites for research in cognitive science.

Composition is a form of cognitive activity that generates a visible residue of that activity; that residue is also a cognitive artifact that affects cognitive processes and structures. I want to make it clear that the term *cognitive* in this context does not refer exclusively to mental processes "inside" an individual. Rather, as Hutchins puts it, "the very same processes that constitute the conduct of the activity and that produce changes in the individual practitioners . . . also produce changes in the social, material, and conceptual aspects of the setting" (*Cognition* 374). Composition does not consist in transferring what is inside the head onto paper or a computer screen. It is a manifestation of the coordination between internal and external structures, which are constituted by and expressed through cultural and cognitive dimensions of every human activity.

This book introduces theories of complex systems currently being studied in diverse disciplines. As we have seen, *complex systems* are described by theorists as adaptive, self-organizing, and dynamic; they are systems that are neither utterly chaotic nor entirely ordered, but exist on the boundary between these two states. *Ecological systems* are metasystems composed of interrelated complex systems. I have proposed that we consider that writers, readers, and texts, together with their environments, constitute one kind of ecological system. In the process, I argue, we might gain a new understanding of composing situations. I have described four attributes of complex systems that provide a theoretical framework for this study. *Distribution* refers to the concept that processes in complex systems are distributed (in both senses; that is, "divided" and "shared") among agents and structures in the environment. *Emergence* refers to the self-organization that arises globally in networks of simple components connected to each other and acting locally—readers, writers, and texts, for instance. *Embodiment* refers to the grounding of complex systems in physical experience and interactions. *Enaction* refers to the situated practices and activities that structure the composing situation as it unfolds over time, from microscale (e.g., drawing letters on a page, tapping a keyboard) to global (e.g., the development of the Internet).

> *Principle:* Readers, writers, and texts are interdependently specified and embedded in particular historical, cultural, and physical ecologies. These ecological systems have dynamic, self-organizing properties that cannot be adequately understood through analysis of individual components or processes.

This exploratory study originated with a question: What might we learn by applying theories of complex systems and distributed cognition to composing situations? To test the possibilities for the general application of these theories, I selected three very different writing situations. Each one presents special challenges to the theories. The case study of Reznikoff's poetic passage, for example, addresses a common objection to theories of distributed cognition: How can such theories account for manifestations of individual genius? The case study of a group of students collaborating on a single essay addresses the challenge of understanding learning as a process of coordination and adaptation in complex systems. The case study of a computer forum of social scientists during the Gulf War addresses the challenge of understanding conflict in ecological systems as more sensitive to perturbation, more dynamic, and much more complex than our taken-for-granted individualist models of binary oppositions or well-defined sequences of logical argumentation would suggest. Even this limited sample shows the promise of an ecological approach to understanding composing. If we recognize theories of complex systems and distributed cognition as productive for studying three such diverse situations, it is likely that there is real potential for their application to other composing situations as well. There should be justification for further research that might expand our application of the theories, as well as our understanding of their limitations.

> *Principle:* Current interdisciplinary research on complex systems, distributed cognition, and situated cognition can provide us with important new perspectives, methods, and analytical tools for understanding composing situations.

Promising New Directions for Research in Composition Studies

This exploratory study suggests exciting possibilities for future research in composition studies, as well as new approaches to writing instruction and evaluation. The necessity, significance, and urgency of changes in our research agendas and our pedagogical practices are intensified by the rapid deployment of new technologies:

- technologies for composing, such as computer word-processing and page-layout programs, as well as integrated programs that enable mixed media constructions
- technologies for communication, such as computer networks and

software for email, discussion groups, remote database access, and real-time online communication

• technologies for reading or "experiencing" compositions, including the World Wide Web, hypertexts, and hypermedia, as well as "virtual environments," such as MOOs and MUDs designed for exploration, construction, and interaction.

Academics, writers, students, artists, musicians, and children, as well as corporations, politicians, and government agencies have embraced these technologies and developed an astonishing variety of uses for them. And in turn, new technologies have been created or adapted to meet the emerging needs and desires of users. Hutchins points out,

> Computers are the most plastic medium ever invented for the representation and propagation of information. In fact, they are so adaptable and can manifest such a wide range of behaviors, that little but the hardware itself may be easily identifiable as an enduring property of the device. ("Metaphors" 11)

New technologies have not only opened up new territory for composing and communicating, however; they have also called into question many of our assumptions about more conventional discourse arenas.

The three cases in this study provide support for a theory of composing situations as complex adaptive systems of readers, writers, and texts in dynamic interaction with each other and with their environments. They also suggest promising new directions for research in composition studies, but they go beyond merely suggesting possibilities for research to offer examples of how such research might proceed. There are signs of interest in our field: some research in the application of theories of complex systems is already underway; Paul Taylor, Martin Rosenberg, and Stuart Moulthrop, for example, are actively applying these concepts in their work; and Louise Wetherbee Phelps has even described the field of composition studies as a self-organizing complex system.[1]

This study is itself an example of emergent properties in the field of composition studies. It reflects dynamic changes in research among three major areas: cognitivist approaches, ethnographic approaches, and technology studies. Recent trends suggest that researchers in each of these once parochial specialties have expanded their "domain of scrutiny," bringing them closer together in their interests. For example, current work by Linda Flower and by Charles Bazerman on "socially negotiated" or "socially constructed" meaning in reading and writing suggests that cognitivists in our field are increasingly interested in exploring sociocultural influences in composing. In turn, the research of Walvoord and McCarthy, who studied students' writing and thinking in college courses in four subjects, shows how ethnographers might inform our understanding of cognitive development, while Shirley Brice Heath's work on differences in schooling in two southern communities begins to map the environmental interactions that shape the literacy practices of young writers and readers (*Ways*). Susan Peck MacDonald examines the linguistic practices of disciplinary cultures through analysis of recurring structures in professional academic texts. Finally, researchers such as Denise Murray, Stuart Moulthrop, Lester Faigley, Cynthia Selfe, and John Slatin, who focus on the influence of new technologies, have become increasingly interested in the role of culture and social interaction in the use and development of technology. This recent work in composition studies seems to reflect a kind of convergence of once isolated areas of specialization, and creates a space of possibilities for ecological approaches to composing situations.

Challenges for Literacy Research, Pedagogy, and Assessment

We should bear in mind that, appealing as it may seem, the concept of an ecology of composing presents serious challenges to our existing approaches to research, pedagogy, and writing assessment—challenges that may demand radical changes not only in our taken-for-granted assumptions but in our entrenched practices and institutions as well.

Challenges for research. Probably the greatest challenge for research raised by an ecological approach to composing is that the subjects of inquiry are not primarily objects or objectified subjects but relationships and dynamic processes. Consequently we are confronted with complexity of subject, method, and approach in our research. While we have, for some time now, worked to enlarge the unit of analysis in composition studies beyond the individual—through studies of collaborative writing and through ethnographic projects, for example—we have continued to focus on readers, writers, and texts as independent objects. It is extremely difficult to observe, interpret, and represent relationships and dynamic processes in composing situations. We are immediately overwhelmed by the richness of data and the pace of interactions in even small-scale settings. As noted in chapter 1, conventional research methods may not be effective, or they may need to be adapted; single-methodology approaches may be inadequate. We need to guard against the distortions caused by our own romantic notions, tacit assumptions, disciplinary socialization, methodological biases, and perceptual artifacts, while recognizing that these are necessarily the conditions from which we must begin our studies. The difficulties, however, will compel us to continue to scrutinize the dynamics of knowledge construction in our field, probably a healthy outcome.

I have presented three case studies here because I believe that case studies represent our most promising avenue for ecological research on composing. I have deliberately chosen diverse examples that show the utility of case studies across a range of research methods: archival research, ethnography, and discourse analysis. If we hope to understand composition as an ecological system, we need to look carefully at a wide range of writing situations. In my opinion, case studies are the best means to accomplish this goal. It should be clear that the value of these cases lies not in their generalizability to other populations or composing situations but in their ability to inform our theories.[2] The case study of Reznikoff's poem does not provide us much insight into how other poems are constructed; rather, it supports a theory of composing situations as ecologies. The study of students writing collaboratively tells us little about how other students might collaborate; instead, it gives insight into some of the problems of adaptation for writers in new composing environments. And the Gulf War conversation on xlchc is not a typical example of conversation in computer forums; rather, it illuminates some features of conflicts in complex systems of readers, writers, and texts. These case studies do not typify larger populations but contribute to the development of a theory. If, as I suspect, writing situations are far more diverse than we have been led to believe by the preponderance of studies in our field, then case studies are absolutely essential for this project.[3]

Another complexity involved in ecological research is the fundamentally interdisciplinary nature of the work. This study illustrates the generative effect of seeing composing situations through another discipline's spectacles, asking different questions, and observing different phenomena. Frankly, I find this interdisciplinary quality bracing: it prevents a dangerous insularity and hyperspecialization, which can result in an elite few talking only to and for each other. But there are also dangers in taking an interdisciplinary approach: the almost overwhelming quantity of unfamiliar information to be assimilated, the risk of dilettantism, and the chance of falling prey to the "harmony of illusions" of a different thought collective. It would be a pity, though, if these dangers kept us timidly paddling in the shallows close to familiar shores rather than setting forth on a bold mission of exploration and communication with other disciplinary cultures.

Challenges for pedagogy. Theories of composing as ecological systems also present certain challenges to our established pedagogical approaches. We may be ready, even eager, to give up the concept of the solitary writer/reader, for example, without recognizing how that loss complicates instruction and evaluation, particularly within institutional structures still wedded to individual sorting and grading. Furthermore we are not accustomed to considering the physical environment as an active participant in the learning situation, particularly in college-level instruction. We tend to think of classrooms as fixed containers, which serve as a backdrop for, or occasionally as a reflection of, individual intellectual activity (as in bulletin boards that spotlight student work). Therefore, we find ourselves teaching and learning in physical environments that hamper interaction and promote isolation: lecture halls with auditorium seating; writing classrooms with tiny desks bolted to the floor in rows; computers installed in single-student cubicles yet, oddly enough, networked together.

We have difficulty coming to terms with the embodiment of students and teachers. We have difficulty understanding learning as a nonlinear process of dynamic parallel relationships between students, teachers, and their environments. We continue to overvalue products and undervalue development. And we cling to a narrow view of writing and reading and learning, with rigid expectations about how these activities are accomplished. But the deep questions raised by an ecological view have long been harbored by thoughtful, observant teachers: If writing and reading are distributed processes, how can we give a paper or a student an individual grade? If they are embodied processes, how should teachers think about the differences between a hungry student and one who is well fed, an exhausted student and one who is rested, a battered student and one who is well loved, a disabled student and one who is "normal"—and the whole complex range of physical conditions that lie between or among these poles? If they are emergent processes, when should we give feedback on students' work, and in what ways would that feedback help the student develop as a reader and a writer? If they are enactive processes, what practices and activities should we establish and encourage in the course of instruction? To what should I attach a grade—to the paper, to the paper with all of its drafts, to its writers, or to the class itself in which it was produced? How do we know whether we are in fact supporting students' development as readers and writers? What environments increase opportunities for this development, and how can we help construct them? How can we develop our own capabilities as coparticipants in students' self-determination? These are only a few of the pedagogical questions raised by an ecological approach to composing. Resolving these questions depends on our recognition that teachers, as well as students, are embedded in ecological systems that both enable and constrain their activities and practices, rather than viewing teachers as standing outside of the ecological system and somehow "constructing" it.

Challenges for assessment. Finally, theories of composing as ecological systems present real challenges to our established assessment practices. In this chapter, I focus particular attention on these challenges because methods of classroom evaluation and large-scale assessment have an enormous impact on teaching and learning environments and activities. Some of the intentions motivating assessment practices are supportive. For example, we want to know whether students are developing as capable readers and writers. We hope to identify students who need extra support in their development, students who are not being well served by our educational institutions, and students who are thriving. We want to monitor the effects of our current methods of instruction and the relative strengths of individual programs, schools, and districts. We also want to prevent inequities in opportunities to learn and to accurately reflect progress and growth among diverse student populations. The most optimistic view of the assessment process is that it tries to ensure that we (teachers, administrators, and educational institutions) are doing the best job that we can for all of the students in our charge. These are the premises that serve as a mandate for some form of writing assessment. However, writing assessment has also had some tremendously damaging effects, particularly when scores are used as a weapon to batter already-beleaguered students, teachers, schools, and districts, or to rank students by reading and writing "ability" or "performance." Increasingly, these malignant effects are drawing fire from researchers, teachers, administrators, and parents. At this time, there are few people who continue to maintain that writing can be adequately assessed through standardized multiple-choice testing. In many states, large-scale writing assessment is now based on samples of student writing. Typically, students are asked to respond to a short piece of reading or a prompt; for example, the following is one writing prompt for such an assessment:[4]

Taking a Position on Banning Toy Guns

Writing Situation

Recently, a police officer shot a youngster who was holding a realistic-looking toy gun. Now state lawmakers have proposed a law banning the sales of realistic-looking toy guns. Toy shop owners have argued against the law; police officials and PTA groups support it. The students at your school seem divided on the issue.

You decide to write a letter to your local newspaper presenting your position on this controversial issue. Do you think sales of realistic-looking toy guns should be banned? Think about this issue and decide which position you will support.

Directions for Writing

Write a letter to your local newspaper taking a position on the issue of whether sales of realistic-looking toy guns should be banned. Begin your letter "Dear Editor:" Develop a clear position and support your position with reasons and evidence. Your readers may have a different view, so your position will need to be supported by more than a strong feeling. Try to convince your readers that you have thought carefully about your position, and that it is a reasonable one.

Student writing for assessments like these is collected and sent to a central location where readers (usually teachers) are paid to read and score the writing, generally using holistic scoring or feature-based rubrics. The scores are then subjected to statistical analysis and interpretation and ultimately can have profound political, social, and economic consequences for schools, districts, and states.

Obviously, under these circumstances writing assessment becomes an arena for high-stakes, bitterly contested, and continuously fought battles. Issues of fairness and equity, reliability, resource allocation, educational opportunities, accommodation for cultural and linguistic diversity, and support for special needs are negotiated and renegotiated to no real resolution. And we still know very little about how to tell not only how well students are writing, but how students are writing at all.

Recently, one-shot individual writing assessments have come under fire for inadequately representing students' writing development. Critics have argued that we need to look at a larger range of student reading and writing, gathered over time and based on contextualized classroom and out-of-class activities. Such work might include, for example, collaborative work, informal writing, and extended projects with multiple revisions, rather than the special-purpose, narrowly focused activities contrived solely for large-scale assessments (Barr and Cheong; Barrs et al.; Falk and Darling-Hammond; González; Thomas). It would seem that we are growing closer to an ecological view of student writing in assessment practices. However, in spite of recent efforts by testing services and agencies to construct reading and writing situations that are closer to typical classroom activities (incorporating some collaborative work, annotations of reading, and revisions of writing, for example, and even allowing writing activities to be spread over several days), large-scale writing assessment is still a long way from capturing the salient features of reading and writing ecologies "in the wild."

Formidable challenges remain, and there are real questions about how they can be resolved. Some challenges are inherent in the concept of writing assessment, others are methodological, and still others are strategic. Here is a sampling of some unresolved questions for assessment:

- What are we observing, and what regularities in what we observe represent developmental stages in writing?
- How can we administer the assessment, monitor the collection of data, and abstract what we need to know from it?
- How can we ensure reasonable reliability of our measures and fairness in how they are applied?
- How can we prevent writing assessments from being used unfairly for punitive or gatekeeping purposes?
- How can we construct writing assessments that serve to support and enrich teaching and learning rather than merely score it ex post facto?
- How can assessment be integrated into the learning environment and emerge naturally from it rather than be superimposed upon that environment from the outside?

An ecological perspective is necessary to even begin to address questions such as these. It should be clear that our research, pedagogical, and assessment goals are interdependent, yet too often we have treated these aspects of composition in isolation.

Bringing Theory into Practice: The Learning Record

Teachers, researchers, and scholars are likely to agree that an ecological approach to composition is promising, but they may well wonder how such an approach could be productively applied in actual teaching practices, research projects, and evaluation methods. Do the challenges for research, pedagogy, and assessment presented by an ecological view of composing create insurmountable obstacles to its implementation in any practical sense? There is promise in a new approach that integrates literacy research, pedagogy, and assessment. I describe this approach in some detail to clarify its unique contribution to the application of the theories I've presented above.

The Learning Record system, an integrated approach to literacy research, pedagogy, and assessment, provides one model for an ecological account of the development of students as readers and writers. This approach was originally developed in England by Myra Barrs and her colleagues, strongly influenced by the work of James Britton and Lev Vygotsky, and it has since been adapted for use in the United States. In England, it is called the Primary Language Record; the version adapted in California under the direction of Mary Barr is now called the Learning Record (LR), reflecting its expansion beyond the primary level and also its projected extension to other disciplines, such as math and science (See the web site, www.learningrecord.org/lrorg for more information.) More recently, the Online Learning Record has been developed for use in computer-enhanced postsecondary courses.[5] (See www.cwrl.utexas.edu/~syverson/olr for more information). The Learning Record is currently in use in California and New York, where it is being implemented as an alternative to conventional forms of evaluation and large-scale assessment for students K–12, and in Texas, where it is used in college-level composition and literature classes. It has been designated the official alternative to standardized testing for schools administered by the Bureau of Indian Affairs. The Record has also been used as the basis for ethnographic research (Falk and Darling-Hammond; Miserlis; Thomas). I focus on the Learning Record because it is most widely used and also because it is applicable to composition studies from kindergarten to college level. I first ex-

plain how the Learning Record functions as a system that can provide
an ecological account of learning in complex systems, and then I discuss some of the theoretical issues and assumptions that underlie the
Learning Record model.

The Learning Record's method of investigation and inquiry follows sound practices that have grounded research across many disciplines, from biology to economics to anthropology:

- observations of phenomena we wish to understand, over time and
  under diverse conditions
- collection of diverse kinds of data from multiple sources
- informed interpretations based on these observations and data
  samples
- theory and practice mutually informing and regulating each other
- public reporting for confirmation or challenge by peers investigating similar phenomena

The Learning Record model integrates evaluation and assessment
from the microlevel (the development and achievements of an individual student) to the macrolevel (the performance of schools and districts statewide). How does it achieve these effects?

The Learning Record document. The Learning Record is based on an
eight-page document that provides a convenient format for gathering
information about the student's development in reading and writing
from diverse sources over the course of the school year, semester, or
term. These sources include interviews with parents or caregivers, interviews with the student, and observations and interpretations of the
student in ongoing classroom activities by the teacher, together with
samples of student work that provide evidence of literacy development. (See the example of a completed CLR in appendix F.) The
format does not dictate the kinds of classroom, reading, or writing
activities or products to be included. Instead, teachers and students
may include a wide variety of different kinds of materials, observations, and interpretations. The Learning Record is a public document: it is made available to students, parents, resource teachers,
administrators, and anyone who has an interest in the student's
literacy development.

The LR is intended to accompany samples of student work, which
provide evidence in support of the teacher's observations and interpretations; this work typically consists of a student portfolio or selections from a portfolio. Standard measures, such as miscue analysis

and running records in reading, can also be incorporated into the record as supporting evidence of development or as diagnostic tools to help teachers recognize what help is needed. The only "rule" for using the Record is that teachers must focus their observations and interpretations on what students demonstrate they know and can do, rather than reporting their assumptions about the students' deficits. The rule comes from an obvious fact of observation: we cannot observe what isn't there, only what is there. When we talk about what students don't know or can't do, we are speculating, not observing. The Learning Record model is based on students' development, not their presumed deficits. This simple rule has had the effect of qualitatively and globally changing the ecology of instruction and evaluation in ways that support student learning.

The procedures. Early in the year, teachers gather information about the students' experiences and activities outside of school for Part A of the LR. At the elementary level, this is usually done through brief interviews with parents or caregivers; at the secondary level and above, teachers may assign students to conduct these interviews. The interview focuses on the background and development of the student; it also provides information about the student's literacies in English and other languages. In addition, teachers interview the students themselves, either face-to-face or through an informal piece of writing. Throughout the course of the year, the teacher (and often the student, as well) records brief observations of the student in a variety of reading, writing, and speaking or listening activities: alone, with one or two other students, with a large group, with the teacher. For students fluent in other languages, teachers also observe and record evidence of growth in the student's other language literacies.[6] It is not necessary for the teacher to be fluent in these other languages to support and observe their development.

The teacher observations form the basis for the interpretive summaries in Part B of the record. Toward the end of the year, teachers review the student's development over the year with the parents and the student and make suggestions in Part C for supporting the student's next stage of development as a reader and writer. They also determine (often in consultation with the student) where to place the student's level of development on a reading scale and a writing scale.

How is it possible to interpret or assess student literacy development on the basis of such diverse activities and materials? The key lies in the use of developmental scales that describe patterns of activities we typically see as students move through stages in their development as readers and writers. These scales are not rubrics, which describe some mythical ideal at the high end and progressively greater deficits as the scale descends. Rather, they describe observable features of development in which each stage represents positive growth based on five interdependent dimensions of learning: confidence and independence; knowledge and understanding; skills and strategies; use of prior and emerging experience; and reflectiveness, or *metacognition*. The materials gathered in the Learning Record provide evidence in support of the teacher's assessment of the student's placement on these developmental scales.

Teachers are supported in the use of the LR through seventy-five hours of staff development spread over three years. Staff development is provided by teacher-leaders who are experienced LR users, through workshops, seminars, and on-site visits. These experienced teachers help teachers new to the LR resolve some questions about how and what to observe, how to describe what is observed, how to build in class time for observation, and how to manage the record keeping for the LR. In anthropological terms, the new teachers are introduced to ethnographic field research, data collection methods, and issues in interpretation; in practical terms, the Learning Record simply supports and legitimizes what has long been recognized as good teaching practice.

The Learning Record, therefore, since it collects data from diverse sources and multiple perspectives, is an excellent vehicle for research, whether conducted by an outside researcher or by the teacher as researcher. It is grounded in informed observations of situated activities, samples of student work, interviews, and interpretive summaries sustained over an extended period of time, providing, by the end of the year, an in-depth case study. Because it engages teachers in careful observation to discover what students can actually do, it is also an important catalyst for instructional transformation and enhanced learning.[7] As teachers pay close attention to how students are learning, it becomes easier to tailor instruction to students' real needs and to provide support in meaningful ways.

Effects on instruction. During the first year, when teachers keep a record for only three to five students, it is common for teachers to feel overwhelmed at the thought of using the Learning Record with all their students. The procedures are unfamiliar, and they sometimes seem like an extra burden on teachers already overloaded with competing demands for accountability. By the end of the first year, however, they have gained a deeper understanding of and respect for the students they are observing, and they generally begin to reconceive their methods and practices. Often they entirely rearrange the classroom environment as well. Although using the LR does not dictate these changes, teachers typically break desks out of rows, replacing them with learning centers stocked with resources for independent group and individual activities. Teachers begin to talk less, and listen more. They develop more collaborative activities where students can work with partners and with small and large groups. They often describe themselves as moving from "telling" to "facilitating." Teachers also experience many struggles in learning to see students differently; they commonly meet with other teachers to share their growing understanding, their problems and questions, and most of all, their unfolding records. By the third year, teachers have internalized the process of keeping the LR, and by this time they usually begin to keep records for the whole class.

But the Learning Record would be just another utopian dream of educational reform if it did not offer a practical, reliable, and equitable means for fostering learning and assessing reading and writing. And it would be of minor interest as a helpful system for college-level composition research and instruction if it did not also offer the potential for assessment to determine special instructional needs of students. Large-scale assessment is possible through the use of moderation readings, a process unique to the Learning Record model.

The Learning Record system of assessment. Since the spring of 1994, the Learning Record has been tested and used for large-scale assessment of reading and writing through a system of *moderation readings*. The testing has established the validity of the LR as an alternative to norm-referenced standardized testing; in fact, it has been recommended for this purpose by the State Department of Education in California. Moderation readings are held to assure that claims for the consistency, equity, and reliability of teacher judgments about student progress can be supported. The moderations are conducted first at the school level, then at the regional level.

Teachers attend the moderation readings with a statistically selected sample of their completed Learning Records together with selected samples of the students' work. The last names of the students and the teacher's placement of each student on the developmental scales are masked. In pairs, the teachers, each experienced with using the LR, read the completed records and the student work. They discuss the observations, samples of work, and interpretations and, based on the evidence, come to agreement about where they would place the student on the developmental scales. They note their placement on a data form; there is also a space on the data form for providing feedback about the record for the classroom teacher. If there is a correlation between the readers' placement and the teacher's placement, nothing further need be done. If there is a difference between the two placements, both placements are masked and another pair of readers reviews the evidence in the record and makes an independent placement.

In any event, because the classroom teacher (or, at the regional level, the Learning Record teacher-leader) is present at the moderation readings, there is an opportunity to discuss special circumstances that may not be apparent to readers and for teachers to learn directly some ways to improve their observations and interpretations or to ask questions about a difficult or problematic record. This is a revolutionary approach to assessment, both in terms of the direct involvement of teachers closest to the learning situation and also in the concept of returning to those teachers something of value: an opportunity to deepen their understanding of their work as teachers. Further, it strips the mask from the "impartial," "distanced," and "objective" judgment of student (and teacher) performance claimed for tests that use standardized tasks and situates assessment in a productive conversation among students, parents, and teachers about how to improve instruction and student achievement. It reduces the increasingly baroque apparatus of writing assessment to a minimum intrusion on learning situations, yet it manages to provide much richer answers to the real questions at the heart of assessment: What are students learning? What are they able to do? Are we providing opportunities for learning equitably? It also provides some answers to a question that conventional assessments can't hope to address: What kinds of environments support student development as readers and writers?

Several principles guide the moderation process.

1. People who have a stake in the process are integral to the moderation readings, which are public. Typically, teachers bring records to moderations, where they read the records brought by other teachers. In college-level moderations, where students are responsible for their own Learning Records, they are often involved as

readers. In addition, parents, administrators, community members, and students are welcome and often serve as observers.

2. Learning Records are read and discussed by pairs of readers, who reach an agreement about the student's level of achievement indicated by the Record's observations, interpretations, and samples of student work. Where they have questions about the Record, they may consult with the classroom teacher or the teacher's representative to clarify a key point. For example, readers at one moderation noted that a research paper, typically assigned in sixth grade, was not mentioned in a student's LR. The classroom teacher was able to explain that, because of funding cuts, the school library had been closed the entire year, and research projects were canceled.

3. It is assumed that more, rather than less, contextual information about the learner and about teaching and learning situations is desirable. Although quantitative data can be abstracted and aggregated to provide large-scale accountability across classrooms or programs or regions, all data—numerical and narrative—are structurally coupled and interdependent.

4. It is assumed that the student and the classroom teacher, who are closest to the learning situation over the longest period of time, are the most qualified "experts" to make evaluations about an individual student's progress and achievement.

Moderation readings are held for multiple purposes: to ensure the quality, consistency, equity, and reliability of teacher judgments about student progress; to share best practices and inform instruction; to provide quantitative information for large-scale analysis; and to support professional development.

While it remains to be seen whether the Learning Record model will gain wide or lasting acceptance, it has already demonstrated the surprising impact of an ecological theory of literacy. The Learning Record itself provides an example of the dynamics of complex systems. Classrooms are ecological systems of students, teachers, resources, and physical environments in continuous interaction. In an educational system marked by a welter of explicit and implicit rules and a blizzard of record-keeping documents, changing just one rule (that is, teachers must account for what students know and can do rather than their deficits) and introducing just one document (the LR form) propagates changes that have a global effect on the entire system, including the physical environment.

Furthermore, the Learning Record is itself an example of a distributed, embodied, emergent, and enactive ecological system. More important, it takes into account the ecology of literacy development in a rich sense. It is *distributed* in the sense that parents, students, and teachers contribute to the evidence provided in the Learning Record, with students taking over more and more of the observation, analysis, and evaluation of their own development as they progress through grade levels. The document *embodies* texts from both students and teachers; that is, it physically incorporates such texts into the document itself. It recognizes developmental stages of literacy learning and provides a way to account for the student's progress through those stages, allowing for comparative analysis or identification of special needs. Consequently, it is a particularly rich and portable source of information about students who are persistently under-represented, such as migrant or transient students. The Learning Record *emerges* over time through the collaborative interactions of students with parents, other students, and teachers. And it is *enacted* in daily practice not only of reading, writing, speaking, and listening but of observation, interpretation, analysis, and evaluation as learning unfolds.

The Learning Record directly addresses the practical question that might be raised by theories of complex systems and distributed cognition in composing: Even if these theories are true, how can we possibly apply them in meaningful ways in teaching and learning environments?

Significance of the Learning Record Model

My purpose in introducing this model in such detail is not necessarily to argue that it should be universally adopted or mandated. Rather, I believe the Learning Record model demonstrates the conceptual work needed to implement a theory of composing situations as ecological systems in any real sense. It also demonstrates that it is possible to achieve revolutionary changes in entrenched institutions without razing them and starting over. The entire educational project has been reconceived via the Learning Record, yet the transformational effects have not been achieved by destroying existing social and institutional structures, nor have they been achieved by top-down mandate; they have been achieved through local, situated practices in everyday classrooms, in both rich and poor schools. The Learning Record originated in and drew its strength from classrooms, emerging out of the frustrations of teachers looking for richer and more authentic means of accounting for learning across diverse student populations and a wider variety of activities. However, educational administrators and teacher educators have also been very responsive to the LR model, and some state departments of education have not only expressed interest but have successfully lobbied for the LR as an alternative to their existing models of reading and writing assessment.

The conceptual work indicated by this model involves rethinking our whole approach to literacy education, requiring, in this case, close observation of naturally occurring activities, a regular practice of recording observations, summary interpretations of the meaning of the observations in terms of literacy development, and open sharing of those interpretations with the participants in the situation, who also contribute their perspectives. If this sounds like good ethnomethodology, it is because that is what it most closely resembles. But it also, for the first time, seamlessly integrates literacy research, pedagogy, and assessment on a common theoretical foundation and grounds it in situated practice. Instead of setting arbitrary standards for achievement, it attempts to help the development of students toward their goals of coordination with the social and physical structures in their environments.

Challenges to an Ecological Theory of Composing

While an ecological theory of composing seems promising for composition research, pedagogy, and assessment, there are still some unresolved issues that pose challenges for the theory. Here is a representative sample:

1. In a complex system, it can be difficult to determine the extent of individual responsibility or agency. In theory, responsibility is distributed among individuals in a system. Problems in complex systems are difficult to predict, analyze, prevent, or repair. Consequently, individuals in the system may view a troublesome condition or situation as "not my problem" or "the fault of the system," leading to a diminished sense of personal responsibility or even capability for preventing or repairing the problem. Problems may be viewed as "too complex" to attempt a solution (e.g., the cultural and linguistic diversity that destabilizes traditional approaches to literacy), or they may seem either too local to merit attention (the substitution of *it's* for *its* in a rough draft) or too

global for one individual to affect (the underappreciation of composition studies in the field of English). However, it would be an error to assume that an ecological theory of composing negates the significance of the individual in favor of the "system" simply because the theory situates individuals within networks of physical and social structures and processes, subject to historically emerging conditions and events. As Roy Bhaskar, the British philosopher of critical realism, puts it,

> According to the transformational understanding of social activity, the existence of social structure is a necessary condition for any human activity. Society provides the means, media, rules and resources for everything we do. . . . We do not create society—the error of voluntarism. But these structures which pre-exist us are only reproduced or transformed in our everyday activities; thus society does not exist independently of human agency—the error of reification. The social world is reproduced or transformed in daily life.
>
> . . . On this transformational and relational conception, society is a skilled accomplishment of active agents. But the social world may be opaque to the social agents upon whose activity it depends in four respects, in that these activities may depend on or involve a) unacknowledged conditions, b) unintended consequences, c) the exercise of tacit skills, and/or d) unconscious motivation. (*Reclaiming Reality* 6)

2. There is a danger of replacing objectification (treating texts, writers, and readers as objects) with the reification of processes. We have recent evidence of this in composition studies with the enormous influence of a simplified model of composing introduced by Linda Flower and John Hayes and generally referred to as "the writing process." If an exclusive focus on objects and objectified subjects is inadequate, an exclusive focus on process dynamics is equally inadequate; we need to integrate our approach to include both structures and processes.

3. Complex systems breed complex problems, which tend to require complex solutions. More significantly, the solutions are themselves likely to be ongoing and locally situated dynamic processes rather than finite universal determinations. Our system of law is a good example: decisions in a court case rarely answer the questions raised by the particulars of the case. New circumstances demand new interpretations; changes in the values of a culture differentially shape the way justice is decided. Ultimately, there will be no agreement about the perfect writing situation, no resolution to the

question of how best to teach writing, no optimal configurations of technologies for composing and communication, no settled interpretation for a literary work. Rather, it is more likely that there will be local, temporary solutions. Many people find the uncertainty generated by such dynamic processes intolerable.

4. If complex systems "never get there," how do we decide whether we are moving in the right direction? How do we interpret our present position? More important, how do we figure out where we want to go? And what constraints prevent us from chaotic wandering? (This is fundamentally the same set of questions faced by Hutchins's navigators.)

5. If complex systems are not controlled by a central "brain" or processor, how do some agents—particular readers, writers, or texts, for instance—come to have a greater influence on such systems and why? How is that influence situated and exerted? Where complex systems do take a hierarchical form, how is the hierarchy structured and maintained—and at what costs and benefits to the system?

6. A theory of composing as an ecological system is particularly vexing because it challenges our present investment in and assumptions about the ownership of intellectual work, such as creative ideas and textual productions. Much has been written about the commodification of ideas and the relatively recent construction of the individual author (e.g., Gere; Lunsford and Ede). Many interdependent institutions, from publishers to broadcast media to academic institutions, are structured around cultural beliefs concerning the individual ownership of expressions of ideas. Even poststructuralists, who refute the notion of "originality," and social constructivists, who argue that our ideas and practices are entirely the product of social interactions, nevertheless continue to issue books and articles under their own names and to protect their rights of ownership with copyrights.

In my opinion, these unresolved issues do not diminish the importance of a theory of composing situations as ecological systems; rather, they suggest worthwhile topics for continued research in the development and application of the theory.

The Value of an Ecological Approach to Composition

What does a theory of composing situations as ecological systems buy us? How does it improve on current views of composing? It seems to me that this theory offers greater explanatory power than existing theories and has the potential to help us better understand composing. Furthermore, as new technologies for composing and communication evolve and proliferate, new discourse arenas are emerging and existing ones are fundamentally and permanently changed. We need to account for not only the social situatedness of composition but its material, physical situatedness as well. An ecological approach to composing could illuminate aspects of composing that are of particular interest to a wide range of scholars right now, including the emergence of genre (Irv Peckham, David Russell, Ritva Engestrom), the development of literacy in diverse situations (Shirley Brice Heath, Barbara Walvoord, Lucille McCarthy), the connection between the cognitive and the social in composing (Deborah Brandt, Linda Flower, Charles Bazerman), the social construction of disciplinary knowledge (Susan Peck MacDonald, Lucille McCarthy), the impact of new technologies on composing situations (Cynthia Selfe, Stuart Moulthrop, Paul Taylor, Paul LeBlanc), and the equitable and authentic assessment of composing (Charles Cooper, Myra Barrs, Mary Barr, Wynne Harlen, Pamela Moss, Grant Wiggins, Royce Sadler).

> *Principle:* A theory of composing situations as ecological systems is necessary and timely for resolving some perplexing questions and intransigent problems in composition studies.

Because theories of complex systems, distributed cognition, and situated cognition provide a complex view of composing and present formidable methodological challenges, researchers are certain to raise these questions: What do these theories add to our existing understanding of composing? In what ways is this approach to research methodologically defensible? In what ways does it fairly represent the complexity of actual composing situations? How can what we learn from one composing situation through this approach inform our understanding of other composing situations?

I believe that the theories of complex systems, distributed cognition, and situated cognition I have drawn on in developing the concept of an ecology of composing provide useful analytical tools for studying what might otherwise seem chaotic, incomprehensible, and overwhelming: the ecologies of readers, writers, and texts situated in particular environments, for example. The work of ethnographers in our field has opened our eyes to the richness and specificity of writing situations. This work has proven invaluable in balancing more closely focused empirical studies of composing, which factored out context in a search for structured regularities common across writing situations. In my view, however, ethnographic studies of composition present us with a different set of problems: how will we use the wealth of observations and interpretations demonstrating the complexity and situatedness of every composing situation? The theories I have presented here have great promise, I believe, for accommodating both empiricist and ethnographic approaches to composing. They offer a way to acknowledge the unpredictability, the social and physical and historical contextuality, the specificity, and the diversity of composing situations. Yet they also offer a way to acknowledge and formally account for some regularities across diverse composing situations.

Cognitive scientists studying complex systems and distributed cognition recognize the difficulties inherent in moving beyond the individual as a unit of analysis. A central problem is how to fix the boundaries of the study if we view individuals and their environment as co-originating. One solution is for researchers to select systems bounded in time and space. For example, Hutchins (*Cognition*) has studied navigation crews in cockpits of planes and on ships engaged in a specific navigational task with a well-defined goal, such as landing a plane or maneuvering a ship safely into harbor; Jean Lave has studied shoppers as they engage in "supermarket arithmetic" during a shopping trip; King Beach has studied how bartenders learn their trade in a bartending course, and so on. D. E. Rumelhart has called this "setting the boundary where the traffic is low."[8]

Writing situations, however, do not always offer such well-defined boundaries for researchers. It can be difficult to establish just where "the traffic is low." Perhaps this is why the scope of research in composition initially focused on texts, only gradually broadening out to encompass authors (typically conceived as solitary figures), individual readers, particular writing tasks, and social and historical contexts. In circumscribing an arena of study (a domain of scrutiny), we must be much more discriminating in our definition of what is "included" and what is "excluded." This task is not as difficult as we might imagine; but it is nearly impossible to try to construct some standard unit of analysis that will apply in every case. Instead, we must establish, for each study, some bounds that make sense, that open a reasonable space for analysis, and that do not exclude parts of the terrain that are significant to our understanding. In this way, we may be able to more closely and rigorously articulate the properties and dynamics of ecologies of composing, as I have only begun to sketch out here.

When you enlarge the unit of analysis from the individual to the ecological system, you are not merely asking, How do individuals function in this system? or How does this system affect individuals? You are asking fundamentally different questions. Instead of asking, for example, How did going to law school affect Reznikoff? or, What kind of law student was Reznikoff? you might ask, How is Reznikoff's poetry an expression of law? What does a culture need with this kind of expression? How does the culture make room for it? and What does it contribute to the overall knowledge making and knowledge retrieval project of the culture? From this standpoint, we can acknowledge the unique perspective on legal history that his stripped-down, poetically arranged law cases provide the culture—an unconventional view of history, law, memory, and social organization. And in the larger culture, this work also provides a different insight into the construction of cultural history and social interaction.

The understanding we gain from studying composing situations as complex ecological systems should help us as we consider the changes wrought by new technologies. In composition studies, we have, until very recently, viewed computers as extensions of typewriters: a more sophisticated means of accomplishing the goal of putting words on a page. We've studied the effects of composing on a computer versus composing by hand, the effects of computers on revision strategies, quantity of writing, and mechanical correctness. We've hailed the new applications that make text production easier: spelling checkers, page-layout programs, font packages, word processors. We've agonized over whether students' writing was getting better or worse as they began composing with computers. The text-based worldview has even been favored by computer interface designers. We work on metaphorical desktops, creating "files," "folders," and "documents"; we post email; we quickly and easily print out pages and pages of text. But the children who have grown up with computers, along with a few visionaries in the field, have a radically different perspective on the technology; for these people, the computer serves as a construction site, an alternative universe for exploration, a toolkit for the imagination, and a direct connection to other people. They no longer recognize our taken-for-granted boundaries between text and graphics, sound, video, and animation; and they navigate easily across networks, computer bulletin boards, chat rooms, databases, and other remote resources.

Until very recently, the notion that an individual would own a "personal computer" seemed as likely as the notion that an individual would own a "personal aircraft carrier"; the notion that a child would own a computer was simply inconceivable. Now the technology is becoming nearly ubiquitous. While computers are fundamentally altering composing environments, other kinds of computer programs and networks create their own environments as well—databases, spreadsheets, hypertexts and hypermedia, video production, sound editing, 3-D modeling and rendering, animation, and online collaborative environments called MOOs and MUDs are just a few diverse examples—and we live in these environments with their affordances and constraints as surely as we live among our cities, suburbs, and countrysides.

Yet, just as there are inequities in access to other social and material resources, there continue to be inequities in both access to new technologies and the ways they are being used. We need to be mindful of how computers, readers, writers, and compositions will shape and be shaped by their ecosystems, while there is still time to influence emerging social and physical structures surrounding their use. How will computer-supported classrooms be arranged? What hardware, software, and network access will be provided, and how often can it be serviced and upgraded? What kinds of support can we provide for multimedia, hypermedia, virtual reality, and other experimental compositions? How will we ensure that access to technological resources— not just hardware and software but human resources as well—will be equitable? What will we want students to know and know how to do when they leave our computer-based classes in rhetoric, composition, creative writing, and literature? Furthermore, the impact of technological changes in our field affords us a rare opportunity to step back and reconsider more conventional composing environments as well, to rethink our research programs, and to reconceptualize our goals for educating writers and readers.

In my opinion, the real value in taking an ecological perspective is that it compels us to ask a better set of questions about the dynamic relationships among writers, readers, and texts and drives us toward a deeper understanding of composition. As the example of the Learning

Record demonstrates, the consequences are transformational, in terms described best by Bhaskar, who argues that human emancipation depends on the transformation of structures rather than the amelioration of states of affairs:

> Indeed, in present and foreseeable circumstances, the transformation of structures may be a practically necessary condition for more humane states of affairs. But this transformation does not involve a magic transportation into a realm free of determination, as imagined by both utopian and so-called 'scientific' socialists. Rather, it consists in the move or transition from unneeded, unwanted and oppressive to needed, wanted, and empowering sources of determination. (*Reclaiming Reality* 6)

He also reminds us, however, that "social structure[s are] embedded in, conditioned by and in turn efficacious on the rest of nature, the ecosphere. . . . [W]e have to see the natural and social dimensions of existence as in continuous dynamic causal interaction" (6).

This book is an extended speculation about what we might discover if we apply current theories of complex systems and distributed cognition to composing situations. It is only a beginning. As Gertrude Stein put it, the problem from this time on becomes more definite.

Appendixes
Notes
References
Index

Appendix A
Syllabus and Journal Questions for Third College Writing Program, 1A, Winter, 1989

TCWP 1A: Explanation and Argument

Syllabus

Instructor: Peg Syverson
Office: TCHB 135
Mailbox: TCHB 132
TCWP Office: TCHB 132 (M–F 8–4:30)
Phone: 534-2742 (Leave message)

Important!

Do not lose this handout. It will serve as a guideline throughout this quarter, and you are responsible for knowing and following the directions it contains.

Things to Buy

- *The Saint Martin's Guide to Writing (SMGW)*
- *Myths to Live By,* Joseph Campbell
- *GAIA: An Atlas of Planet Management,* GAIA Staff
- *Ellis Island and Other Stories,* Mark Helprin
- Six manila folders (one for each of the four assignments, one to keep your journals in, and one for your four revisions at the end of the quarter)

Things to Bring to Each Class Meeting

- *SMGW*
- the book(s) we're reading
- any work that is due to be discussed in workshops or turned in
- your journals

Attendance

In Class: Because the success of the workshops and class discussions depends on your participation at every class meeting, attendance is absolutely vital. The TCWP attendance policy is strict: you are allowed a maximum of two absences, and these must be for legitimate reasons. Arriving in class late or leaving early will count as one-half absence.

Please note: If you absolutely must miss a class, it is up to you to find out what you missed and to make up the work. This includes having a friend critique your draft outside of class if you miss a workshop. It's a good idea to have the phone numbers of a few of your classmates.

Conferences: Conferences are an extremely important part of this course. The conferences are meant to help you uncover and address problems with your own drafts. You may expect to do most of the thinking and talking about these problems in the conference. My role is that of a coach; I can't go out there and play the game for you, but I can work with you to develop some strategies that might help. Conferences replace class meetings in the fourth, sixth, and ninth weeks of the quarter. One missed conference is the equivalent of two missed class meetings. If, for a very good reason, you can't keep a scheduled conference appointment, call a classmate and switch times. The conference schedule, including times, names, and phone numbers, will be posted on my office door during conference weeks. If all else fails, call me to schedule an alternate time. Note: *If you come to a conference unprepared, we will not be able to meet, and this will count as a missed conference.*

Assignments

You will be writing four papers this quarter. The first will be an evaluation of something with which you are familiar, the second will be an analysis of the causes of a trend, the third will be a proposal to solve a problem, and the last will be a literary analysis of a short story. The causal and literary analyses will each be seven to ten pages long, while the evaluation and proposal will be somewhat shorter.

When you complete each assignment, you will turn in all the writing you did for it in one of the manila folders. Your name and the assignment should be written on the folder, and it should contain the following:

- **Invention:** a minimum of four pages of rough notes, labelled according to the invention sequence for that assignment in SMGW.

- **Documentation:** photocopies of any pages of published material from which you have quoted, paraphrased, or summarized within your own text. Each photocopied page should include complete bibliographical information (i.e., author's name, book or article title, date of publication, etc.). Note: This is in addition to proper citation of each source within your manuscript.

- **Drafts:** one to three rough drafts, depending on the assignment. Label these "First Draft," "Second Draft," etc.

- **Workshop Response:** commentary written by a classmate in the workshop, using the critical reading section of the appropriate chapter of SMGW. Please make sure that your reader's name appears on his or her response.

- **Revision:** the final version of the paper, substantially revised from earlier drafts. It must be prepared this way:
    Typed on one side of the paper only, in clear, readable type.
    Double spaced
    Proofread, with errors neatly corrected
    Your name and the page number at the top of each page
    Stapled or paper clipped (do NOT bend corners to fasten papers)
  You will also need a title page labeled as follows:
    Your name
    The title of your essay
    Revision: Evaluation Essay (or whichever essay is assigned)
    Date

- **Self-Evaluation (Learning from your own writing process):** a letter or memo from you to me, telling me what you were trying to do in the paper, what worked, what didn't, how the paper developed and changed from invention through drafts to revision; what major decisions you made in composing it, what parts you want me to look at in particular, what you learned from the assignment, etc. This self-evaluation should be detailed, honest, and thoughtful. It will tell me a lot about your level of involvement with the writing process.

I will return each package to you after I have read it and written some comments about it. Keep the package in a safe place! Don't throw any part of it away, because at the end of the quarter you will need to turn in all your packages again so that I can take a final look at them before evaluating your work for a grade.

At the end of the quarter, TCWP keeps the revisions of each essay for the program records. If you want to keep any of your essays for your own records, photocopy them before the end of the quarter.

Journals

In addition to the four papers, you will be keeping a writer's journal, making from two to four entries in it each week. Most of these entries will be directly related to the other reading and writing you will be doing in the course. You will be asked to share some of these in class during discussions of the reading.

Don't think of the journal as a formal assignment—feel free to play around. Journal entries should be thoughtful and insightful, but they need be no more formal than a letter to a friend. Don't worry too much about spelling, grammar, etc., but do write legibly.

I may not comment on every journal entry, but I will read each one. I will generally respond and try to answer any questions you might raise. As I return journal assignments to you, keep them in a folder until the end of the quarter.

The answer to each journal question should be about one page long, written on separate sheets of paper, and stapled together. Head each entry with your name, the week number, and the entry number.

Grading Policy

The main goal of this writing class is to give you more control over your writing by helping you to see why writing works well or not so well, and by showing you the range of options available to you in a given writing situation. Gaining control over your writing requires time, effort, and experience, which is why TCWP courses are so intensive.

Your grade will be based mainly on the quality of your work and the progress you make during the quarter. All students should be sure to use the course materials to develop a greater awareness of the elements of good writing. The course materials include *The St. Martin's Guide,* the readings, the journal, in-class workshops and discussions, and my own instruction.

Finally, here is a very general description of my grading scale:

A   Consistently excellent work, outstanding performance in *all* areas of the course.
A- Consistently fine work, occasionally excellent.
B+ Very good work, lots of effort and some significant achievements.
B   Good work, good effort, and some achievement.
B- Generally good work that exhibits some weaknesses.
C+ Adequate work.
C   Fair work that is weak in significant areas.
C- Barely adequate work.

D   Poor work. I try to advise people to drop the course if they seem headed for this area of the grading scale.

F   Failing work.

Please remember that if you expect to get at least a C grade you must attend class regularly, participate in class discussions and activities, and complete *all* assigned work on time. If you put in extra effort, make regular, thoughtful contributions to class discussion, give helpful, thorough responses to other students' drafts in workshops, and submit writing that is engaging, original, perceptive, ambitious, and typically free of error, you can expect to earn a grade in the B or even the A range. These standards are high but not unrealistic for UCSD undergraduates. TCWP courses are demanding, and they take considerable time each week, but if you are prepared to work hard in TCWP 1A, you can expect to learn much and to profit greatly from your experience this term.

TCWP 1A
Week 6. Journal Questions

Note: These questions deal specifically with your group writing experience. You may answer them briefly, in a few sentences or a paragraph about each one, or at length, as you like.

1. How did your group go about planning the work? How did you decide how you would schedule your meetings?
2. How did your group divide the workload?
3. How did the group do the invention work?
4. How did your group decide on a topic?
5. Do you feel comfortable with the topic? Why or why not?
6. How is the group planning to accomplish the research? Who is responsible for the research?
7. How was the first draft prepared?
8. Who is responsible for accuracy of facts, the logic of the argument, and errors of the text?

TCWP 1A
Week 7. Journal Questions

Note: Again, these questions deal specifically with your group writing experience. You may answer them briefly, in a few sentences or a paragraph about each one, or at length, as you like.

1. How were workshop responses to the draft handled by the group?
2. How did your group decide which revisions to make? Who actually made the revisions?
3. Do you feel satisfied with the organization of the essay?
4. How are disagreements or differences of opinion handled in the writing group?
5. Does your group have a single leader, or do you share leadership of the group? Does the leader change at times?
6. Can you describe some of the obstacles or problems your group has faced in working on this essay? How have you overcome these?
7. What kinds of distractions occur? How does the group handle distractions?
8. In what ways did other group members contribute toward your sense of the audience for this essay? That is, did they point out arguments that you might have overlooked, or discover weaknesses that you might not have spotted?
9. Do you feel that writing this way is slowed by the interactions and decision-making done by the group?

TCWP 1A
Week 8. Journal Questions

Note: Again, these questions deal specifically with your group writing experience. You may answer them briefly, in a few sentences or a paragraph about each one, or at length, as you like.

1. How was the final draft prepared?
2. Who was responsible for proofreading the final revision?
3. How did your group handle different writing styles in order to make the essay coherent?
4. Do you feel that this is a stronger argument than you might have produced alone?
5. Do you feel there are fewer errors of fact, mechanics, or style as a result of the group work?
6. What did you learn about your role on a team? Did you feel strongly active, moderately active, responsive, supportive, passive, or uninterested? Were there times when you took a leadership role?
7. How willing would you be to repeat the collaborative writing experience? Do you plan to collaborate for the literary analysis essay?
8. What parts of the writing task do you feel most comfortable collaborating on?
9. How do you feel the group treated your ideas? Did they value them as

much as you felt they should? Do you feel your ideas made a real contribution to the essay?

10. How would you rate the value of the ideas supplied by other members of your group? How did those ideas help you in your thinking about the essay?

11. How would you compare the amount of work that was done individually to the amount of work done communally? That is, looking at the whole process from beginning to end, were certain tasks assigned to individuals and then incorporated later, or was the majority of the work accomplished together?

TCWP 1A
Week 9. Journal Questions

Note: Again, these questions deal specifically with your group writing experience. You may answer them briefly, in a few sentences or a paragraph about each one, or at length, as you like.

1. Do you feel that the collaborative proposal essay "belongs" to you? That is, how much does it reflect your thinking, style, and effort?
2. How do you feel you handled your responsibilities toward the group?
3. How did others in your group handle their responsibilities? Did they contribute equally to the ideas, the organization, the work, and the style of the essay?
4. What obstacles and problems did you experience working within the group situation?
5. Overall, do you feel that your group was able to produce a better essay than you might have produced alone?
6. Do you think it is fair to share the evaluation of this text among your group members?
7. How has this experience changed the way you think about writing?
8. Did you find this way of writing more or less satisfying than writing alone? Why?
9. What recommendations would you make to another writer in this situation?
10. How might the instructor provide more support for collaborative writers?
11. Think about the whole process from beginning to end. What worked particularly well for you? What would you do differently on your next collaborative writing task?
12. Did anything surprise you about this experience?

Appendix B
Workshop Handout

Reading with a Critical Eye:
Proposing a Solution to a Problem

After you have read the writer's draft and made notes on the copy, think about the ways that the draft might be improved. Each reader should write out responses to the questions below, and then discuss them with the writer. Try to be as specific and detailed as possible in your responses, giving the writer the kind of help you would like to get with your own drafts.

1. **General impressions.** Write a few sentences stating your immediate reaction to the draft.
2. **Audience.** Is it clear to you who is the audience for this essay? Describe the audience the writer is addressing. Does the writer's tone seem persuasive for this particular audience? Does it seem to you that this audience can take action to solve the problem?
3. **Defining the Problem.** Is the problem clearly defined? Are you convinced that the problem exists? Write down in one or two sentences exactly what the problem is.
4. **Convincing the Audience of the Seriousness of the Problem.** Has the writer presented the problem in a way that will convince *the identified audience* that the problem is serious and that something should be done about it?
5. **Proposed solution.** Has the writer clearly presented a way the problem could be solved? Is this solution described in enough detail so that the readers will be able to take action on it? Does the solution seem reasonable?
6. **Argument and Counterarguments.** Has the writer argued well for the proposed solution? Does the writer provide enough evidence in the form of reasons, examples, facts, statistics, and so on to support the proposed solution? What other evidence might be provided? Has the writer anticipated the audience's counterarguments?
7. **Alternative Solutions.** Are alternative solutions clearly and fairly presented? Is the argument against them convincing? Why or why not? Indicate any alternative solutions that seem plausible to you.
8. **Frame.** Look at the beginning and the ending. Is the beginning effective? Does it capture your interest? Suggest some alternate ways to open the essay. Is the ending graceful and satisfying? Suggest some alternate ways to conclude the essay.

Appendix C
Conference Worksheet

TCWP 1A
Conference Worksheet
Proposal Essay

The basic features of a proposal are as follows:

1. a well-defined problem, discussed in enough detail to establish both its existence and its seriousness
2. a proposed solution
3. an argument that demonstrates that the proposed solution will solve the problem, is feasible, and is preferable to alternative solutions
4. a reasonable tone of voice that establishes the writer's credibility and authority.

Before the conference you will need to prepare brief written answers to the questions below:

1. What problem are we trying to solve? Why is it significant? Does it affect anyone other than our writing group? How large a group does this problem affect?
2. Who is our audience? Is it an individual, a committee, a large segment of the population? What is our present attitude toward this audience? What are our expectations of this audience?
3. What is our proposed solution to the problem? How did we arrive at it? What other possible solutions have we considered (and rejected)? Why is this the best possible solution?
4. How much authority do we have in this issue? Do we need to look into the problem more deeply (i.e., should we do more research)?

Appendix D
Correlations Between Events
of the Gulf War and XLCHC Messages

The following tables and message maps show the correlations between some key historical events related to the Gulf War and the messages posted to xlchc during the same period. On the left page is a timeline of major historical events of the Gulf War, month by month. On the right page is a map showing the distribution of messages on xlchc for the same month. The map diagrams the relationships among messages posted to xlchc over time during the Gulf War episode.

Email messages on the topic of the Gulf War are shown with the sender's three-letter initial code in black; messages on other topics are shown with the sender's initials in gray (see the following legend of names and codes). There were no messages on the topic between September 1990 and January 1991. The maps are arranged by month, with the days of the month indicated vertically in the left column and the hours of each day across the top row. The effect is of a timeline that has been folded like a carpenter's rule.

Names and Codes for Participants in the Conversation about the Gulf War on XLCHC[2]

ABR	Anne Brice	LGO	Larry Goldman
AEN	Armand Endicott	LLA	Lauren Lane
ALO	Art Lopetsky	LMO	Lisa Moffett
AMI	Ana Milano	LNI	Lars Nilsson
AWO	Amy Wood	MBU	Martha Bunker
BRE	Bob Reasoner	MCO	Matt Connors
DCO	Dave Covey	MGR	Mark Green
DJE	Donna Jensen	MSC	Michael Schwartz
EJU	Elena Juarez	MTA	Martin Taylor
EMO	Ethan Morse	NSA	Nora Sanders
FSI	Frank Simpson	PBE	Pat Benson
GLA	George Lakoff	PGR	Penny Grolier
GPA	Gerald Parsons	RFO	Roger Forrest
GSA	Gene Saltzman	RSE	Richard Sessions
HRA	Hans Rausch	RWE	Robert Werman
JBA	Jim Barrett	SEM	Sarah Emerson
JOL	Jake Olson	SSC	Steven Schnell
KGR	Katherine Grayson	STR	Sam Trautman

Historical Events Related to the Gulf War: September 1990

1   Libya, having consulted Iraq, Jordan, and Sudan, unveils a seven-point peace plan, including the withdrawal of Iraqi troops from Kuwait and U.S. and other non-Muslim troops from Saudi Arabia, the lifting of the embargo against Iraq, the ceding of Warba and Bubiyan Islands to Iraq, and the people of Kuwait deciding their own political system through a plebiscite. Kuwait and Saudi Arabia reject it.

5   Saddam Hussein renews his call to "the Iraqi people, faithful Arabs and Muslims everywhere" to wage a holy struggle against Saudi rulers and their backers.
Tariq Aziz meets President Gorbachev in Moscow.

6   Jordan says that an estimated 605,000 people have entered the kingdom since August 2 and that 105,000 are being held in 17 refugee camps.

8   Saddam Hussein urges "the concerned politicians" worldwide to "choose this critical issue and time to restore the Soviet Union to its superpower status" by "a just and fair position" on the Gulf crisis and rejecting "America's shunning" of his August 12 peace initiative.

9   At the end of a summit meeting in Helsinki, Bush and Gorbachev call on Iraq to withdraw unconditionally from Kuwait, allow the restoration of the legitimate government of Kuwait, and free all hostages held in Iraq and Kuwait.

10   Iraq and Iran decide to renew diplomatic relations.

11   Saddam Hussein offers Third World countries free oil as long as they can arrange the transportation at their own expense.

12   Ayatollah Khamenei condemns the U.S. military presence in the gulf and declares that those who confront "American aggression and greed" in the Persian Gulf will have participated in a holy war in the path of Allah.
The Saudi-funded World Muslim League declares at the end of a three-day conference in Mecca that the foreign help sought by Saudi Arabia to boost self-defense was necessitated by "a legitimate need."

16   U.N. Security Council adopts Resolution 667 by unanimous vote, condemning Iraq's acts of violence against diplomats and their personnel in Kuwait.
In a *Washington Post* interview, General Michael Dugan, U.S. Air Force chief of staff, says that U.S. air power is the only effective way of expelling Iraq from Kuwait, that Baghdad will be on "the cutting edge" of the bombing, and that, according to Israeli advice, Saddam Hussein should be at "the focus of our efforts."

17   U.S. defense secretary Cheney sacks General Dugan.
Iraq's deputy prime minister, Taha Yassin Ramadan, says Iraq is prepared to withdraw from Kuwait if it leads to an international conference to solve the Palestinian problem.

19   King Hassan II of Morocco, after consulting Jordanian and Algerian rulers, offers a peace plan, including Iraqi evacuation of Kuwait, withdrawal of non-Arab troops from Saudi Arabia, a "special relationship" between Iraq and Kuwait, and an international conference to consider the Palestinian and Lebanese problems.
Washington and Riyadh reject the proposal.

21   The Popular Forces Conference for Solidarity with Iraq, attended by 20 radical Arab parties in Amman, condemns the Saudi alliance with the U.S.

23   In Tehran, Syrian president Assad reiterates his call for the withdrawal of Iraqi troops from Kuwait. While endorsing this demand, Iran's president Rafsanjani says that the presence of foreign force in the Persian Gulf is hindering the regional Arab countries from finding a solution to the crisis.

24   At the U.N. General Assembly, President Mitterrand proposes a four-phase peace plan, including an Iraqi declaration of "intent" to withdraw from Kuwait; tackling the problems of Lebanon, the Palestinians, and security for Israel; and reduction of arms in the region. Iraq and China respond positively.

25   U.N. Security Council adopts Resolution 670, 14 votes to none, extending the applicability of sanctions against Iraq to all means of transport, including aircraft, and threatens Iraq with "potentially severe consequences" if it fails to withdraw from Kuwait.
At the U.N. General Assembly, Soviet foreign minister Eduard Shevardnadze says that the U.S.S.R. may support the use of force if Iraq continues to occupy Kuwait.

27   Following a statement by Shaikh Yamani, former Saudi oil minister, that in case of war the Kuwaiti oil wells will be set on fire and that Iraq can inflict damage on Saudi oil installations, the price of oil rises to $40 a barrel, the highest in 12 years.

29   A senior White House official says, "Our message number one, two, and three to Israel is to keep out of this [crisis] at all costs."

EMAIL MESSAGES ON XLCHC: SEPTEMBER 1990

Hour → (columns 0–23), Day ↓ (rows 1–30)

Day	0	1	2	3	4	5	6	7	8	9	10	11	12	13	14	15	16	17	18	19	20	21	22	23
1																								
2																				MCO	KGO			
3																								
4											LBA													
5																								
6									EMO															
7												RRU												
8								HRA																
9																						KGO		
10			JOL						MCO / MCO	DJE		MCO	JOL / JOL	MBU	PBE		PBE							
11										OHA												KKU		
12												KGO		JOL				RHU	MCO					
13										AMI / MCO								**RSE** / RSE	RHU		JOL			
14			HRA						LBA / TBE	**MCO** / **MBU** / AMI	FRN							SHR				HRA		
15							HRA																	
16																		GWE			GWE			
17							DNO						MCO											
18																								
19							GBU		MCO					JJA	MCO							KGO		
20												MCO		MCO / EMO	MCO	GWE								
21												MCO	MCO	MCO / MCO	HRA / RGE / MCO	MCO								
22								RGL / RSE			JTU			JOL		MBE								
23										SST						MCO	JAM							
24							HRA	HLI	MCO			KBE									RSE			
25				SST								MCO									KGO / KGO			
26									DNO	GWE / SST														
27								BBE		FSI														
28						LBA			HRA			DNO			HLI			CGO						
29				HRA						BHU / DNO														
30													RHU					JOL	MCO / TWE					

Historical Events Related to the Gulf War: January 1991

3   Bush offers to send Baker to Geneva for talks with Aziz between January 7 and 9.
4   Iraq agrees to Aziz–Baker talks in Geneva on January 9.
6   On Iraqi Army Day, Saddam Hussein says that the "Mother of All Battles" will be waged under experienced, cohesive military leadership.
7   Baker meets British foreign minister Hurd in London, and they reject the idea of extending the January 15 deadline.
9   Baker–Aziz talks fail. Baker says there is no flexibility from Iraq. Aziz says Iraq is prepared "for the worst."
10   Baker tours the capitals of the Arab and Western allies, confirming the launching of a U.S.-led attack on Iraq soon after the January 15 deadline.
11   Lawrence Eagleburger arrives in Israel to urge Prime Minister Shamir not to retaliate if Israel is attacked by Iraq. Shamir refuses. In turn, Eagleburger rejects his request for tactical coordination between the Israeli military and U.S. forces in the Gulf.
     The Third Popular Islamic Conference in Baghdad calls for a holy war if Iraq is attacked.
12   Congress authorizes Bush to use U.S. military pursuant to U.N. Security Council Resolution 678. The vote in the Senate is 53–47; in the House of Representatives, 250–183.
12–13   Antiwar demonstrations are held in all major European cities.
14   Iraqi parliament unanimously decides to go to war rather than withdraw from Kuwait and gives President Saddam Hussein constitutional powers to conduct it.
15   At the Security Council, facing strong American and British opposition, France withdraws its four-point peace plan. The U.S.-led coalition has fielded 680,000 troops to confront 545,000 Iraqi troops in Kuwait and southern Iraq.
16   The air campaign of the U.S.-led coalition, code named Operation Desert Storm, begins at 23:30 GMT involving aerial bombing and the firing of Tomahawk cruise missiles from U.S. warships.
17   Foreign ministers in Paris combine an appeal to Iraq to withdraw from Kuwait with an endorsement of French calls for an international peace conference on the Middle East.
     Baghdad Radio broadcasts a defiant speech by Saddam Hussein.
18   Twelve Iraqi Scud ground-to-ground missiles land in Tel Aviv and Haifa.
19   Allied air sorties reach 4,000. Allied bombing of Iraq's water, fuel, and electrical supplies has caused shortages in Baghdad and other cities.
     Antiwar demonstrations are staged in American cities.
20   Iran calls for an emergency meeting of the 45-member Islamic Conference Organization. Only 10 members support its initiative.
21   Iran protests that the allied attacks on Iraq far exceed the U.N. mandate to liberate Kuwait.
22   Three Iraqi Scuds hit populated areas in Tel Aviv, killing 3 and injuring 70.
23   Germany offers Israel $170 million in humanitarian aid. Later additions raised to $670 million.
     Total allied air sorties in the first week amount to more than 12,000; Tomahawk cruise missile firings, 216.
26   The first 7 of the 135 Iraqi aircraft seek refuge in Iran.
     Large antiwar demonstrations are held in American and European cities.
27   War damage creates an oil slick 35 miles long and 10 miles wide.
     Iraq's RCC says that any Iraqi, Arab, or Muslim taking part in "a commando attack" against U.S.-led coalition members will be considered a martyr in the "Mother of All Battles."
28   General Mirza Aslam Beg, military chief of staff in Pakistan, with troops in Saudi Arabia, accuses the West of a conspiracy to undermine the Muslim world by encouraging Iraq to invade Kuwait to provide it with a justification to start a war against Iraq to destroy it. In an interview with CNN, Saddam Hussein says that any chance of "negotiations to end the conflict" is up to Bush.
29   French defense minister Chévenement resigns, saying that the allies now aim to overthrow Saddam Hussein's regime and decimate much of Iraq.
     In Moscow, President Gorbachev's spokesman repeats Soviet fears that the conflict may escalate into a broader war and says that time may be right for a new peace initiative.
29   After talks in Washington, Baker and the Soviet foreign minister state that a cease-fire in the Gulf War will be possible only if Iraq follows its commitment to withdraw with concrete steps and add that the U.S.-U.S.S.R. efforts to promote Arab–Israeli peace will be enhanced in the aftermath of the cease-fire.
30   Israel denounces the Baker–Bessmertnykh statement. The White House says that there are no differences between it and the State Department.

JANUARY 1991

Hour → / Day ↓	0	1	2	3	4	5	6	7	8	9	10	11	12	13	14	15	16	17	18	19	20	21	22	23
1										FSI								JWE		ANI	RSE MPA PAG			
2	KAM		SWH											ANI							JBA			
3											LGO				LNI LNI				JBA					
4													EMO	MPA	MCO	EMO MCO							LNI	
5											KGO										PSA PSA			
6							EFO								MCO									
7																								
8																								
9			LMA						PDA		JWE	MCO PDA								RFO RFO/ GLA				
10							MCO								NSA/ SEM								PDA	
11							SON						LHO		MPA									
12						LLA					HRA	DNO				PDA								JZH
13												HRA				ANI	MPA DNO							
14										HRA											PDA			
15												MCO				MCO		BZE			MCO	RSE		
16	VND																							
17																								
18		SST																						
19																								
20																						HME		
21								RGL																
22									GSA/ STR															
23												PBE												TSK
24												GSA/ STR												
25																								
26																								
27															PPO									
28															LMO	MCO		FRE			ABR GHU			
29								SRA DJE	ECH	LMO MCO PBE	GHU GHU	RDU RDU			LNI	GSA/ RWE		LMO TSC	GPA				ABR	
30									JWE			GHU				GWE		AWO						
31																					MCO			

Historical Events Related to the Gulf War: February 1991

3   Allied air missions reach a total of 41,000.
5   Bush sends a letter to President Rafsanjani saying that America has no plans to stay in the region for long and will leave "as soon as the crisis is over."
    U.N. secretary-general protests the death of eight Jordanian truck drivers by allied bombing of the Baghdad–Amman highway.
6   Iraq severs diplomatic relations with the U.S., Britain, Canada, France, Italy, Egypt, and Saudi Arabia.
7   Allied air missions reach 49,000 in 3 weeks, with the U.S. responsible for 84% of the total.
11 Allies bomb Iraq and Kuwait in the largest land-sea-air operation to date.
13 Allied bombing of an air-raid shelter in Baghdad kills 1,000+ civilians, the majority women and children.
15 Iraq's RCC expresses readiness to "deal with Security Council Resolution 660" provided the subsequent resolutions are abrogated.
    Bush calls the Iraqi offer "a cruel hoax."
    Soviet foreign minister says that Iraq's offer opens up "a new stage in the development of the conflict."
17 Iraq starts secretly withdrawing its best troops from Kuwait; the withdrawing forces set Kuwaiti oil wells on fire.
18 In Moscow, Aziz meets Gorbachev, who forwards his peace plan to Bush.
    In a message to Gorbachev, Bush outlines minimum conditions for a truce. Britain and France back Bush's peace plan.
19 In an interview with an Iranian newspaper, Hamadi says that in the first 26 days of the war allied bombing killed 20,000 Iraqis and injured 60,000, and caused estimated damage of $200 billion to Iraq's infrastructure.
21 Iraq responds positively to Gorbachev's eight-point peace plan.
22 At 6:00 GMT, Bush rejects the Gorbachev peace plan. He gives Saddam Hussein until 17:00 GMT on 23 February to accept publicly the conditions to be listed by the White House spokesman.
22 At 15:45 GMT, the White House press secretary, Fitzwater, lists 12 conditions for Iraq; in return, the coalition forces will not attack retreating Iraqi soldiers.
    At 19:00 GMT, the Kremlin announces a refined six-point plan agreed to by Gorbachev and Aziz.
    At 20:45 GMT, Iraqi government accepts the Soviet plan.
23 At 12:00 GMT, Aziz says that following the acceptance of the Soviet peace plan, the Iraqi government has decided to withdraw from Kuwait immediately and unconditionally.
    At 15:00 GMT, the White House dismisses the latest Soviet plan, repeating Bush's ultimatum.
    At 15:30 GMT, Gorbachev tries and fails to convince Bush to postpone the ground attack on the Iraqi forces.
23 At 18:00 GMT, Bush orders Schwarzkopf to eject the Iraqis from Kuwait.
24 At 1:00 GMT, the U.S.-led coalition launches its ground offensive, Operation Desert Saber.
25 At 21:30 GMT, the Soviet Union presents a new peace plan.
    At 22:30 GMT, accepting the Soviet plan, Iraq's RCC orders an Iraqi withdrawal from Kuwait.
26 At 4:25 GMT, the U.S. rejects the latest Soviet peace initiative.
    At 4:30 GMT, disputing Saddam Hussein's statement that the Iraqi forces were withdrawing, Bush says, "His defeated forces are retreating."
    At 8:20 GMT, Saddam Hussein announces on Baghdad Radio that Iraq is withdrawing from Kuwait in compliance with U.N. Security Council Resolution 660.
    At 9:15 GMT, the Soviet Union proposes a cease-fire.
    At 11:50 GMT, Iraqi forces are out of Kuwait City and suburbs.
    At 12:00 GMT, the Pentagon says that all exits for the Iraqi troops in the Kuwaiti theater of operations are blocked. Slaughtering of the retreating Iraqis along Jahra–Basra highway, Jahra–Umm Qasr road, and Umm Qasr–Nasiriyeh–Baghdad road continues until the cease-fire 40 hours later.
27 At 1:30 GMT, the Pentagon says that Kuwaiti and Saudi troops control Kuwait City.
    At 5:30 GMT, Baghdad announces that it has completed its withdrawal from Kuwait.
    At 18:00 GMT, the U.N. Security Council receives a letter from Aziz in which he accepts Resolutions 660, 662 and 674, and rejecting 661, 665, and 670.
    Total allied air sorties reach 106,000 in 42 days of war.
28 At 2:00 GMT, Bush delivers a victory speech to the nation and orders a cease-fire at 5:00 GMT if Iraq puts down its arms.
    At 4:40 GMT, Iraq accepts Bush's conditions for a cease-fire.
    At 5:00 GMT, a temporary cease-fire comes into effect after 209 days of the Gulf crisis and warfare.

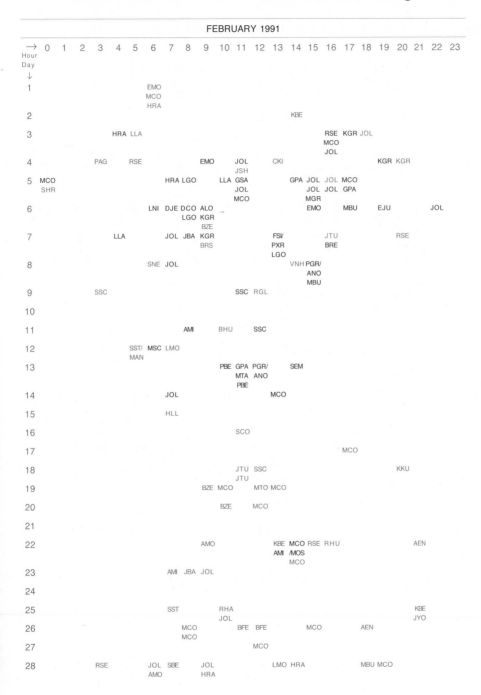

FEBRUARY 1991

Historical Events Related to the Gulf War: March 1991

2   The U.N. Security Council adopts Resolution 686, 11 votes to 1 (Cuba), with 3 abstentions (China, India, and Yemen), setting out the steps Iraq should take to consolidate the temporary cease-fire.
    A revolt by Shia dissidents begins at Nasiriyeh.
3   Iraqi commanders Ahmad and Mahmoud meet Schwarzkopf and Khalid at Safwan airstrip six miles from the Kuwait–Iraq border.
4   The town of Ranya is taken over by Kurdish nationalists.
    Shia rebellion spreads to other urban centers, including Basra, Najaf, and Karbala.
6   In Damascus, the foreign ministers of Egypt, Syria, and the Gulf Cooperation Council agree to form a joint peacekeeping force to maintain postwar security in the Gulf.
7   Rafsanjani calls on Saddam Hussein to resign.
9   Reassembled government forces launch a counterattack against Shia insurgents.
13 Ayatollah Khamenei urges the Iraqi army not to fire on the people.
    In Beirut, a three-day conference of the Joint Action Committee of Iraqi Opposition ends with a program to overthrow Saddam Hussein's regime.
14 Iraqi troops retake Karbala.
    Kuwaiti emir Shaikh Jaber III al Sabah returns to Kuwait.
    The defection of the 100,000-strong Iraqi army auxiliary force of Kurds enables the Kurdish nationalists to take over 12 major towns in a 100-mile-long arc.
15 Bush warns Saddam Hussein to desist from combat operations against Iraqi insurgents.
16 In a radio and television speech, Saddam Hussein accuses "rancorous traitors" of spreading terror and devastation in southern towns and cities. He attributes the Kurdish uprising to infiltration of armed elements from "the same place" (meaning Iran) as in the south.
17 Iraqi troops regain Najaf.
20 The Kuwaiti government, with seven al Sabahs running the most important ministries, resigns.
21 Kurdish nationalists control the Suleimaniya, Arbil, and Dohak provinces of the Autonomous Region of Kurdistan and parts of Tamim province, including its capital, Kirkuk, altogether forming 10% of the Iraqi territory.
22 Saddam Hussein dispatches Ali Hassan Majid to Mosul to reorganize the government troops in the Kurdish region.
23 Saddam Hussein makes seven major changes in the government, promoting Hamadi, a Shia, as the prime minister, and the army chief of staff, Lt.-General Abbas, as the defense minister.
24 Bush says, "We're playing no part in [the Iraqi uprising], but it shows great unrest with the rule of Saddam Hussein."
26 King Fahd has secret talks with U.S. national security adviser Scowcroft in Saudi Arabia.
28 Iraqi troops retake Kirkuk.
30 Kurdish exodus begins.

MARCH 1991

Hour → (columns 0–23), Day ↓ (rows 1–31)

Day	0	1	2	3	4	5	6	7	8	9	10	11	12	13	14	15	16	17	18	19	20	21	22	23
1											JBA													
2								MBU																
3					HRA			RSE																
4							ECH	JTU	MCO									TPY			GPA	MCO		
									MCO										MCO			TSC		
									TSC													JBA		
5						JOL				SAE		HRA		JOL		AMI					LAG	MCO		
																						KGO		
6					ECH	AKA									AMI									HRA
7					SST					MCO		JTU	RHU											
										MCO			SAE											
										/ZCH														
8							DBA																	
9																								
10																								
11																								
12											AMI		PGR	EDI	SAE	GHU	GRA	RGL/		KGR				
															PBE		YSA	SAE						
13				SST			MCO	MCO																
								CHE																
14				HRA														LAG	AEN	LAG/	LAG			
																			JYO	RSE				
15				PDA	JOL			MCO						PXR			AEN	EDM		AEN				AEN
16								PAG			AEN													
17																								
18					SST			RRU									PGR							AMI
19																			RSE					
20										RGL		TWE								AEN				
21											MCO			MCO			MBE		CRA					
														EFO										
22						LLA			JWE	GHU								AEN	MCO			AEN		
					KAM					MCO														
23															JYO		MCO							
																	MCO							
																	SBE							
24							MCO			SEM	LAG													
25													JTU								BZE			
26								MCO												MCO				
																				MCO				
27																								
28																								
29																								
30																								
31																								

Historical Events Related to the Gulf War: April 1991

1   Kurdish leader Masud Barzani appeals to the U.S., Britain, and France to act through the U.N. to save the Kurds from "genocide and torture."

3   U.N. Security Council adopts Resolution 687, 12 votes to 1. A 34-paragraph document, it deals with the details of the cease-fire and war reparations and sets out the main condition for the complete lifting of economic sanctions against Iraq: destruction of its nonconventional weapons.

6   Iraq accepts Resolution 687.

7   Kuwait's emir says that a parliamentary election will be held "next year" according to the constitution.

11   U.N. Security Council president informs the Iraqi ambassador that a cease-fire in the Gulf conflict is now in effect, with a U.N. peacekeeping force of 1,400 soldiers deployed to monitor it.

16   At 8:30 GMT, an undeclared cease-fire between the Iraqi military and Kurdish guerrillas comes into force.

17   Complying with Resolution 687, Iraq provides information to the U.N. Security Council about its chemical, nuclear, and missile programs.

18   An Amnesty International report details instances of scores of murders and widescale torture mainly of the Palestinians and Iraqis since the recapture of Kuwait by the allied forces on February 26.

19   Saddam Hussein deputes two Iraqi generals to meet the U.S. commander in charge of Operation Provide Comfort to set up safe havens for the Kurdish refugees inside Iraq.

21   Robert Gates, the director-designate of the CIA says, "All possible sanctions [against Iraq] will be maintained until Saddam Hussein is gone."

22   In his meeting with the Kuwaiti emir, Baker points out the violations of human rights in Kuwait.

24   Talabani announces tentative agreement with Saddam Hussein's government on Kurdish autonomy, designed to encourage the return of 1.5 million Kurdish refugees.

29   In Riyadh, Prince Khalid says that Saudi history, traditions, and culture weigh against substantial American presence in the Saudi kingdom.

APRIL 1991

Hour → / Day ↓	0	1	2	3	4	5	6	7	8	9	10	11	12	13	14	15	16	17	18	19	20	21	22	23
1													PDA PDA PDA			MCO		LNI			**AEN**			
2						TPY	SST	**MBU**				AMI												
3				JOL																				
4											MBU													
5																			JYO					
6																								
7																								
8												JTU				MCO								
9													GSA											
10			ROE																					
11															JOL TSC JOL			JTU						
12																								
13																								
14																								
15																				MCO	MCO			
16															MCO				AEN					
17																								
18																								
19																								
20																								
21																								
22								MCO				ALI	JOL MCO	RRU					JYO MCO	MCO				
23														MCO		JYO					MBE			
24								DCO								YSA								
25																			MPA					
26																								
27																								
28																								
29															AEN									
30																								

Appendix E
Distribution of Participants by Location, Discipline, and Gender

Name	Location	Discipline	Gender
Pat Benson	San Diego, CA	staff, LCHC	F
Armand Endicott	Argentina	psychology	M
Anne Brice	San Diego, CA	communications	F
Lauren Lane	Worcester, MA	education	F
Matt Connors	Palo Alto, CA	communication & psychology	M
Nora Sanders	Denver, CO	education	F
Martin Taylor	not known	not known	M
Ana Milano	New York, NY	cognitive science	F
Dave Covey	Idaho	physicist	M
Lars Nilsson	San Diego, CA	educational psychology	M
Larry Goldman	Cincinnati, OH	psychology	M
Jim Barrett	New York, NY	education	M
Roger Forrest	San Diego, CA	cognitive science	M
Bob Reasoner	Worcester, MA	education	M
Katherine Grayson	Berkeley, CA	education	F
Jake Olson	Denmark	cognitive science	M
Frank Simpson	Toronto, Canada	education	M
Penny Grolier	New York, NY	psychology	F
Art Lopetsky	not known	not known	M
Michael Schwartz	New York, NY	psychology	M
George Lakoff	Berkeley, CA	linguistics	M
Ethan Morse	Chicago, IL	anthropology	M
Donna Jensen	Nova Scotia, Canada	education	F
Hans Rausch	Hamburg, Germany	psychology	M
Gerald Parsons	Berkeley, CA	education	M
Gene Saltzman	Arizona	communications	M
Steven Schnell	Innsbruck, Austria	education	M
Richard Sessions	Baltimore, MD	psychology	M

Name	Location	Discipline	Gender
Sarah Emerson	Denver, CO	education	F
Sam Trautman	Tel Aviv, Israel	psychology	M
Mark Green	San Diego, CA	psychology/ cognitive science	M
Lisa Moffett	San Diego, CA	communication	F
Martha Bunker	New York, NY	ethology	F
Elena Juarez	San Diego, CA	communications	F
Robert Werman	Jerusalem, Israel	physician/writer	M
Amy Wood	San Diego, CA	applied math	F

Appendix F
Example of a Completed
California Learning Record

Following is a copy of the California Learning Record for Michelle, a sixth-grade student in San Diego. It was published in 1993 as a component of Portfolio Assessment and Chapter 1: The California Learning Record, a project funded by the Compensatory Education Office, California Department of Education. It is printed here by permission of the Center for Language in Learning, El Cajon, California. The California Learning Record was adapted by permission from the Primary Language Record, developed and copyrighted by the Centre for Language in Primary Education, Webber Row Teachers' Centre, Webber Row, London SE1 8QW, in 1988 and distributed in the United States by Heinemann Educational Books, Inc. ISBN 0-435-08516-6. In 1998, the California Learning Record became the Learning Record, to better reflect its extension beyond California.

California Learning Record (for Secondary Schools)

This record form is adapted with permission from the Primary Language Record, developed and copyrighted by the Centre for Language in Primary Education, Webber Row Teachers' Centre, Webber Row, London SE1 8QW, in 1988 and distributed in the U.S. by Heinemann Educational Books, Inc. ISBN 0-435-08516-6

School __Middle School__   School Year __1992-93__   Grade Level __6__

Name __Michelle__   Languages read __English__

Languages understood

Languages spoken __English__   Languages written __English__

Teacher(s) responsible for recording

__Barbara__

PART A To be completed during the first quarter

A1 Record of discussion between student's parent(s) and class teacher (Discussion may have taken place in writing, by phone or in face-to-face conference)   (See CLR Handbook for Teachers, A1).

Michelle has always enjoyed school and in particular language arts. She reads at any opportunity. Mom says that Mr.   enjoys reading and that both parents read to Michelle as a child. There are many magazines and books at home, and Mrs.   often take both daughters to the library. Michelle had the same teacher in 4th and 5th grade. She sparked Michelle's interest in writing and since that time, Michelle has written at home. She writes poems, short stories, mini books and journals. Michelle is very theatrical and enjoys acting and performing.

Date __10/14/92__

A2 Record of language/literacy conference with student   (See CLR Handbook for Teachers, A2).

Michelle says she loves school and that her favorite subject has always been English. She prefers mystery books and she especially likes books by Susan Galforth. Michelle exchanges books with her friend and likes to discuss them. She and her cousin enjoy writing —especially mysteries. They exchange stories, discuss them and revise them. She has many copies of her writing at home.

Date __10/20/92__

PART B To be completed during the second and/or third quarter by the teacher and student, using evidence of student progress collected on the Data Collection Form.

Student as a language user (one or more languages)

Teachers may want to refer to the Bilingual Education Handbook, published by and available from the California Department of Education, ISBN 0-8011-0890-X, in completing each section of the record.

B1 Talking and listening Consider evidence of this student's development and use of spoken language in different contexts, in English and/or other languages: use of oral language in collaborative groups or presentations to communicate experience and ideas, to listen actively to the ideas of others, to apply subject matter content in performing classroom tasks, etc. (See CLR Handbook for Teachers, B1)

During group discussions Michelle speaks in complete, thoughtful sentences. She uses notes or visuals to clarify her points with others in the group. She has been a facilitator in groups and encourages others to contribute ideas by saying, "What do you think? Should we say this?" She smiles often and assists ESL students with their speech. In impromptu situations, Michelle is at ease and has good eye contact. In these cases, she relies upon her teammates to support or add information to her statements. In each group activity which required a verbal report from the group, Michelle was selected as the spokesperson. Her explanations are broken down into simple steps and are easy to follow. When stating opinions, she supports her ideas with facts or examples.

What learning experiences have helped/would help development in this area?

Michelle uses notes and visuals in small group settings. She says she feels nervous when doing large group. More opportunities to do large group would be valuable as well as using visuals or models with bigger groups, also.

B2 Reading Please comment on the student's progress and development as a reader in English and/or other languages: the stage at which the student is operating (Refer to the CLR Reading Scale 2 included in the CLR); the range, quantity and variety of text; the student's pleasure and involvement in reading, individually or with others; the range of strategies used when reading; and the student's ability to reflect critically on what is read. (See CLR Handbook for Teachers B2)

Michelle has strong tastes in reading... her preference is mystery. She has strong skills which enable her to sort out details and make inferences. She is able to grasp the author's intent and humor. She uses punctuation cues to assist her in reading fluently and with expression. Her research skills are strong and enable her to work independently. She is a reflective reader who is willing to try different genre. On the secondary reading scale I would place Michelle at the level of an beginning experienced reader.

(continued)

B3 Writing Please comment on the student's progress and development as a writer in English and/or other languages: the degree of confidence and independence as a learner who writes; the range, quantity and variety of writing; for both personal and academic purposes; the student's pleasure and involvement in writing and thinking, both narrative and non-narrative text, alone and in collaboration with others. (See CLR Teachers Handbook, B3)

What learning experiences have helped/would help development in this area?

To strengthen her skills as an experienced reader I would encourage Michelle to use such research materials as the reader's Guide. She has, I feel, the foundation needed to begin formal footnotes. I encourage her to use them in her reports. I would also recommend that she become more diverse in her reading... perhaps including biographies and historical novels in her reading. Michelle says that writing about herself is difficult. Perhaps if she read more autobiographies, it would become more easy.

B3 Writing

Please comment on the student's progress and development as a writer in English and/or other languages: the degree of confidence and independence as a writer; the range, quantity and variety of writing; the student's pleasure and involvement in writing, both narrative and non-narrative, alone and in collaboration with others. Use the CAP scoring guides, as

Michelle has received a score of 4 on her autobiogrical incident and a 5 on the CAP rubric for her 1st hand biography sketch. She has a strong vocabulary which enables her to express herself clearly. Her conventions allow the reader to read her works without interfering with meaning. Michelle enjoys writing and sharing her work with others! I would encourage her to work with some of equal writing ability or slightly better. This will help michelle to stretch and grow and to try new techniques. I would also encourage her not just to save her work but to revisit them and revise them from time to time. On the writing scale : Being a writer I would identify michelle as an experienced writer.

What learning experiences have helped/would help development in this area? Record outcomes of any discussion with other staff or parent(s).

Since Michelle likes to read and to write, I recommend that she read short stories poems and plays. These are types of writing that would broaden her repertoire.

Signed: Student _Michelle_ _____ Date: _5-19-93_

Signed: Teacher _Barbara_ ___ Date: _5/19/93_

Part C To be completed during the fourth quarter

C1 Comments on the record by the student's parent(s) (See CLR Handbook for Teachers, C1)

This type of grading allows the teacher a more personal evaluation of the student. It also gives the parents specific things they can do to help the child improve their weak areas.

C2 Record of a culminating language/literacy conference with the student (See CLR Handbook for Teachers, C2)

I like this type of grading. It lets me find out what my weak writing and reading skills are; and how I can improve them. It's helpful to find out how to write better essays by learning what you could improve by looking it cross written.

C3 Update on this year's portfolio This section is to ensure that information about student progress as illustrated by by work in the student's portfolio is as up to date as possible. Please comment on changes and development in any aspect of the student's learning since Part B was completed. (See CLR Handbook for Teachers, C3)

Michelle is a confident speaker and courteous listener. She emerges often as a class leader and confidant. She is willing to make changes and risk new things. She LOVES reading. Mother feels guilty about telling her daughter to stop and do other things. Michelle's interest in writing is equally as strong. She has a strong background in the mechanics and conventions of writing which she credits to her 4/5 grade teacher whom she had for 2 yrs. Michelle is a reflective learner who wants to grow and is eager to assist others in their quest for learning.

What learning experiences and teaching have helped/would help development?

I recommend that Michelle have further experiences in public speaking with the use of visuals & note cards. She is willing to read and write in different genres, therefore, I recommend more self-selection opportunities for her. She is ready, I feel, to explore the more formal dynamics of formal reporting — quotes, footnotes. Also, she is ready to explore resources such as computer services & reader's guide.

Signed: Parent(s) _Barbara_   Date: _5-18-93_

Teacher _Barbara_   Date: _5/18/93_

Observations and Samples (California Learning Record)
Secondary English Language Arts

Grade Level: _6_ Name: _Michelle_

1. Talking & Listening: diary of observations

(Refer to taped documentation, if available)

The diary below is for recording examples of your use of talk for learning and for interacting with others in English and/or other languages.

Include different kinds of talk (e.g., planning an event, solving a problem, expressing a point of view or feelings, reporting on the results of an investigation, interpreting a poem...)

Document your experience and confidence in handling social dimensions of talk (e.g., initiating a discussion, listening to another contribution, qualifying former ideas, encouraging others...)

The matrix on the right sets out some possible contexts for observing talk and listening. Observations made in the diary can be plotted on the matrix to record the range of social and curriculum contexts sampled.

LEARNING CONTEXTS	SOCIAL CONTEXTS			
	pair	small group	student with adult	large group
collaborative reading and writing activities	4-1-93	2-16-93 3-10-93 3-17-93		12-7-92
dramatic/visual interpretation		2-4-93		4-14-93
formal presentation		3-18-93		11-4-92
non-literary discussion		10-27-92 10-29-92 4-18-93		
literary discussion		3-17-93		
other:	3-19-93		11-10-92	12-1-92

Dates	Name of observer (you and others)	Observations and their contexts
10-27-92	B.	10/27/92 Planning session with 3 other students to discuss cultural universal (communication) for DIG. Her eyes focus on group members as ea. speaks. Assumes leadership by offering ideas to consider before next meet.
10-29-92	"	10/29/92 Michelle comes to meeting with notes to share with group. She is open to suggestions to revising her list. Gr. members agree to her proposal and add ideas to hers.
11-4-92	"	11-4-92 Michelle presents her groups' ideas to the entire class using the over-head for the first time. Her transparency helps with understanding. She answers questions clearly and has good eye contact with students.
11-10-92	"	11-10-92 Michelle has developed the "Rosetta Stone" for our culture – a diary from the Princess. Class is pleased with her story and has few questions about it. M. answers questions thoroughly.

Adapted with permission from the Primary Language Record (PLR), developed and copyrighted by the Centre for Language in Primary Education, Webber Row Teachers' Centre, Webber Row, London SE1 8QW, in 1988 and distributed in the U.S. by Heinemann Educational Books, Inc. ISBN 0-435-08516-6

2. Reading and Writing: observations (Reading and writing in English and/or other languages)

Date	Name of observer	Reading Record observations of your development as a reader across a range of contexts and kinds of reading. Consider growth in confidence/independence, experience, strategies, knowledge/understanding. (see CLR Handbook for Teachers B2)
12-7-92	B.	12-7-92 1st oral reading of "5 Under Cover" play. Reads with expression + understands stage directions. Reads "musing" + "adamately" 2/16/93 Group reading — Michelle assists others with pronunciation of difficult words, pauses for commas + end marks. Understands quotation marks + alters voice tone for different speakers. 2/4/93 - Rd's theater; michelle fre- adently looks up from script + looks at class. She reads clearly with ex-pression and stands relaxed before the class, she is confident.

(Attach another page for additonal entries.)

Date	Name of observer	Writing Record observations of your development as a writer across a range of contexts and kinds of writing. Consider growth in confidence/independence, experience, strategies, knowledge/understanding. (See CLR Handbook for Teachers B3)
11-3-92	B.	Partner Talk for autobiographical incident; open to partner's suggestions
1-12-92	"	In discussion with teacher Michelle comments, "The more I write, the better I get."
1-4-93	"	Learned that inside address is needed in a business letter. In self evaluation - commented, "I learned that you have to put the business adress on the inside of the letter which I never knew before."
3-26-93	"	Michelle says the partner talks are valuable because talking with another student helps her to clarify her ideas and correct errors. (Attach another page for additonal entries.)

3. Reading Sample 1 2 3 Circle one. (Reading in English and/or other languages)

Attach a photocopied sample of the text used to indicate its complexity unless the text is a familiar one to most teachers at the grade level. (See CLR Handbook for Teachers, B2)

Dates	2-16-93	3/5/93	3/29/93
Title of book/text	Cleopatra of Egypt	Zeely	"I" is for Innocent Sue Grafton
Context for this sample of your reading • Known/unknown text • Pair, small group • Alone • Assigned/self chosen • Literary/efferent stance	• Unknown Text • Alone • Assigned	• Unknown • pair + small group • assigned	• Known - author Read A-H in a series • alone • self selected • mystery
Your impressions about your reading • what did you have to know or understand to read this well? • what did you do if you did not understand? • how did this kind of reading add to your power as a reader?	• I had to know a little bit about Egypt • If I didn't understand, I asked my mom about it. • This book had a lot of big words in it. It also told a lot about Egypt	• This book was dull and confusing in parts • It was difficult to know when Geeder was daydreaming and what was reality. • To understand she went back and reread a few times slowly • Vocabulary was not very challenging. • It made her aware of various writing styles - not one but she's read books	• figuring out why characters act as they do • reread more slowly because • adds to general knowledge of laws + court system + helps her to pay more attention to little details in all books
What this sample selected for your portfolio shows about your development as a reader • how it fits into the range of your previous reading • experiences/support needed to further development (Use Reading Scale 2 to help teacher and student decide on next steps.)	• I usually choose young adult books to do my book reports on because their easier to tell about • I think that knowing about the time period the body takes place in helps me alot	• This type of book is not one she'd chose. Prefers mysteries with more developed plot. Likes the challenge of the figuring out clues rather than someone's thoughts. • Keep a literature log helps to sort out michelle's thoughts about the characters. • Teacher can support also by providing more stream of conciousness type of reading.	• Read mostly mysteries to "kid stuff" • read other types of literature - especially biographies and autobiographies

4. Writing Samples (writing in English and/or other languages)

Attach the writing sample described below. (See CLR Handbook for Teachers, B3)

Dates	11-12-92	3/18/93	3/26/93
Title/topic	Autobiographical Incident	The Empty Pot	
Context for this sample of your writing • how the writing arose, self-assigned or assigned by another • whether you wrote alone or with others • whether the writing was discussed with anyone while you were working on it • kind of writing (e.g., poem, journal writing, essay, story) • complete piece of work or extract	• teacher assigned • alone with read-around with 2 others • discussed with classmates + teacher • essay • complete piece	• assigned by teacher • with others • it was discussed • play • complete	teacher/student- • alone with partner talk • discussed with Laurale • friendly letter • completed
Your own response to the writing • to the content of the writing • to your ability to handle this particular kind of writing • overall impressions	• She selected river rafting because it was fun and memorable. She'll remember it forever. • This was more difficult to write because there were so many different feelings. It's easier to tell about others or make up a story. • Michelle says, "The more she (I) write the better I get."	• I enjoyed working in a group - I enjoyed writing a play • it was easy • it was fun, I enjoyed it	• Interested because she's your favorite author. Things Michelle really wants to know. • Easy because it was informal + something she's done often • Liked better than formal letter because it sounded more like herself — more natural
Development of use of writing conventions	• Punctuates subordinate clauses • uses expressive verbs • capitalize Aunt when part of name	• Understand commas for use of direct address	• understands format • Concludes abruptly. • Thoughtful questions
What this sample selected for your portfolio shows about your development as a writer • how it fits into the range of your previous writing • experience/support needed to further development (Use Writing Scale 2 to help teacher and student to decide on next steps.)	• This style of writing is more challenging. • Michelle has not written many such essays. • Michelle needs to read more autobiographies and biographies as models for writing	• it's the first play I've written • I like to be able to talk to the teacher if I have a question • good understanding of play format	• comfortable because she's done business + friendly last yr. + this year. • "important to work with a partner because they tell you how it sounds + catch mistakes"

Notes

1
Introduction: What Is an Ecology of Composition?

1. For a general introduction to complexity theory and its theorists, see M. Mitchell Waldrop's *Complexity: The Emerging Science at the Edge of Order and Chaos*, and Roger Lewin's *Complexity: Life at the Edge of Chaos*, which also includes interviews with some critics of complexity theory. For a more technical introduction to the theoretical concepts, see *Exploring Complexity: An Introduction*, by Grégoire Nicolis and Ilya Prigogine, and the various proceedings and lectures published in series as the Santa Fe Inst. Studies in the Sciences of Complexity. These volumes, published by Addison Wesley, often focus on research on a particular topic, such as economics, information theory, or linguistics.
2. See, for example, Paul C. Davies, ed., *The New Physics*; Anderson, Arrow, and Pines, eds., *The Economy as an Evolving Complex System*; Stuart Kauffman, *Origins of Order: Self-Organization and Selection in Evolution*; John H. Holland, *Adaptation in Natural and Artificial Systems*.
3. Donald Norman has a great deal to say about these physical interactions with environmental structures in *The Psychology of Everyday Things*.
4. For an idea of what such a disciplinary practice might involve, as well as a fascinating view of the socialization of novice practitioners in archaeology, see Goodwin and Goodwin, "Professional Vision."

2
Thinking with the Things As They Exist: Ecology of a Poem

1. See, for example, Brandt; Bruffee; and LeFevre, among others.
2. At the beginning of *Charles Reznikoff: Man and Poet*, ed. Milton Hindus, is an epigraph from Franz Kafka: "You have always relied only upon yourself and thus built up the strength to be alone."
3. See Lakoff and Johnson's analysis of metaphorical connections: *health and life are up; sickness and death are down.*
4. See Bak and Chen; and see Kauffman, "Antichaos," *Origins*, and "Sciences."
5. Lakoff and Johnson refer to this as the metonymic substitution of *producer for product*, an example of *part-whole* metonymy.
6. See Kauffman, *Origins*; Prigogine and Stengers; and Wolfram.
7. Marie claimed that he never read a modern novel and read few contemporary poets; yet, while he was working in Hollywood, he sent her a letter in which he wrote, "Do not buy Joyce's new book, Finnegan's Wake since I had to buy it.

247

You won't like it anyway; at a glance it looks like short and long-distance pun-ning—verbal music and all the sense in overtones, some of which are very faint: horns of (Ireland) . . . faintly blowing" (Syrkin 50).

8. A great deal of popular culture mirrored this shift from the confrontational politics of the 1960s to an aesthetic of togetherness, peace, and harmony (marked in such songs as "Bridge over Troubled Water," "You've Got a Friend," and "Celebrate") in the 1970s.

3
"Next Time We're Not Giving Steve Our Essay to Read": Ecology of Writers

1. While it is common for scholars and researchers in many fields to publish col-laborative journal articles, books, and monographs, academic institutions con-tinue to insist on individually authored papers from undergraduates. And some departments at most institutions continue to require an individually authored book for scholars' advancement to tenure. This internal contradiction is all the more striking in the face of strong evidence, dating back at least to the 1930s, for the social basis of learning and knowledge construction as well as more recent evidence for the social basis of composing.

2. There are a variety of conventions for representing conversation used by dis-course analysts, indicating pause length, variations in pronunciation and em-phasis, repairs, pitch, and overlaps. To avoid overcomplicating the reader's task, I have kept to the normal conventions of written dialogue, indicating pauses with ellipses, rising inflections with question marks, and interruptions with dashes. Often, a second speaker will take advantage of a pause in the first speaker's conversation to initiate a new turn. These occasions are marked by ellipses at the end of the first speaker's turn.

3. Lucy Suchman refers to face-to-face conversation as "the richest form of human communication," arguing that it "incorporates the broadest range of possible resources for communication, with other forms of interaction being characteriz-able in terms of particular resource limitations or additional constraints" (69).

4
Desert Storm on the Network: Ecology of Readers

1. With the exception of George Lakoff, whose widely distributed essay on meta-phor and war is mentioned in this chapter, all names of participants in the Gulf War conversation on xlchc are pseudonyms.

2. Throughout this chapter, I have preserved the original texts of email messages, although I have abbreviated the headers to save space. The misspellings and

other flaws of punctuation, syntax, and grammar are a feature of this communication medium, where informality and immediacy take priority over correctness. Further, some mail systems severely limit writers' ability to edit online. Typically, they may be able to make corrections in a line only while in that line.

3. However, different groups establish their own levels of "comfort" by convention, with norms ranging from quiet civility to discourse marked by vivid confrontation and extremes of emotion.

5
Conclusion: Implications and Proposals for an Ecology of Composition

1. The opening chapter of Christina Haas's *Writing Technology: Studies on the Materiality of Literacy* also argues for the kind of research I am advocating here.

2. This point is cogently argued by Yin.

3. A good starting place is Odell and Goswami's edited collection, *Writing in Nonacademic Settings*.

4. This prompt was developed in 1991 for use in the California Assessment Program (CAP) Direct Writing Assessment, which is no longer administered.

5. The Learning Record was originally known as the California Learning Record (CLR). It is developed and supported by the Center for Language in Learning, El Cajon, California.

6. Roseann Dueñas González argues that "equity begins with an educational curriculum that promotes the use of students' native language as a medium of instruction and incorporates their home culture, history, and literacy." And, she adds, "To address the issue of equity, standards alone will not be sufficient. The quality of teaching, the physical surroundings in which children learn, the quality of equipment, textbooks, and classroom materials must also be addressed" (14).

7. See the 1993 article by Susan Miserlis, "The Classroom as an Anthropological Dig," which argues for the value of teacher research using the CLR.

8. This quotation is from a conversation reported by Hutchins in a personal communication.

Appendix D
Correlations Between Events
of the Gulf War and XLCHC Messages

1. I am indebted to Dilip Hiro's history, *Desert Shield to Desert Storm: The Second Gulf War,* for the following timetables of events, which have been edited from the original to conserve space.
2. As mentioned in chapter 4, these names are pseudonyms, with two exceptions: George Lakoff and Robert Werman, both of whom published their texts under their own names.

References

Anderson, Philip W., Kenneth J. Arrow, and David Pines, eds. *The Economy as an Evolving Complex System*. Reading: Addison, 1988.

Assessment, N. F. O. *Principles and Indicators for Student Assessment Systems*. Cambridge: FairTest, 1995.

Axelrod, Rise, and Charles Cooper. *The St. Martin's Guide to Writing*. 2nd ed. New York: St. Martin's, 1988.

Axelrod, Robert. *The Evolution of Cooperation*. New York: Basic, 1984.

Badger, E. "The Effect of Expectations on Achieving Equity in State-Wide Testing: Lessons from Massachusetts." *Equity and Excellence in Educational Testing and Assessment*. Ed. Michael T. Nettles and Arie L. Nettles. Boston: Kluwer, 1995. 289–308.

Bak, Per, and Kan Chen. "Self-Organized Criticality." *Scientific American* Jan. 1991: 46–53.

Bakhtin, M. M. *The Dialogic Imagination*. Trans. Caryl Emerson and Michael Holquist. Austin: U of Texas P, 1981.

Ball, A. F. "Incorporating Ethnographic-Based Techniques to Enhance Assessments of Culturally Diverse Students' Written Exposition." *Educational Assessment* 1 (1993): 255–81.

Barker, Thomas T. "Computers and the Instructional Context." *Computers and Writing: Theory, Research, Practice*. Ed. Deborah H. Holdstein and Cynthia L. Selfe. New York: MLA, 1990. 7–17.

Barker, Thomas T., and Fred O. Kemp. "Network Theory: A Postmodern Pedagogy for the Writing Classroom." *Computers and Community: Teaching Composition in the Twenty-first Century*. Ed. Carolyn Handa. Portsmouth: Boynton/ Cook, 1990. 1–27.

Barnes, D., J. Britton, and M. Torbe. *Language, the Learner and the School*. 3rd ed. Harmondsworth, UK: Penguin, 1987.

Barr, Mary A. *California Learning Record: A Handbook for Teachers, Grades 6–12*. Portsmouth: Heinemann, 1999.

———. "Who's Going to Interpret Performance Standards? A Case for Teacher Judgment." *Claremont Reading Conference Yearbook*. Ed. P. H. Dreyer. Claremont: Inst. for Developmental Studies of The Claremont Graduate School, 1995. 22–45.

Barr, Mary, and Jacqueline Cheong. "Achieving Equity: Counting on the Classroom." *Equity and Excellence in Educational Testing and Assessment*. Ed. M. T. Nettles and A. L. Nettles. Boston: Kluwer, 1995. 161–84.

Barr, M[ary]. A., and P. J. Hallam. "Assessing, Teaching and Learning through the California Learning Record." *Writing Portfolios in the Classroom: Policy and Practice, Promise and Peril*. Ed. R. A. Calfee and P. Perfumo. Hillsdale: Erlbaum, 1996. 285–302.

Barrs, M[yra]. "The Primary Language Record: Reflection of Issues in Evaluation." *Language Arts* 67 (1990): 244–53.

———. *Words Not Numbers: Assessment in English*. Exeter: Natl. Assn. of Teachers of English, 1990.

Barrs, M[yra]., S. Ellis, H. Hester, and A. Thomas. *Patterns of Learning: The Primary Language Record and the National Curriculum.* London: Centre for Lang. in Primary Educ., 1988.

Barrs, Myra, Sue Ellis, Hilary Hester, Anne Thomas. *The Primary Language Record: Handbook for Teachers.* Portsmouth: Heinemann, 1989.

Barrs, M[yra], and A. Thomas, eds. *The Reading Book.* London: Centre for Lang. in Primary Educ., 1991.

Bateson, Gregory. *Mind and Nature: A Necessary Unity.* New York: Bantam, 1979.

Bauer, Henry H. *Scientific Literacy and the Myth of the Scientific Method.* Urbana: U of Illinois P, 1992.

Bazerman, Charles. *Constructing Experience.* Carbondale: Southern Illinois UP, 1994.

Beach, King. "Challenges at Work: A Microgenetic Perspective on the Development of Symbolic Representation." Annual Symposium of the Jean Piaget Society. Philadelphia, 1986.

Bennett, Charles H. "Dissipation, Information, Computational Complexity and the Definition of Organization." *Emerging Syntheses in Science: Proceedings of the Founding Workshops of the Santa Fe Institute, Santa Fe, New Mexico.* Ed. David Pines. Redwood City: Addison, 1988. 215–31.

Bereiter, Carl, and Marlene Scardamalia. "Levels of Inquiry in Writing Research." *Research on Writing.* Ed. Peter Mosenthal, Lynne Tamor, and Sean A. Walmsley. New York: Longman, 1983. 3–25.

Berger, Peter, and Thomas Luckman. *The Social Construction of Reality: A Treatise in the Sociology of Knowledge.* New York: Doubleday, 1966.

Berkenkotter, Carol. "Paradigm Debates and Sociocognitive Inquiry." *College Composition and Communication* 42 (1991): 151–69.

Bhaskar, Roy. "Emergence, Explanation, and Emancipation." *Explaining Human Behavior: Consciousness, Human Action and Social Structure.* Ed. Paul F. Secord. Beverly Hills: Sage, 1982. 275–310.

____. *The Possibility of Naturalism.* Brighton, UK: Harvester, 1979.

____. *Reclaiming Reality.* London: Verso, 1989.

____. *Scientific Realism and Human Emancipation.* London: Verso, 1986.

Black, Stephen D., et al. "Real and Non-real Time Interaction: Unraveling Multiple Threads of Discourse." *Discourse Processes* 6 (1983): 59–75.

Boiarsky, Carolyn. "Computers in the Classroom: The Instruction, the Mess, the Noise, the Writing." *Computers and Community: Teaching Composition in the Twenty-first Century.* Ed. Carolyn Handa. Portsmouth: Boynton/Cook, 1990. 47–67.

Bolter, Jay David. *Writing Space: The Computer, Hypertext, and the History of Writing.* Hillsdale: Erlbaum, 1991.

Boster, James S. "The Information Economy Model Applied to Biological Similarity Judgment." *Perspectives on Socially Shared Cognition.* Ed. Lauren B. Resnick, John M. Levine, and Stephanie Teasley. Washington, D.C.: Amer. Psychological Assn., 1991. 203–25.

Boulding, Kenneth E. *Ecodynamics: A New Theory of Societal Evolution.* Beverly Hills: Sage, 1978.

Brandt, Deborah. "The Cognitive as the Social." *Written Communication* 9 (1992): 315–55.

Briggs, Charles. "Questions for the Ethnographer." *Semiotica* 46.2 (1983): 233–61.

Britton J. *Language and Learning.* 2nd ed. Portsmouth: Boynton/Cook, 1992.

Brodwin, Stanley. "Edward Smith King's *Joseph Zalmonah:* The Romance of Immigration." *Immigration and Ethnicity: American Society—"Melting Pot" or*

"Salad Bowl"? Ed. Michael D'Innocenzo and Josef P. Sirefman. Westport: Greenwood, 1992. 121–46.

Bruffee, Kenneth. "Collaborative Writing and the 'Conversation of Mankind.' " *College English* 46 (1984): 635–52.

Bruner, Jerome. *Acts of Meaning.* Cambridge: Harvard UP, 1990.

Calfee, Robert. "Authentic Assessment of Reading and Writing in the Elementary Classroom." *Elementary School Literacy: Critical Issues.* Ed. Mariam Jean Dreher and Wayne H. Slater. Norwood: Gordon, 1992. 211–26.

Calkins, Lucy McCormick. *Lessons from a Child: On the Teaching and Learning of Writing.* Exeter: Heinemann, 1983.

Callon, Michael, John Law, and Arie Rip, eds. *Mapping the Dynamics of Science and Technology: Sociology of Science in the Real World.* London: Macmillan, 1986.

Chafe, Wallace L. "Integration and Involvement in Speaking, Writing, and Oral Literature." *Spoken and Written Language: Exploring Orality and Literacy.* Ed. Deborah Tannen. Norwood: Ablex, 1982. 35–54.

Chandrasekaran, B. "Natural and Social System Metaphors for Distributed Problem Solving: Introduction to the Issue." *IEEE Transactions on Systems, Man, and Cybernetics* SMC-11 (1981): 1–5.

Chase, William G. *Spatial Representations of Taxi Drivers.* Learning Research and Development Center, U of Pittsburgh, 1982.

Chi, Michelene T. H., Robert Glaser, and M. J. Farr. *The Nature of Expertise.* Hillsdale: Erlbaum, 1988.

Chiseri-Strater, Elizabeth. *Academic Literacies: The Public and Private Discourse of University Students.* Portsmouth: Boynton/Cook, 1991.

Cicourel, Aaron V. "The Integration of Distributed Knowledge in Collaborative Medical Diagnosis." *Intellectual Teamwork: Social and Technological Foundations of Cooperative Work.* Ed. Jolene Galegher, Robert E. Kraut, and Carmen Egido. Hillsdale: Erlbaum, 1990. 221–42.

Claggett, F. *A Measure of Success: From Assignment to Assessment in English Language Arts.* Portsmouth: Boynton/Cook, 1996.

Clark, Herbert H., and Susan E. Brennan. "Grounding in Communication." *Perspectives on Socially Shared Cognition.* Ed. Lauren B. Resnick, John M. Levine, and Stephanie Teasley. Washington, D.C.: Amer. Psychological Assn., 1991. 127–49.

Clifford, James. "Introduction: Partial Truths." *Writing Culture.* Ed. James Clifford and George E. Marcus. Berkeley: U of California P, 1986. 1–26.

———. "On Ethnographic Allegory." *Writing Culture.* Ed. James Clifford and George E. Marcus. Berkeley: U of California P, 1986. 98–121.

———. "On Ethnographic Authority." *Representations* 1 (1983): 51–76.

———. *The Predicament of Culture: Twentieth-Century Ethnography, Literature, and Art.* Cambridge: Harvard UP, 1988.

Cohen, Robert S., and Thomas Schnelle, eds. *Cognition and Fact: Materials on Ludwik Fleck.* Dordrecht: Reidel, 1986.

Cole, Michael. "Conclusion." *Perspectives on Socially Shared Cognition.* Ed. Lauren B. Resnick, John M. Levine, and Stephanie Teasley. Washington, D.C.: Amer. Psychological Assn., 1991. 398–417.

Cole, Michael, and Yrjö Engström. *A Cultural-Historical Approach to Distributed Cognition.* Laboratory of Comparative Human Cognition, U of California.

Cole, Michael, et al. *The Cultural Context of Learning and Thinking: An Exploration in Experimental Anthropology.* New York: Basic, 1971.

Collins, Allan, and Dedre Gentner. "How People Construct Mental Models." *Cul-

tural Models in Language and Thought. Ed. Dorothy Holland and Naomi Quinn. Cambridge, UK: Cambridge UP, 1987. 243–68.

Collins, James L. "Computerized Text Analysis and the Teaching of Writing." *Critical Perspectives on Computers and Composition Instruction*. Ed. Gail E. Hawisher and Cynthia L. Selfe. New York: Teachers College P, 1989. 30–43.

Comrie, Bernard. "Before Complexity." *The Evolution of Human Languages: Proceedings of the Workshop on the Evolution of Human Languages, Held August 1989 in Santa Fe, New Mexico*. Ed. John A. Hawkins and Murray Gell-Mann. Santa Fe Inst. Studies in the Sciences of Complexity. Redwood City: Addison, 1992. 194–211.

Cooper, Charles R. *Measuring Growth in Appreciation of Literature*. Newark, DE: Intl. Reading Assn., 1972.

____, ed. *The Nature and Measurement of Competency in English*. Urbana: NCTE, 1981.

Cooper, Charles R., and Lee Odell, eds. *Evaluating Writing: Describing, Measuring, Judging*. Urbana: NCTE, 1977.

Cooper, Charles R., and Alan C. Purves. *A Guide to Evaluation. Responding*. Ginn Inter-related Sequences in Literature: Evaluation Sequence. Lexington, MA: Ginn, 1973.

Cooper, Marilyn M. "The Ecology of Writing." *College English* 48 (1986): 364–75.

Corson, D. J. "Old and New Conceptions of Discovery in Education." *Educational Philosophy and Theory* 22.2 (1990): 1–27.

Corson, David. "Bhaskar's Critical Realism and Educational Knowledge." *British Journal of Sociology of Education* 12 (1991): 223–41.

Crook, Charles. "Electronic Messaging and the Social Organization of Information." *Quarterly Newsletter of the Laboratory of Comparative Human Cognition* 7.3 (1985): 65–69.

Crowley, Sharon. "Reimagining the Writing Scene: Curmudgeonly Remarks about *Contending with Words*." *Contending with Words: Composition and Rhetoric in a Postmodern Age*. Ed. Patricia Harkin and John Schilb. New York: MLA, 1991. 189–97.

Cyganowski, Carol Klimick. "The Computer Classroom and Collaborative Learning: The Impact on Student Writers." *Computers and Community: Teaching Composition in the Twenty-first Century*. Ed. Carolyn Handa. Portsmouth: Boynton/Cook, 1990. 68–88.

Damon, William. "Problems of Direction in Socially Shared Cognition." *Perspectives on Socially Shared Cognition*. Ed. Lauren B. Resnick, John M. Levine, and Stephanie Teasley. Washington, D.C.: Amer. Psychological Assn., 1991. 384–97.

D'Andrade, Roy. "A Folk Model of the Mind." *Cultural Models in Language and Thought*. Ed. Dorothy Holland and Naomi Quinn. Cambridge, UK: Cambridge UP, 1987. 112–50.

D'Andrade, Roy, and Claudia Strauss, eds. *Human Motives and Cultural Models*. Cambridge, UK: Cambridge UP, 1992.

D'Andrade, R[oy] G., and M. Wish. "Speech Act Theory in Quantitative Research on Interpersonal Behavior." *Discourse Processes* 8 (1985): 229–59.

Darling-Hammond, L[inda]. "Equity Issues in Performance-Based Assessment." *Equity and Excellence in Educational Testing and Assessment*. Ed. M. T. Nettles and A. L. Nettles. Boston: Kluwer, 1995. 89–114.

____. "Policy for Restructuring." *The Work of Restructuring Schools*. Ed. A. Lieberman. New York: Teachers College P, 1995.

Davidson, Michael. "Palimtexts: Postmodern Poetry and the Material Text." *Genre* 20.3–4 (1987): 307–27.

Davies, Paul C., ed. *The New Physics.* New York: Cambridge UP, 1989.

de Certeau, Michel. *The Practice of Everyday Life.* Berkeley: U of California P, 1984.

Delany, Paul, and George P. Landow, eds. *Hypermedia and Literary Studies.* Cambridge: MIT P, 1991.

DeLawter, Jayne, and Carol Hendsch. "California Learning Record: Observations and Samples of Learning." *Whole Language Catalog: Supplement on Authentic Assessment.* Ed. Kenneth S. Goodman, Lois Bridges Bird, and Yetta M. Goodman. Santa Rosa: American School, 1992.

Dembo, L. S. "Charles Reznikoff: A Talk with L. S. Dembo." *Charles Reznikoff: Man and Poet.* Ed. Milton Hindus. Man and Poet Ser. Orono: Natl. Poetry Foundation, 1984. 97–108.

Dennett, Daniel C. *Consciousness Explained.* Boston: Little, 1991.

Dobrin, David N. "A Limitation on the Use of Computers in Composition." *Computers and Writing: Theory, Research, Practice.* Ed. Deborah H. Holdstein and Cynthia L. Selfe. New York: MLA, 1990. 40–57.

Doheny-Farina, Stephen, and Lee Odell. "Ethnographic Research on Writing: Assumptions and Methodology." *Writing in Nonacademic Settings.* Ed. Lee Odell and Dixie Goswami. New York: Guilford, 1986. 503–36.

Dorinson, Joseph. "The Educational Alliance: An Institutional Study in Americanization and Acculturation." *Immigration and Ethnicity: American Society— "Melting Pot" or "Salad Bowl"?* Ed. Michael D'Innocenzo and Josef P. Sirefman. Westport: Greenwood, 1992. 93–108.

Douglas, Mary. *How Institutions Think.* Syracuse: Syracuse UP, 1986.

Dunlop, Charles, and Rob Kling, eds. *Computerization and Controversy.* Boston: Academic, 1991.

Eccles, J. S., and C. Midgly. "Stage-Environment Fit: Developmentally Appropriate Classrooms for Young Adolescents." *Research on Motivation in Education.* Ed. C. Ames and R. Ames. New York: Academy, 1989. 139–85.

Edelman, Gerald M. *Bright Air, Brilliant Fire: On the Matter of the Mind.* New York: Basic, 1992.

Eldred, Janet M. "Computers, Composition Pedagogy, and the Social View." *Critical Perspectives on Computers and Composition Instruction.* Ed. Gail E. Hawisher and Cynthia L. Selfe. New York: Teachers College P, 1989. 201–18.

Emig, Janet. *The Composing Processes of Twelfth Graders.* Urbana: NCTE, 1971.

Falk, Beverly, and Linda Darling-Hammond. *The Primary Language Record at P.S. 261: How Assessment Transforms Teaching and Learning.* NCREST, 1993.

Falk, B[everly], S. MacMurdy, and L[inda] Darling-Hammond. *Taking a Different Look: How the Primary Language Record Supports Teaching for Diverse Learners.* New York: Natl. Center for Restructuring Educ., Schools and Teaching, 1995.

Feltovich, Paul J., Rand J. Spiro, and Richard Coulson. "Learning, Teaching, and Testing for Complex Conceptual Understanding." *Test Theory for a New Generation of Tests.* Ed. Norman Frederiksen, Robert J. Mislevy, and Isaac I. Bejar. Hillsdale: Erlbaum, 1993. 181–217.

Ferrara, Kathleen, Hans Brunner, and Greg Whitemore. "Interactive Written Discourse as an Emergent Register." *Written Communication* 8 (1991): 8–34.

Fiske, Donald W., and Richard A. Schweder, eds. *Metatheory in Social Science: Pluralisms and Subjectivities.* Chicago: U of Chicago P, 1986.

Fleck, Ludwik. *Genesis and Development of a Scientific Fact.* Trans. Fred Bradley and Thaddeus J. Trenn. Chicago: U of Chicago P, 1979.

____. "On the Crisis of 'Reality.'" 1929. *Cognition and Fact: Materials on Ludwik Fleck*. Ed. Robert S. Cohen and Thomas Schnelle. Dordrecht: Reidel, 1986. 39–46.

____. "The Problem of Epistemology." 1936. *Cognition and Fact: Materials on Ludwik Fleck*. Ed. Robert S. Cohen and Thomas Schnelle. Dordrecht: Reidel, 1986. 59–78.

____. "Problems of the Science of Science." 1946. *Cognition and Fact: Materials on Ludwik Fleck*. Ed. Robert S. Cohen and Thomas Schnelle. Dordrecht: Reidel, 1986. 79–112.

____. "Scientific Observation and Perception in General." 1935. *Cognition and Fact: Materials on Ludwik Fleck*. Ed. Robert S. Cohen and Thomas Schnelle. Dordrecht: Reidel, 1986. 47–58.

____. "Some Specific Features of the Medical Way of Thinking." 1927. *Cognition and Fact: Materials on Ludwik Fleck*. Ed. Robert S. Cohen and Thomas Schnelle. Dordrecht: Reidel, 1986. 39–46.

____. "To Look, to See, to Know." 1947. *Cognition and Fact: Materials on Ludwik Fleck*. Ed. Robert S. Cohen and Thomas Schnelle. Dordrecht: Reidel, 1986. 113–28.

Flower, Linda. *The Construction of Negotiated Meaning: A Social Cognitive Theory of Writing*. Carbondale: Southern Illinois UP, 1994.

____. *Problem-solving Strategies for Writing*. 2nd ed. New York: Harcourt, 1985.

Flower, Linda, and John Hayes. "A Cognitive Process Theory of Writing." *College Composition and Communication* 32 (1981): 365–87.

____. "Images, Plans, and Prose: The Representation of Meaning in Writing." *Written Communication* 1 (1984): 120–60.

Forman, Janis. "Computing and Collaborative Writing." *Evolving Perspectives on Computers and Composition Studies: Questions for the 1990s*. Ed. Gail E. Hawisher and Cynthia L. Selfe. Urbana: NCTE, 1991. 65–83.

Fortune, Ron. "Visual and Verbal Thinking: Drawing and Word-Processing Software in Writing Instruction." *Critical Perspectives on Computers and Composition Instruction*. Ed. Gail E. Hawisher and Cynthia L. Selfe. New York: Teachers College P, 1989. 145–61.

Freedman, S. W. "Linking Large-Scale Testing and Classroom Portfolio Assessments of Student Writing." *Educational Assessment* 1 (1993): 27–52.

Gadamer, Hans-Georg. *Truth and Method*. Trans. Joel Weinsheimer and Donald Marshall. Rev. ed. New York: Crossroad, 1991.

Galegher, Jolene, Robert E. Kraut, and Carmen Egido, eds. *Intellectual Teamwork: Social and Technological Foundations of Cooperative Work*. Hillsdale: Erlbaum, 1990.

Gardner, Howard. *The Mind's New Science: A History of the Cognitive Revolution*. New York: Basic, 1985.

Geertz, Clifford. "Blurred Genres: The Refiguration of Social Thought." *Critical Theory since 1965*. Ed. Hazard Adams and Leroy Searle. Tallahassee: Florida State UP, 1986. 514–23.

Gell-Mann, Murray. "Complexity and Complex Adaptive Systems." *The Evolution of Human Languages: Proceedings of the Workshop on the Evolution of Human Languages, Held August 1989 in Santa Fe, New Mexico*. Ed. John A. Hawkins and Murray Gell-Mann. Santa Fe Inst. Studies in the Sciences of Complexity. Redwood City: Addison, 1992. 3–18.

Gere, Anne Ruggles. *Writing Groups: History, Theory, and Implications*. Studies in Writing and Rhetoric. Carbondale: Southern Illinois UP, 1987.

Gerrard, Lisa. "Computers and Basic Writers: A Critical View." *Critical Perspectives on Computers and Composition Instruction.* Ed. Gail E. Hawisher and Cynthia L. Selfe. New York: Teachers College P, 1989. 94–108.

Ginzburg, Carlo. "Morelli, Freud and Sherlock Holmes: Clues and Scientific Method." *History Workshop* 9 (1980): 5–36.

Gleick, James. *Chaos: Making a New Science.* New York: Penguin, 1987.

Gomez, Mary Louise. "The Equitable Teaching of Composition with Computers: A Case for Change." *Evolving Perspectives on Computers and Composition Studies: Questions for the 1990s.* Ed. Gail E. Hawisher and Cynthia L. Selfe. Urbana: NCTE, 1991. 318–35.

González, Roseann Dueñas. *National Standards and Culturally/Linguistically Diverse Students: A Question of Equity.* Urbana: NCTE, 1993.

Goodman, J. "Change Without Difference." *Harvard Educational Review* 65 (1995): 1–29.

Goodman, Nelson. *Ways of Worldmaking.* Indianapolis: Hackett, 1978.

Goodwin, Charles, and Marjorie Harness Goodwin. "Professional Vision." *American Anthropologist* 96 (1994): 606–33.

Goody, Jack R. "Alternative Paths to Knowledge in Oral and Literate Cultures." *Spoken and Written Language: Exploring Orality and Literacy.* Ed. Deborah Tannen. Norwood: Ablex, 1982. 201–16.

Graves, Donald H. "What Children Show Us about Writing." *Language Arts* 56 (1979): 312–19.

———. *Writing: Teachers and Children at Work.* Portsmouth: Heinemann, 1983.

Haas, Christina. "'Seeing It on the Screen Isn't Really Seeing It': Computer Writers' Reading Problems." *Critical Perspectives on Computers and Composition Instruction.* Ed. Gail E. Hawisher and Cynthia L. Selfe. New York: Teachers College P, 1989. 16–29.

———. *Writing Technology: Studies on the Materiality of Literacy.* Hillsdale: Erlbaum, 1996.

Hall, Edward T. *The Dance of Life: The Other Dimension of Time.* New York: Anchor, 1983.

Hall, S. "The Four Stages of National Research and Education Network Growth." *Educom Review* 26 (1991): 18–25.

Halliday, M. A. K. *Spoken and Written Language.* Oxford: Oxford UP, 1989.

Hamill, James F. *Ethno-Logic: The Anthropology of Human Reasoning.* Urbana: U of Illinois P, 1990.

Handa, Carolyn, ed. *Computers and Community: Teaching Composition in the Twenty-first Century.* Portsmouth: Boynton/Cook, 1990.

———. "Politics, Ideology, and the Strange, Slow Death of the Isolated Composer, or Why We Need Community in the Writing Classroom." *Computers and Community: Teaching Composition in the Twenty-first Century.* Ed. Carolyn Handa. Portsmouth: Boynton/Cook, 1990. 160–84.

Hargreaves, A. "Transforming Knowledge: Blurring the Boundaries between Research, Policy, and Practice." *Educational Evaluation and Policy Analysis* 18 (1996): 105–22.

Harkin, Patricia, and John Schilb, eds. *Contending with Words: Composition and Rhetoric in a Postmodern Age.* New York: MLA, 1991.

Harlen, W[ynne]. "Concepts of Quality in Student Assessment." Amer. Educ. Research Assn. New Orleans, 1994.

———, ed. *Enhancing Quality in Assessment.* London: Chapman, 1994.

Harré, Rom. *Varieties of Realism: A Rationale for the Natural Sciences.* Oxford: Blackwell, 1986.

Hartman, Karen, et al. "Patterns of Social Interaction and Learning to Write: Some Effects of Network Technologies." *Written Communication* 8 (1991): 79–113.

Hastie, Reid, and Nancy Pennington. "Cognitive and Social Processes in Decision Making." *Perspectives on Socially Shared Cognition.* Ed. Lauren B. Resnick, John M. Levine, and Stephanie Teasley. Washington, D.C.: Amer. Psychological Assn., 1991. 308–27.

Hatano, Giyoo, and Kayoko Inagaki. "Sharing Cognition through Collective Comprehension Activity." *Perspectives on Socially Shared Cognition.* Ed. Lauren B. Resnick, John M. Levine, and Stephanie Teasley. Washington, D.C.: Amer. Psychological Assn., 1991. 331–48.

Hawisher, Gail E. "Reading and Writing Connections: Composition Pedagogy and Word Processing." *Computers and Writing: Theory, Research, Practice.* Ed. Deborah H. Holdstein and Cynthia L. Selfe. New York: MLA, 1990. 71–83.

____. "Research and Recommendations for Computers and Composition." *Critical Perspectives on Computers and Composition Instruction.* Ed. Gail E. Hawisher and Cynthia L. Selfe. New York: Teachers College P, 1989. 44–74.

Hawisher, Gail E., and Paul LeBlanc, eds. *Re-imagining Computers and Composition: Teaching and Research in the Virtual Age.* Portsmouth: Boynton/Cook, 1992.

Hawisher, Gail E., and Cynthia L. Selfe, eds. *Critical Perspectives on Computers and Composition Instruction.* New York: Teachers College P, 1989.

____, eds. *Evolving Perspectives on Computers and Composition Studies: Questions for the 1990s.* Urbana: NCTE, 1991.

Hawkins, John A., and Murray Gell-Mann, eds. *The Evolution of Human Languages.* Redwood City: Addison, 1992.

Hayes, John, and Linda Flower. "Identifying the Organization of Writing Processes." *Cognitive Processes in Writing.* Ed. Lee Gregg and Erwin Steinberg. Hillsdale: Erlbaum, 1980. 3–30.

Heath, Shirley Brice. "Protean Shapes in Literacy Events: Ever-shifting Oral and Literate Traditions." *Spoken and Written Language: Exploring Orality and Literacy.* Ed. Deborah Tannen. Norwood: Ablex, 1982. 91–118.

____. *Ways with Words: Language, Life, and Work in Communities and Classrooms.* London: Cambridge UP, 1983.

Hejinian, Lyn. *My Life.* Los Angeles: Sun and Moon, 1987.

Helprin, Mark. *Ellis Island and Other Stories.* New York: Delacorte, 1981.

Hendriks-Jansen, Horst. *Catching Ourselves in the Act: Situated Activity, Interactive Emergence, Evolution, and Human Thought.* Cambridge: MIT P, 1996.

Herrmann, Andrea W. "Computers and Writing Research: Shifting Our 'Governing Gaze.' " *Computers and Writing: Theory, Research, Practice.* Ed. Deborah H. Holdstein and Cynthia L. Selfe. New York: MLA, 1990. 124–34.

____. "Evaluating Computer-Supported Writing." *Evolving Perspectives on Computers and Composition Studies: Questions for the 1990s.* Ed. Gail E. Hawisher and Cynthia L. Selfe. Urbana: NCTE, 1991. 150–72.

Hildyard, Angela, and David R. Olson. "On the Comprehension and Memory of Oral vs. Written Discourse." *Spoken and Written Language: Exploring Orality and Literacy.* Ed. Deborah Tannen. Norwood: Ablex, 1982. 19–34.

Hillis, W. Daniel. "Intelligence as Emergent Behavior; or, the Songs of Eden." *Daedalus* 117.1 (1988): 175–89.

Hiltz, S. R. *Online Scientific Communities: A Case Study of the Office of the Future.* Norwood: Ablex, 1984.

Hiltz, S. R., and M. Turoff. *The Network Nation: Human Communication via Computer.* Reading: Addison, 1978.

Hindus, Milton. "Introduction." *Charles Reznikoff: Man and Poet*. Ed. Milton Hindus. Man and Poet Ser. Orono: Natl. Poetry Foundation, 1984. 15–36.

Hiro, Dilip. *Desert Shield to Desert Storm: The Second Gulf War*. New York: Routledge, 1992.

Hofstadter, Douglas. *Godel, Escher, Bach, an Eternal Golden Braid*. New York: Basic, 1979.

Holdstein, Deborah H. "A Theory of One's Own? An Introduction to Theoretical and Critical Contexts for Composition and Computers." *Computers and Writing: Theory, Research, Practice*. Ed. Deborah H. Holdstein and Cynthia L. Selfe. New York: MLA, 1990. 31–39.

———. "Training College Teachers for Computers and Writing." *Critical Perspectives on Computers and Composition Instruction*. Ed. Gail E. Hawisher and Cynthia L. Selfe. New York: Teachers College P, 1989. 126–44.

Holdstein, Deborah H., and Cynthia L. Selfe, eds. *Computers and Writing: Theory, Research, Practice*. New York: MLA, 1990.

Holland, Dorothy, and Naomi Quinn, eds. *Cultural Models in Language and Thought*. Cambridge, UK: Cambridge UP, 1987.

Holland, John H. *Adaptation in Natural and Artificial Systems: An Introductory Analysis with Applications to Biology, Control, and Artificial Intelligence*. Ann Arbor: U of Michigan P, 1975.

———. "Complex Adaptive Systems." *Daedalus* 121.1 (1992): 17–30.

Howard, Tharon. "The Rhetoric of Electronic Communities." Diss. Purdue U, 1992.

———. "WANS, Connectivity, and Computer Literacy." *Computers and Composition* 9.3 (1992): 41–58.

Hutchins, Edwin. *Cognition in the Wild*. Cambridge: MIT P, 1995.

———. "Metaphors for Interface Design." *The Structure of Multimodal Dialogue*. Ed. M. M. Taylor, F. Néel, and D. G. Bouwhuis. North-Holland: Elsevier, 1989. 11–28.

———. "Myth and Experience in the Trobriand Islands." *Cultural Models in Language and Thought*. Ed. Dorothy Holland and Naomi Quinn. Cambridge, UK: Cambridge UP, 1987. 269–89.

———. "The Social Organization of Distributed Cognition." *Perspectives on Socially Shared Cognition*. Ed. Lauren B. Resnick, John M. Levine, and Stephanie Teasley. Washington, D.C.: Amer. Psychological Assn., 1991. 283–307.

Hutchins, Edwin, and Brian Hazlehurst. "Learning in the Cultural Process." *Artificial Life II*. Ed. C. G. Langton et al. Santa Fe Inst. Studies in the Sciences of Complexity. Redwood City: Addison, 1991. 689–706.

Hutchins, Edwin L., and James A. Levin. *Point of View in Problem Solving*. San Diego: Center for Human Information Processing, U of California, 1981.

IRA/NCTE. *Standards for the Assessment of Reading and Writing*. Urbana: Intl. Reading Assn, Joint Task Force on Assessment, 1995.

Johnson, Mark. *The Body in the Mind: The Bodily Basis of Meaning, Imagination, and Reason*. Chicago: U of Chicago P, 1987.

Johnston, P. H. *Constructive Evaluation of Literate Activity*. New York: Longman, 1992.

Kaplan, Nancy. "Ideology, Technology, and the Future of Writing Instruction." *Evolving Perspectives on Computers and Composition Studies: Questions for the 1990s*. Ed. Gail E. Hawisher and Cynthia L. Selfe. Urbana: NCTE, 1991. 11–42.

Kauffman, Stuart. "Antichaos and Adaptation." *Scientific American* Feb. 1991: 78–84.

____. *The Origins of Order: Self-Organization and Selection in Evolution.* New York: Oxford UP, 1993.

____. "The Sciences of Complexity and 'Origins of Order.' " *Creativity: The Reality Club.* Ed. John Brockman. New York: Simon, 1993. 75–107.

Kay, Paul. "Linguistic Competence and Folk Theories of Language: Two English Hedges." *Cultural Models in Language and Thought.* Ed. Dorothy Holland and Naomi Quinn. Cambridge, UK: Cambridge UP, 1987. 67–77.

Keesing, Roger M. "Models, 'Folk' and 'Cultural': Paradigms Regained?" *Cultural Models in Language and Thought.* Ed. Dorothy Holland and Naomi Quinn. Cambridge, UK: Cambridge UP, 1987. 369–94.

Kiefer, Kathleen. "Computers and Teacher Education in the 1990s and Beyond." *Evolving Perspectives on Computers and Composition Studies: Questions for the 1990s.* Ed. Gail E. Hawisher and Cynthia L. Selfe. Urbana: NCTE, 1991. 117–31.

Kiesler, Sara, Jane Siegel, and Timothy W. McGuire. "Social Psychological Aspects of Computer-Mediated Communication." *American Psychologist* 39 (1984): 1123–34.

Kiesler, Sara, and Lee Sproull. *Computing and Change on Campus.* Cambridge, UK: Cambridge UP, 1987.

Kitcher, Philip. *The Advancement of Science: Science without Legend, Objectivity without Illusions.* New York: Oxford UP, 1993.

Klem, Elizabeth, and Charles Moran. "Computers and Instructional Strategies in the Teaching of Writing." *Evolving Perspectives on Computers and Composition Studies: Questions for the 1990s.* Ed. Gail E. Hawisher and Cynthia L. Selfe. Urbana: NCTE, 1991. 132–49.

Kohn, Alfie. *Punished by Rewards: The Trouble with Gold Stars, Incentive Plans, A's, Praise, and Other Bribes.* Boston: Houghton, 1993.

Krauss, Robert M., and Susan R. Fussell. "Constructing Shared Communicative Environments." *Perspectives on Socially Shared Cognition.* Ed. Lauren B. Resnick, John M. Levine, and Stephanie Teasley. Washington, D.C.: Amer. Psychological Assn., 1991. 172–200.

Kuhn, Thomas S. *The Structure of Scientific Revolutions.* 2nd ed. Chicago: U of Chicago P, 1970.

Lakoff, George. *Women, Fire, and Dangerous Things: What Categories Reveal about the Mind.* Chicago: U of Chicago P, 1987.

Lakoff, George, and Mark Johnson. *Metaphors We Live By.* Chicago: U of Chicago P, 1980.

Lakoff, George, and Mark Turner. *More Than Cool Reason: A Field Guide to Poetic Metaphor.* Chicago: U of Chicago P, 1989.

Lakoff, Robin Tolmach. "Some of My Favorite Writers Are Literate: The Mingling of Oral and Literate Strategies in Written Communication." *Spoken and Written Language: Exploring Orality and Literacy.* Ed. Deborah Tannen. Norwood: Ablex, 1982. 239–60.

Landow, George P. *Hypertext: The Convergence of Contemporary Critical Theory and Technology.* Baltimore: Johns Hopkins UP, 1992.

Langston, M. Diane. *Searching for Unity in Composition Pedagogy: Persona in Electronic Discourse.* New York: New York Inst. of Technology, 1991.

Langston, M. Diane, and Trent W. Batson. "The Social Shifts Invited by Working Collaboratively on Computer Networks: The ENFI Project." *Computers and Community: Teaching Composition in the Twenty-first Century.* Ed. Carolyn Handa. Portsmouth: Boynton/Cook, 1990. 140–59.

Latour, Bruno. *Science in Action.* Cambridge: Harvard UP, 1987.

____. "Visualization and Cognition: Thinking with the Eyes and Hands." *Knowledge and Society: Studies in the Sociology of Culture Past and Present* 6 (1986): 1–40.

Lave, Jean. "Situating Learning in Communities of Practice." *Perspectives on Socially Shared Cognition.* Ed. Lauren B. Resnick, John M. Levine, and Stephanie Teasley. Washington, D.C.: Amer. Psychological Assn., 1991. 63–82.

Lave, Jean, Michael Murtaugh, and Olivia de la Rocha. "The Dialectic of Arithmetic in Grocery Shopping." *Everyday Cognition: Its Development in Social Context.* Ed. Barbara Rogoff and Jean Lave. Cambridge: Harvard UP, 1984. 67–94.

Lave, Jean, and Etienne Wenger. *Situated Learning: Legitimate Peripheral Participation.* Ed. Roy Pea and John Seely Brown. Cambridge, UK: Cambridge UP, 1991.

LCHC Staff. "XLCHC—Some Stories about Its Origins, Conventions, and Operation." UCSD, *XLCHC,* 1991.

LeFevre, Karen Burke. *Invention as a Social Act.* Studies in Writing and Rhetoric. Carbondale: Southern Illinois UP, 1987.

Levine, John M., and Richard L. Moreland. "Culture and Socialization in Work Groups." *Perspectives on Socially Shared Cognition.* Ed. Lauren B. Resnick, John M. Levine, and Stephanie Teasley. Washington, D.C.: Amer. Psychological Assn., 1991. 257–79.

Lewin, Roger. *Complexity: Life at the Edge of Chaos.* New York: Macmillan, 1992.

Libo, Kenneth. "A People in Print: Jews and Journalism in America." *Immigration and Ethnicity: American Society—"Melting Pot" or "Salad Bowl"?* Ed. Michael D'Innocenzo and Josef P. Sirefman. Westport: Greenwood, 1992. 109–20.

Lieberman, Philip. "On the Evolution of Human Language." *The Evolution of Human Languages: Proceedings of the Workshop on the Evolution of Human Languages, Held August 1989 in Santa Fe, New Mexico.* Ed. John A. Hawkins and Murray Gell-Mann. Santa Fe Inst. Studies in the Sciences of Complexity. Redwood City: Addison, 1992. 21–47.

Louis, K. S. "Beyond Managed Change: Rethinking How Schools Improve." *School Effectiveness and School Improvement* 5.1 (1994): 2–24.

Lunsford, Andrea, and Lisa Ede. *Singular Texts/Plural Authors: Perspectives on Collaborative Writing.* Carbondale: Southern Illinois UP, 1990.

MacDonald, Susan Peck. *Professional Academic Writing in the Humanities and Social Sciences.* Carbondale: Southern Illinois UP, 1994.

Marcus, George E. "Contemporary Problems of Ethnography in the Modern World System." *Writing Culture.* Ed. James Clifford and George E. Marcus. Berkeley: U of California P, 1986. 165–93.

Marcus, George E., and Michael M. J. Fischer. "Two Contemporary Techniques of Cultural Critique in Anthropology." *Anthropology as Cultural Critique: An Experimental Moment in the Human Sciences.* Ed. George E. Marcus and Michael M. J. Fischer. Chicago: U of Chicago P, 1986. 137–64.

Mason, Robin, and Anthony Kaye, eds. *Mindweave.* New York: Pergamon, 1989.

Maturana, Humberto, and Francisco Varela. *Autopoiesis and Cognition: The Realization of the Living.* Dordrecht: Reidel, 1980.

____. *The Tree of Knowledge: The Biological Roots of Human Understanding.* Boston: Shambhala, 1992.

McDaid, John. "Toward an Ecology of Hypermedia." *Evolving Perspectives on Computers and Composition Studies: Questions for the 1990s.* Ed. Gail E. Hawisher and Cynthia L. Selfe. Urbana: NCTE, 1991. 203–23.

McDonald, Joseph P. "Three Pictures of an Exhibition: Warm, Cool, and Hard." *Phi Delta Kappan* Feb. 1993: 480–85.

Merton, Robert K. *On the Shoulders of Giants: A Shandean Postscript.* New York: Free, 1965.

Middleton, David, and Derek Edwards. *Collective Remembering*. London: Sage, 1990.

Miller, Carolyn R. "Rhetoric and Community: The Problem of the One and the Many." *Defining the New Rhetorics*. Ed. Theresa Enos and Stuart Brown. Newbury Park: Sage, 1992. 79–94.

Minsky, Marvin. *The Society of Mind*. New York: Simon, 1985.

Miserlis, Susan. "The Classroom as an Anthropological Dig: Using the California Learning Record (CLR) as a Framework for Assessment and Instruction." *Claremont Reading Conference Yearbook*. Ed. P. H. Dreyer. Claremont: Inst. for Developmental Studies of The Claremont Graduate School, 1993. 103–18.

Mislevy, R. "What Can We Learn from International Assessment?" *Educational Evaluation and Policy Analysis* 17 (1995): 419–37.

Moss, P. A. "Can There Be Validity without Reliability?" *Educational Researcher* 23.2 (1994): 5–12.

____. "Enlarging the Dialogue in Educational Measurement: Voices from Interpretive Research Traditions." *Educational Researcher* 25.1 (1996): 20–28, 43.

Moulthrop, Stuart. "The Politics of Hypertext." *Evolving Perspectives on Computers and Composition Studies: Questions for the 1990s*. Ed. Gail E. Hawisher and Cynthia L. Selfe. Urbana: NCTE, 1991. 253–74.

Murray, Denise E. "The Composing Process for Computer Conversation." *Written Communication* 8 (1991): 35–55.

____. *Conversation for Action: The Computer Terminal as Medium of Communication*. Pragmatics and Beyond, New Series. 180. Amsterdam: Benjamins, 1991.

Neill, M. "Using Language Records (PLR/CLR) as Large-Scale Assessments." *FairTest Examiner* (Summer 1995): 8–9.

Neill, M., P. Bursh, B. Schaeffer, C. Thall, M. Yohe, and P. Zappardino. *Implementing Performance Assessments: A Guide to Classroom, School and System Reform*. Cambridge: FairTest, 1995.

Nelson, John S., Allan Megill, and Donald N. McCloskey, eds. *The Rhetoric of the Human Sciences: Language and Argument in Scholarship and Human Affairs*. Madison: U of Wisconsin P, 1987.

Nicolis, Grégoire, and Ilya Prigogine. *Exploring Complexity: An Introduction*. New York: Freeman, 1989.

Norman, Donald. *The Psychology of Everyday Things*. New York: Basic, 1988.

Norris, Christopher. "Consensus 'Reality' and Manufactured Truth: Baudrillard and the War That Never Happened." *Southern Humanities Review* 16 (1992): 43–66.

North, Stephen M. *The Making of Knowledge in Composition: Portrait of an Emerging Field*. Upper Montclair: Boynton/Cook, 1987.

Odell, Lee, and Dixie Goswami, eds. *Writing in Nonacademic Settings*. New York: Guilford, 1986.

Olson, David R. *Nature and Origins of Competence in the Everyday World*. Cambridge, UK: Cambridge UP, 1986.

Ong, Walter J. *Orality and Literacy: The Technologizing of the Word*. Ed. Terence Hawkes. London: Methuen, 1982.

Oppen, Mary. "Walking with Charles Reznikoff." *Charles Reznikoff: Man and Poet*. Ed. Milton Hindus. Man and Poet Ser. Orono: Natl. Poetry Foundation, 1984. 79–84.

Ornatowski, Cesar. "Between Efficiency and Politics: Technical Communication and Rhetoric in an Aerospace Firm." U of California at San Diego. *Dissertation Abstracts International*, 1993.

Oyama, Susan. *The Ontogeny of Information: Developmental Systems and Evolution*. Cambridge, UK: Cambridge UP, 1985.

Papert, Seymour. *The Children's Machine: Rethinking School in the Age of the Computer.* New York: Basic, 1993.

Paredes, Americo. "On Ethnographic Work among Minority Groups: A Folklorist's Perspective." *New Directions in Chicano Scholarship.* Ed. Ricardo Romo and Raymond Paredes. Chicano Studies Monograph Ser. La Jolla: U of California at San Diego, 1978. 1–32.

Parkes, Don, and Nigel Thrift. *Times, Spaces, and Places: A Chronogeographic Perspective.* Chichester, UK: Wiley, 1980.

Patomäki, Heikki. "Concepts of 'Action,' 'Structure' and 'Power' in 'Critical Social Realism': A Positive and Reconstructive Critique." *Journal for the Theory of Social Behavior* 12.2 (1991): 220–47.

Paulson, William R. *The Noise of Culture: Literary Texts in a World of Information.* Ithaca: Cornell UP, 1988.

Perl, Sondra. "The Composing Processes of Unskilled College Writers." *Research in the Teaching of English* 13 (1978): 317–36.

Phelps, Louise Wetherbee. *Composition as a Human Science: Contributions to the Self-Understanding of a Discipline.* New York: Oxford UP, 1988.

Pieper, Martha Heineman. "The Heuristic Paradigm: A Unifying and Comprehensive Approach to Social Work Research." *Smith College Studies in Social Work* 60.1 (1989): 8–34.

Polanyi, Livia. "Conversational Storytelling." *Handbook of Discourse Analysis.* Ed. Teun A. van Dijk. Vol. 3. London: Academic, 1985. 183–201.

Polanyi, Michael. "The Republic of Science: Its Political and Economic Theory." *Minerva* 1 (1962): 54–73.

Poovey, Mary. "Cultural Criticism: Past and Present." *College English* 52 (1990): 615–25.

Poster, Mark. *The Mode of Information: Poststructuralism and Social Context.* Cambridge, UK: Polity, 1990.

Pratt, Mary Louise. "Fieldwork in Common Places." *Writing Culture.* Ed. James Clifford and George E. Marcus. Berkeley: U of California P, 1986. 27–50.

Prigogine, Ilya. *From Being to Becoming: Time and Complexity in the Physical Sciences.* San Francisco: Freeman, 1980.

Prigogine, Ilya, and Isabelle Stengers. *Order out of Chaos: Man's New Dialogue with Nature.* New York: Bantam, 1984.

Quarterman, John S. *The Matrix: Computer Networks and Conferencing Systems Worldwide.* Bedford: Digital, 1990.

Quinn, Naomi, and Dorothy Holland. "Culture and Cognition." *Cultural Models in Language and Thought.* Ed. Dorothy Holland and Naomi Quinn. Cambridge, UK: Cambridge UP, 1987. 3–42.

Rabinow, Paul. "Representations Are Social Facts: Modernity and Post-Modernity in Anthropology." *Writing Culture.* Ed. James Clifford and George E. Marcus. Berkeley: U of California P, 1986. 234–61.

Rader, Margaret. "Context in Written Language: The Case of Imaginative Fiction." *Spoken and Written Language: Exploring Orality and Literacy.* Ed. Deborah Tannen. Norwood: Ablex, 1982. 185–98.

Rapaport, Matthew. *Computer Mediated Communications.* New York: Wiley, 1991.

Rasmussen, Jens. "Trends in Human Reliability Analysis." *Ergonomics* 28 (1985): 1185–96.

Ray, Ruth, and Ellen Barton. "Technology and Authority." *Evolving Perspectives on Computers and Composition Studies: Questions for the 1990s.* Ed. Gail E. Hawisher and Cynthia L. Selfe. Urbana: NCTE, 1991. 279–99.

Reither, James A., and Douglas Vipond. "Writing as Collaboration." *College English* 51 (1989): 855–67.

Resnick, Lauren B. "Shared Cognition: Thinking as Social Practice." *Perspectives on Socially Shared Cognition.* Ed. Lauren B. Resnick, John M. Levine, and Stephanie Teasley. Washington, D.C.: Amer. Psychological Assn., 1991. 1–20.

Reznikoff, Charles. Charles Reznikoff Papers, MSS 9. University Library, Mandeville Dept. of Special Collections, Archive for New Poetry. U of California, San Diego.

____. *Family Chronicle.* New York: Wiener, 1963.

____. *Poems 1918–1975: The Complete Poems of Charles Reznikoff.* Ed. Seamus Cooney. Santa Rosa: Black Sparrow, 1989.

Riel, Margaret. "Approaching the Study of Networks." *Computing Teacher* Dec./Jan. 1991–92: 5–7.

Roberts, John M. "The Self-Management of Cultures." *Explorations in Cultural Anthropology.* Ed. Ward H. Goodenough. New York: McGraw, 1964. 433–54.

Roberts, Lawrence G. "Data by the Packet." *IEEE Spectrum* 11.2 (1974): 46–51.

Rogoff, Barbara, and Jean Lave, eds. *Everyday Cognition: Its Development in Social Context.* Cambridge: Harvard UP, 1984.

Rosaldo, Renato. "Where Objectivity Lies: The Rhetoric of Anthropology." *The Rhetoric of the Human Sciences: Language and Argument in Scholarship and Human Affairs.* Ed. John S. Nelson, Allan Megill, and Donald N. McCloskey. Madison: U of Wisconsin P, 1987. 87–110.

Ross, Donald. "Prospects for Writers' Workstations in the Coming Decade." *Evolving Perspectives on Computers and Composition Studies: Questions for the 1990s.* Ed. Gail E. Hawisher and Cynthia L. Selfe. Urbana: NCTE, 1991. 84–112.

Sacks, Oliver. "A Neurologist's Notebook: To See and Not See." *The New Yorker* 10 May 1993: 59–73.

Sadler, D. R. "Specifying and Promulgating Achievement Standards." *Oxford Review of Education* 13 (1987): 191–209.

Schegloff, Emanuel A. "Conversation Analysis and Socially Shared Cognition." *Perspectives on Socially Shared Cognition.* Ed. Lauren B. Resnick, John M. Levine, and Stephanie Teasley. Washington, D.C.: Amer. Psychological Assn., 1991. 150–71.

Schiffer, Reinhold. "Charles Reznikoff and Reinhold Schiffer: The Poet in His Milieu." *Charles Reznikoff: Man and Poet.* Ed. Milton Hindus. Man and Poet Ser. Orono: Natl. Poetry Foundation, 1984. 109–26.

Schilb, John. "Cultural Studies, Postmodernism, and Composition." *Contending with Words: Composition and Rhetoric in a Postmodern Age.* New York: MLA, 1991. 173–88.

Schroeder, Eric James, and John Boe. "Minimalism, Populism, and Attitude Transformation: Approaches to Teaching Writing in Computer Classrooms." *Computers and Community: Teaching Composition in the Twenty-first Century.* Ed. Carolyn Handa. Portsmouth: Boynton/Cook, 1990. 28–46.

Schwartz, Helen J. "Ethical Considerations of Educational Computer Use." *Computers and Writing: Theory, Research, Practice.* Ed. Deborah H. Holdstein and Cynthia L. Selfe. New York: MLA, 1990. 18–30.

Scribner, Sylvia. "Modes of Thinking and Ways of Speaking: Culture and Logic Reconsidered." *Discourse Production and Comprehension.* Ed. R. O. Freedle. Hillsdale: Erlbaum, 483–500.

____. "Studying Working Intelligence." *Everyday Cognition: Its Development in Social Context.* Ed. Barbara Rogoff and Jean Lave. Cambridge: Harvard UP, 1984. 9–40.

Secord, Paul F., ed. *Explaining Human Behavior: Consciousness, Human Action and Social Structure.* Beverly Hills: Sage, 1982.

Selfe, Cynthia. "Computer-Based Conversations and the Changing Nature of Collaboration." *New Visions of Collaborative Writing.* Ed. Janis Forman. Portsmouth: Boynton/Cook, 1992. 147–69.

———. "Computers in English Departments: The Rhetoric of Techno/Power." *Computers and Writing: Theory, Research, Practice.* Ed. Deborah H. Holdstein and Cynthia L. Selfe. New York: MLA, 1990. 95–103.

———. "Redefining Literacy: The Multilayered Grammars of Computers." *Critical Perspectives on Computers and Composition Instruction.* Ed. Gail E. Hawisher and Cynthia L. Selfe. New York: Teachers College P, 1989. 3–15.

———. "Technology in the English Classroom: Computers through the Lens of Feminist Theory." *Computers and Community: Teaching Composition in the Twenty-first Century.* Ed. Carolyn Handa. Portsmouth: Boynton/Cook, 1990. 118–39.

Selfe, Cynthia L., and Paul R. Meyer. "Testing Claims for On-Line Conferences." *Written Communication* 8 (1991): 163–92.

Shapiro, Harvey. "Remembering Charles Reznikoff." *Charles Reznikoff: Man and Poet.* Ed. Milton Hindus. Man and Poet Ser. Orono: Natl. Poetry Foundation, 1984. 85–87.

Shapiro, Norman Z., and Robert H. Anderson. *Towards an Ethics and Etiquette for Electronic Mail.* Prepared for the Natl. Science Foundation. Santa Monica: Rand, 1985.

Shirk, Henrietta Nickels. "Hypertext and Composition Studies." *Evolving Perspectives on Computers and Composition Studies: Questions for the 1990s.* Ed. Gail E. Hawisher and Cynthia L. Selfe. Urbana: NCTE, 1991. 177–202.

Simons, Herbert W., ed. *Rhetoric in the Human Sciences.* London: Sage, 1989.

Skubikowski, Kathleen, and John Elder. "Computers and the Social Contexts of Writing." *Computers and Community: Teaching Composition in the Twenty-first Century.* Ed. Carolyn Handa. Portsmouth: Boynton/Cook, 1990. 89–105.

Smith, Catherine F. "Reconceiving Hypertext." *Evolving Perspectives on Computers and Composition Studies: Questions for the 1990s.* Ed. Gail E. Hawisher and Cynthia L. Selfe. Urbana: NCTE, 1991. 224–52.

Sommers, Nancy. "Revision in the Composing Process: A Case Study of College Freshmen and Experienced Adult Writers." Diss. Boston U School of Educ., 1978.

Sosnoski, James J. "Postmodern Teachers in Their Postmodern Classrooms: Socrates Begone!" *Contending with Words: Composition and Rhetoric in a Postmodern Age.* New York: MLA, 1991. 198–219.

Spitzer, Michael. "Computer Conferencing: An Emerging Technology." *Critical Perspectives on Computers and Composition Instruction.* Ed. Gail E. Hawisher and Cynthia L. Selfe. New York: Teachers College P, 1989. 187–200.

———. "Local and Global Networking: Implications for the Future." *Computers and Writing: Theory, Research, Practice.* Ed. Deborah H. Holdstein and Cynthia L. Selfe. New York: MLA, 1990. 58–70.

Sproull, Lee, and Sara B. Kiesler. *Connections: New Ways of Working in the Networked Organization.* Cambridge: MIT P, 1991.

Sternburg, Janet, and Alan Ziegler. "A Conversation with Charles Reznikoff." *Charles Reznikoff: Man and Poet.* Ed. Milton Hindus. Man and Poet Ser. Orono: Natl. Poetry Foundation, 1984. 127–36.

Stott, William. *Documentary Expression and Thirties America.* New York: Oxford UP, 1973.

Strickland, James. "The Politics of Writing Programs." *Evolving Perspectives on Computers and Composition Studies: Questions for the 1990s.* Ed. Gail E. Hawisher and Cynthia L. Selfe. Urbana: NCTE, 1991. 300–317.

Suchman, Lucy A. *Plans and Situated Actions. Learning in Doing: Social, Cognitive, and Computational Perspectives.* New York: Cambridge UP, 1987.

Sudol, Ronald A. "The Accumulative Rhetoric of Word Processing." *College English* 53 (1991): 920–32.

Sullivan, Patricia. "Taking Control of the Page: Electronic Writing and Word Publishing." *Evolving Perspectives on Computers and Composition Studies: Questions for the 1990s.* Ed. Gail E. Hawisher and Cynthia L. Selfe. Urbana: NCTE, 1991. 42–64.

Suppe, Frederick. *The Semantic Conception of Theories and Scientific Realism.* Urbana: U of Illinois P, 1989.

Syrkin, Marie. "Charles: A Memoir." *Charles Reznikoff: Man and Poet.* Ed. Milton Hindus. Man and Poet Ser. Orono: Natl. Poetry Foundation, 1984. 37–68.

Syverson, M[argaret] A. "The Community of Memory: A Reznikoff Family Chronicle." *Sagetrieb* 11.1–2 (1992): 127–70.

———. "Sarah Reznikoff: Pure Gold in the Archive." *Archive Newsletter* (Winter 1992). 17–20.

Tannen, Deborah. "The Oral/Literate Continuum in Discourse." *Spoken and Written Language: Exploring Orality and Literacy.* Ed. Deborah Tannen. Norwood: Ablex, 1982. 1–16.

Taylor, C. "Assessment for Measurement or Standards: The Peril and Promise of Large-Scale Assessment Reform." *American Educational Research Journal* 31 (1994): 231–62.

Taylor, Paul. "Social Epistemic Rhetoric and Chaotic Discourse." *Re-imagining Computers and Composition: Teaching and Research in the Virtual Age.* Ed. Gail E. Hawisher and Paul LeBlanc. Portsmouth: Boynton/Cook, 1992. 131–48.

Thiesmeyer, John. "Should We Do What We Can?" *Critical Perspectives on Computers and Composition Instruction.* Ed. Gail E. Hawisher and Cynthia L. Selfe. New York: Teachers College P, 1989. 75–93.

Thomas, Sally O. "Rethinking Assessment: Teachers and Students Helping Each Other through the 'Sharp Curves of Life.' " *Learning Disability Quarterly* 16 (1993): 257–79.

Todorov, Tzvetan. *Genres in Discourse.* Trans. Catherine Porter. Cambridge, UK: Cambridge UP, 1990.

Trimbur, John. "Consensus and Difference in Collaborative Learning." *College English* 51 (1989): 602–16.

Turner, Mark. *Reading Minds: The Study of English in the Age of Cognitive Science.* Princeton: Princeton UP, 1991.

Turner, Monica Goigel. "Landscape Ecology: The Effect of Pattern on Process." *Annual Review of Ecology and Systematics.* Ed. Richard F. Johnston, Peter W. Frank, and Charles D. Michener. Vol. 20. Palo Alto: Annual Reviews, 1989. 171–97.

Tyler, Stephen A. "The Poetic Turn in Postmodern Anthropology: The Poetry of Paul Friedrich." *American Anthropologist* 86 (1984): 328–36.

Ulmer, Gregory. *Teletheory: Grammatology in the Age of Video.* New York: Routledge, 1989.

Van Dijk, Teun A., ed. *Handbook of Discourse Analysis.* 4 vols. London: Academic, 1985.

Varela, Francisco J., and Jean-Pierre Dupuy, eds. *Understanding Origins: Contemporary Views on the Origin of Life, Mind and Society.* Dordrecht: Kluwer, 1992.

Varela, Francisco J., Evan Thompson, and Eleanor Rosch. *The Embodied Mind: Cognitive Science and Human Experience.* Cambridge: MIT P, 1991.

Vitanza, Victor J. "Three Countertheses: Or, A Critical In(ter)vention into Composition Theories and Pedagogies." *Contending with Words: Composition and Rhetoric in a Postmodern Age.* New York: MLA, 1991. 139–72.

Vygotsky, L[ev] S. *Mind in Society: The Development of Higher Psychological Processes.* Ed. Michael Cole, Vera John-Steiner, Sylvia Scribner, and Ellen Souberman. Cambridge: Harvard UP, 1978.

____. *Thought and Language.* Trans. Alex Kozulin. Cambridge: MIT P, 1988.

Wahlstrom, Billie J. "Desktop Publishing: Perspectives, Potentials, and Politics." *Critical Perspectives on Computers and Composition Instruction.* Ed. Gail E. Hawisher and Cynthia L. Selfe. New York: Teachers College P, 1989. 162–86.

Waldrop, M. Mitchell. *Complexity: The Emerging Science at the Edge of Order and Chaos.* New York: Simon, 1992.

Walvoord, Barbara E., and Lucille McCarthy. *Thinking and Writing in College: A Naturalistic Study of Students in Four Disciplines.* Urbana: NCTE, 1990.

Weinberger, Eliot. "Another Memory of Reznikoff." *Charles Reznikoff: Man and Poet.* Ed. Milton Hindus. Man and Poet Ser. Orono: Natl. Poetry Foundation, 1984. 77–78.

Wertsch, James V. "A Sociocultural Approach to Socially Shared Cognition." *Perspectives on Socially Shared Cognition.* Ed. Lauren B. Resnick, John M. Levine, and Stephanie Teasley. Washington, D.C.: Amer. Psychological Assn., 1991. 85–100.

____. *Voices of the Mind: A Sociocultural Approach to Mediated Action.* Cambridge: Harvard UP, 1991.

Wertsch, James V., Norris Minick, and Flavio J. Arns. "The Creation of Context in Joint Problem-Solving." *Everyday Cognition: Its Development in Social Context.* Ed. Barbara Rogoff and Jean Lave. Cambridge: Harvard UP, 1984. 151–71.

White, Geoffrey M. "Proverbs and Cultural Models: An American Psychology of Problem Solving." *Cultural Models in Language and Thought.* Ed. Dorothy Holland and Naomi Quinn. Cambridge, UK: Cambridge UP, 1987. 151–72.

White, Sheldon H., and Alexander W. Siegel. "Cognitive Development in Time and Space." *Everyday Cognition: Its Development in Social Context.* Ed. Barbara Rogoff and Jean Lave. Cambridge: Harvard UP, 1984. 238–78.

Whorf, Benjamin Lee. "Language, Mind, and Reality." *Language, Thought, and Reality.* Ed. John B. Carroll. New York: Technology P of MIT, 1956. 246–70.

____. "Languages and Logic." *Language, Thought, and Reality.* Ed. John B. Carroll. New York: Technology P of MIT, 1956. 233–45.

Wiggins, Grant P. *Assessing Student Performance: Exploring the Purpose and Limits of Testing.* San Francisco: Jossey-Bass, 1993.

Wilkins, Harriet. "Computer Talk: Long-Distance Conversations by Computer." *Written Communication* 8 (1991): 56–78.

Wimsatt, William C. "Robustness, Reliability, and Overdetermination." *Scientific Inquiry and the Social Sciences.* Ed. Marilynn B. Brewer and Barry E. Collins. San Francisco: Jossey-Bass, 1981. 124–63.

Winking, D., J. Farley, H. Schweder, and L. Mabry. *The New York City Early Childhood Initiative Year II Evaluation, Learning Together: Children's Progress in Integrative Early Childhood Evaluation.* Oak Brook: North Central Regional Educ. Laboratory, 1995.

Winograd, Terry, and Fernando Flores. *Understanding Computers and Cognition.* Reading: Addison, 1986.

Wolfram, Stephen. "Complex Systems Theory." *Emerging Syntheses in Science: Pro-

ceedings of the Founding Workshops of the Santa Fe Institute, Santa Fe, New Mexico. Ed. David Pines. Redwood City: Addison, 1988. 183–89.

Woods, David D. "Process-Tracing Methods for the Study of Cognition Outside of the Experimental Psychology Laboratory." *Decision Making in Action: Models and Methods.* Ed. Gary A. Klein et al. Norwood: Ablex, 1993. 228–51.

Woods, David D., Leila J. Johannesen, Richard I. Cook, and Nadine B. Sarter. *Behind Human Error: Cognitive Systems, Computers and Hindsight.* Columbus: Crew Systems Ergonomics Information Analysis Center, 1994.

Yin, Robert K. *Case Study Research: Design and Methods.* Applied Social Research Methods Ser. 5. Beverly Hills: Sage, 1984.

Zurek, Wojciech H., ed. *Complexity, Entropy, and the Physics of Information.* Redwood City: Addison, 1990.

Index

academia: and politics, 167–68

academic research: and emotional suppression, 170–71

adaptation, 75–125; in complex systems (or ecological systems), 76; coordination and, 6; defined, 76; learning as, 75–78, 103–4; problems in, 76

Anderson, Philip W., 130; 247n. 2 (chap. 1)

Archive for New Poetry, UCSD, 55

Arrow, Kenneth J., 247n. 2 (chap. 1)

Artistic Millinery Company, 31, 38

assessment: ecological challenges to, 189–92; questions to be answered, 191; sample prompt, 190; writing, large-scale, 192–200

autobiography: ecological approach to 28–74

Autopoeisis and Cognition (Maturana and Varela), 127–28

Axelrod, Rise, 78

Bak, Per, 129, 247n. 4 (chap. 2)

Barrs, Myra, 192

Bazerman, Charles, 185

Beach, King, 204

Bereiter, Carl, 19

Bhaskar, Roy, 57, 201, 207

binary oppositions, 12

biological symmetry, 12

Brennan, Susan, 160–61

Britton, James, 192

Brodwin, Stanley, 64

Bruner, Jerome, 37

By the Waters of Manhattan (C. Reznikoff), 33, 34

By the Waters of Manhattan: An Annual (C. Reznikoff), 39

By the Well of Living and Seeing (C. Reznikoff), 37

case-study research, 187, 195

Chandrasekaran, B., 36

chaos: edge of, 4 ; order and, 4; as social disruption, 50–51, 66–67

Chen, Kan, 128, 247n. 4 (chap. 2)

Churchland, Pat, 26

Clark, Herbert, 160–61

codependent arising, 52, 104

cognition: and composition, 182–83; processes of, 8–10

Cognition in the Wild (Hutchins), 7–8, 21

coherence: in computer forums, 177–78

collaborative writing, xvi; and Reznikoff, 44; student, 75–125

complex adaptive systems: defined, 5

complexity theory. *See* complex systems

complex systems, xv, 2–26, 183; aggregate behavior and, 5–6; anticipation and, 5–6; attributes of, xv; challenges for theories of, 26; compared with simple and complicated systems, 4; complex problems and, 201–2; composition and, 183; defined, 3–4; dimensions of, 18–23; evolution and, 5–6; intellectual property and, 202; the Learning Record and, 198–99; phase transitions in, 59; question of influence in, 202; responsibility in, 200; uncertainty and, 202. *See also* ecological system; ecology

composition: as cognitive process, 25–26, 182–83; as distributed cognition, 9, 36–47; as embodied, 47–56, 12–13; as emergent, 10, 11, 57–67; as enacted, 13, 68–73; ethnographic approaches to, 24; law school as training for, 69–71; physical-material dimension of, 18; psychological approaches to, 24; psycho-

composition *(continued)*
   logical dimension of, 19–20; social
   dimension of, 19; spatial dimension
   of, 20; studies of material and
   physical, 25; temporal dimension of,
   20–22
composition research, 23–27
composition studies, xv; and future
   research, 184–86; as reductionist,
   16–17
computer forum: argument and, 143–
   45, 150, 155–58, 166–67; coherence
   in, 177–78; controversy in, 143;
   coordination and, 160–67; discourse
   rules in, 169; distribution in
   complex systems and, 142–50;
   dynamic process of chaos and order
   in, 143–45; embodiment in complex
   systems and, 151–60; emergence in,
   160–67; explained, 130–31;
   memory and, 177. *See also* xlchc;
   xwar
computers: in composition. *See*
   technology
conflict: in complex systems, 126–30;
   in a computer forum, 126–81;
   perturbation and, 127–30, 180–81
container metaphor: and physical
   experience, 12
Cooper, Charles, 78
coordination, 59; adaptation and, 6;
   common task and, in computer
   forum, 160–67; conference with
   instructor and, 110–11; defined, 76;
   enaction and, 112–14; humor and,
   108–9; physical proximity and,
   107–8; references to email message
   content and, 162–63; references to
   writer's name in email and, 162;
   shared experience and, 109; shared
   language and, 104–7; student
   writers and, 88–89, 94, 103–4;
   subject-line reference in email and,
   161; threat, perceived and, 109–10

Davies, Paul C., 247n. 2 (chap. 1)
Dembo, L. S., 70
dependent co-origination, 17, 57; and
   writing processes, 53

developmental scales: contrasted with
   rubrics, 194–95
dimensions of ecologies of composing,
   18–22
dimensions of learning: and Learning
   Record, 195
discourse rules: in computer forums,
   169; in xlchc, 169
distribution: in complex systems, xv, 7–
   10, 183; embodiment and, 56;
   material environment and, 46–47;
   memory and, 44; the poem, and 36–
   47; readers and, 142–50; reading
   and, 46; student writers and, 88–97
documentary movement: in American
   culture, 65–66
domain of perturbations, 128
domain of scrutiny, 15, 204
Dorinson, Joseph, 48–50

*Early History of a Sewing Machine
   Operator* (C. Reznikoff), 39
"Early History of a Writer," 28–30,
   37–38, 42–43, 48, 58, 60–64, 65,
   66
ecological approach to composition,
   value of, 203
ecological system: defined, 2, 3
ecological theory of composing:
   challenges to, 200–202
ecology: of readers, 179–81; of writers,
   5; of texts, 73–74
Edwards, Derek, 44
email: and argumentation, 155–58
embodiment: in complex systems, xv,
   12–13, 183; distribution and, 56;
   memory and, 51; the poem and, 47–
   56; readers and, 151–60; student
   writers and, 97–103; texts and, 53–
   56; time and, 51
emergence: in complex systems, xv, 10–
   11, 183; in computer forum, 160–
   67; the poem and, 57–67; readers
   and, 160–67; student writers and,
   103–12; ten aspects of in texts, 58–
   59
emigration: Jewish, 48–50
enaction: audience and, 73; in complex
   systems, xv, xvi, 13–18, 183;

composing and, 17; in a computer forum, 174–79; the poem and, 68–73; readers and, 174–79; student writers and, 112–20; technology and, 174–76
entropy: and emergence, 10–11
equity in education: and native languages, 249n. 6
error: as feedback, 124; human, 120–25
ethnomethodology: Learning Record as, 200

Faigley, Lester, 186
fallacy of instructive interaction, 128
Family Chronicle (C. Reznikoff), 33, 38, 41
fatigue: and writing, 97–98
Flores, Fernando, 128
Flower, Linda, 19, 77, 185–86
focused brainstorming, 82

gay activism: and Persian Gulf War, 169–70
Going To and Fro and Walking Up and Down (C. Reznikoff), 52
González, Roseann Dueñas, 249n. 6
Goodwin, Charles, 15, 247n. 4 (chap.1)
Goodwin, Marjorie, 15, 247n. 4 (chap.1)
Goswami, Dixie, 249n. 3 (chap. 5)
Gulf war. *See* Persian Gulf War

Haas, Christina, 249n. 1
Hayes, John, 19, 77
Hazlehurst, Brian, 6
Heath, Shirley Brice, 186
Helprin, Mark, 78
Hendriks-Jansen, Horst, 11
hindsight bias, 122
Hindus, Milton, 34, 247n. 2 (chap. 2)
historical situatedness, 22
Holland, John, 5, 7, 68, 76, 247n. 2 (chap. 1)
Holocaust (C. Reznikoff), 34
human error, 120–25
Hutchins, Edwin, xiv, 6, 7, 21, 47, 180, 185, 204

immigrant fiction, 64–65
immigration: of Russian Jews, 48–51
instructive interaction, 128

Johnson, Mark, 12, 152

Kauffman, Stuart, 58, 130, 243

Laboratory for Comparative Human Cognition (LCHC), 131
Lakoff, George, 12, 134, 137–38, 146, 150, 152, 164, 247n. 5
languages, multiple: and the Learning Record, 194
large-scale assessment: and Learning Record, 196–99; Learning Record moderations and, 196–98. *See also* Learning Record
Lave, Jean, 204
Learning Record, 192–200; complex systems and, 198–99; developmental scales in, 194–95; dimensions of learning and, 195; document format, 193; effect on instruction of, 195–96; as ethnomethodology, 200; moderation readings and, 196–98; multiple language literacies and, 194; one rule for, 194; procedures for, 194–95; as research tool, 195; sample student record, 237–45; significance of, 199–200; staff development, 195
Lewin, Roger, 247n. 1 (chap. 1)
Lewontin, Richard, 24
Lieberman, Philip, 12

MacDonald, Susan Peck, 186
Mandelbrot, Benoit, 130
Maturana, Humberto, 13, 16, 17, 127–28
McCarthy, Lucille, 19, 186
Megabyte University, 151–52
memory: as collaborative, 44; computer forums and, 177; as distributed, 44, 51; embodiment and, 51
metaphor: and war, 137–38
Meyer, Paul R., 151–52
Middleton, David, 44
Miserlis, Susan, 249n. 7

moderation readings: Learning Record
and, 196–98
Moulthrop, Stuart, 185, 186
Murray, Denise, 186

naturalism: and fiction, 64–65
navigation: among email messages,
177; naval, as complex system, 7–8
nervous system: as network, 127–28
New York: immigration and, 29, 31,
48–51, 64–65; as physical environ-
ment, 52
Nicolis, Grégoire, 247n. 1 (chap. 1)
Norman, Donald, 247n. 3 (chap. 1)
Norris, Frank, 64
"Notes for an Autobiography" (C.
Reznikoff), 28, 38, 41, 66

objectivism, 32–33; and law, 70–71
Objectivist Press, 32–33, 72–73
Odell, Lee, 249n. 3 (chap. 5)
Olympian discourse: in academia, 168
Online Learning Record, 192
Oppen, George, 32
oppositions: binary, 12
Oyama, Susan, 57

Paulson, William, 4
pedagogy: ecological challenges to,
188–89
perception: visual, 14–16, 127–28
Persian Gulf War, xvii, 127–81;
academia and, 167–68; administration of old, white men and, 148,
150, 157; American policy as cause
of, 148; antiwar demonstrations
and, 148; argumentation and, 143–
45, 155–58; chemical weapons and,
152–53; compared with other wars,
146–47; as ecological disaster, 149,
151–52; effects on Iraqi civilians,
146–47; email messages from Israel,
139–42; gay activism and, 169–70;
map of email distribution, 222–31;
military contractors and, 149; as
moral war, 149; propaganda and,
150; sanctions and, 148; timeline of
events, 221–31; World War II and,
152–53
perturbation: in complex systems, 127–

30, 180–81; in a computer forum,
138, 142–45, 180–81; conflict and,
180–81; defined, 127–28
phase transitions: in complex systems,
59–60
physical-material dimension of
ecosystems, 18
Pines, David, 247n. 2 (chap. 1)
Pizer, Donald, 64–65
*Poems 1918–1975: The Complete
Poems of Charles Reznikoff,* 37
Pound, Ezra, 32–33
power law: and self-organized criticality, 142–43
Prigogine, Ilya, 58, 247n. 1 (chap. 1)
Primary Language Record, 192
process-tracing methods, 77
professional development of teachers:
and Learning Record, 195
professional vision, 15–16
proposal essay writing task, 81–82
protocols: talk-aloud, 77
psychological dimension of ecosystems,
19

Rasmussen, Jens, 124
reading: as collaborative, 46; law
school as training in, 69–71
reply function: in computer forums,
178
research: case studies, value of, 187; in
composition studies, 184–86, 203–
5; ecological challenges to, 186–88;
and emotion, 170–71; the Learning
Record and, 195
residua: as traces of cognitive activity,
180
revision: as embodied, 53, 55; as
emergent, 60–64, 109–11; as
enaction, 70–71; Reznikoff and; 37–
38; student workshop and, 91–95;
and student writers, 83–84, 86–87,
91–96, 109–11
Reznikoff, Charles, xvi, 28–74;
biographical background, 31–33; *By
the Waters of Manhattan,* 33, 34; *By
the Waters of Manhattan: An
Annual,* 39; *By the Well of Living
and Seeing,* 37; *Complete Poems,*
37; *Early History of a Sewing*

Machine Operator, 39; "Early History of a Writer," 28–30, 37–38, 42–43, 48, 58, 60–64, 65, 66; *Family Chronicle*, 28, 33, 38, 41; *Going To and Fro and Walking Up and Down*, 52; *Holocaust*, 34; law as practice, 69–71; Marie Syrkin on, 32–33, 45–46; "Notes for an Autobiography," 28, 38, 41, 66; objectivism and, 70–71; *Testimony*, 34, 58; walking and, 52–53

Reznikoff, Nathan, 31, 38, 40, 48, 50–51, 60, 72

Reznikoff, Sarah Yetta, 31, 38, 40, 48, 50–51, 56, 60, 72

"Ridiculous" (Verissimo), 173–74

Rosch, Eleanor, 16, 58, 17

Rosenberg, Martin, 185

Rumelhart, David, 204

Sachs, Oliver, 14

Santa Fe Institute, 247n. 1 (chap.1)

Scardamalia, Marlene, 19

Schiffer, Reinhold, 52

Selfe, Cynthia, 151–52, 186

self-organization, 3; in complex systems, 57; and emergence, 10; and Marie Syrkin, 57; and texts, 57

self-organized criticality: theory of, 129–30

ship navigation: as complex cognitive system, 7–8

situated cognition, 9

Slatin, John, 186

social dimension of ecosystems, 19

spatial dimension of ecosystems, 20

St. Martin's Guide to Writing, The (Axelrod and Cooper), 78–79, 121

Stott, William, 65

Suchman, Lucy, 13, 248n. 3

symmetry, biological, 12

Syrkin, Marie, 32, 35, 45, 52

Taylor, Paul, 185

TCWP (Third College Writing Program), 78–84, 121–22; activities, 81, 113–19, 122; case study design, 77–78, 84–85; causes of student error and, 120–25; collaborative writing rationale, 85; conference with instructor 86–87, 114–15, 122; invention work, 79, 82–83, 90; journal questions, 215–17; as "kind work environment," 124; student essay, 87–88; syllabus, 211–17; TCWP 1A course description, 78–84; texts, 78–80, 121; workshop and, 85, 91–95, 109–10; writing conference worksheet, 219

technology: controversy and, 143, 166–67, 179; distribution in complex system and, 142–45; ecologies of composing and, 18–19, 26, 27, 37, 38, 55, 126–81, 166–67, 205–6; embodiment and, 151–55; emergence and, 160–67; emotion and, 155–59, 179; enaction and, 174–79; as external memory, 177–78; historical situatedness, 2–22, 127; as medium for political action, 137–38; methodological problems for research on, 133–35; as news medium, 138–42, 146; Online Learning Record, 192; perturbations and, 130; recent research on composing with 25, 184–85; social structures and, 131–33; student writers and, 95–97, 101–2; Third World and, 173–74

temporal dimension of ecosystems, 20

Testimony (C. Reznikoff), 34

texts: as physical, 53–55

Third College Writing Program. *See* TCWP

Third World: compared with First World, 173–74

Thompson, Evan, 58

Turner, Mark, 12

Varela, Francisco, 13, 16, 17, 58, 127–28

Verissimo, Luis Fernando, 173–74

visual perception, 14–16; in frogs, 127–28

vitalism: and emergence, 57–58

Vygotsky, Lev, 192

Waldrop, M. Mitchell, 3–4, 247n. 1 (chap. 1)

Walvoord, Barbara, 19, 186

war: psychological effects of, 169–70
Werman, Robert, 142
Williams, William Carlos, 32–33
Winograd, Terry, 128
Wolfram, Stephen, 58
Woods, David, 77–78, 122–24
workshop: handout, 218; student
    writers in, 83–84, 85–86, 91–94,
    103, 109–10, 113, 124;
writing assessment. *See* assessment
writing process, 23

xlchc: 126–81; archive, 177; background and history, 130–33;
coordination and, 160–67; minority
scholars and, 132; norms in, 133;
origin myth, 131–32; Persian Gulf
War conflict in, 126–81; proposal to
shut down, 159. *See also* computer
forum
xwar, 133, 154, 157, 160, 167, 172,
174

Yin, Robert K., 249n. 2

Zukofsky, Louis, 32–33

Margaret A. Syverson is the director of the Computer Writing and Research Lab in the Division of Rhetoric and Composition at the University of Texas at Austin. She has served as a research associate and consultant for the California State Department of Education and for the Center for Language in Learning in San Diego, where she is currently the president of the Board of Directors. She is the Web editor for the *Computers and Composition Journal Online* and serves on the national Computers in College Composition and Communication Committee.